CW00323966

Psychology Express

Cognitive
Psychology

Jonathan Ling
University of Sunderland

Jonathan Catling
University of Worcester

Series editor:

Dominic Upton
University of Worcester

Prentice Hall
is an imprint of

Harlow, England • London • New York • Boston • San Francisco • Toronto
Sydney • Tokyo • Singapore • Hong Kong • Seoul • Taipei • New Delhi
Cape Town • Madrid • Mexico City • Amsterdam • Munich • Paris • Milan

Pearson Education Limited
Edinburgh Gate
Harlow
Essex CM20 2JE
England

and Associated Companies throughout the world

Visit us on the World Wide Web at:
www.pearson.com/uk

First published 2012

ISBN 978-0-273-73798-8

British Library Cataloguing-in-Publication Data
A catalogue record for this book is available from the British Library

Library of Congress Cataloging-in-Publication Data
Catling, Jonathan.
  Cognitive psychology / Jonathan Catling, Jonathan Ling.
      p. cm – (Psychology express)
  Includes bibliographical references and index.
  ISBN 978-0-273-73798-8 (pbk.)
  1. Cognitive psychology.   I. Ling, Jonathan.   II. Title.
  BF201.C38 2011
  153—dc23
                                         2011020733

10 9 8 7 6 5 4 3 2 1
15 14 13 12 11

Typeset in 9.5/12.5 Avenir Book by 3
Printed and bound in Great Britain by Henry Ling Ltd, Dorchester, Dorset

Contents

The PsychologyExpress series

→ UNDERSTAND QUICKLY
→ REVISE EFFECTIVELY
→ TAKE EXAMS WITH CONFIDENCE

'All of the revision material I need in one place – a must for psychology undergrads.'
Andrea Franklin, Psychology student at Anglia Ruskin University

'Very useful, straight to the point and provides guidance to the student, while helping them to develop independent learning.'
Lindsay Pitcher, Psychology student at Anglia Ruskin University

'Engaging, interesting, comprehensive ... it helps to guide understanding and boosts confidence.'
Megan Munro, Forensic Psychology student at Leeds Trinity University College

'Very useful ... bridges the gap between Statistics textbooks and Statistics workbooks.'
Chris Lynch, Psychology student at the University of Chester

'The answer guidelines are brilliant, I wish I had had it last year.'
Tony Whalley, Psychology student at the University of Chester

'I definitely would (buy a revision guide) as I like the structure, the assessment advice and practice questions and would feel more confident knowing exactly what to revise and having something to refer to.'
Steff Copestake, Psychology student at the University of Chester

'The clarity is absolutely first rate ... These chapters will be an excellent revision guide for students as well as providing a good opportunity for novel forms of assessment in and out of class.'
Dr Deaglan Page, Queen's University, Belfast

'Do you think they will help students when revising/working towards assessment? Unreservedly, yes.'
Dr Mike Cox, Newcastle University

'The revision guide should be very helpful to students preparing for their exams.'
Dr Kun Guo, University of Lincoln

'A brilliant revision guide, very helpful for students of all levels.'
Svetoslav Georgiev, Psychology student at Anglia Ruskin University

Introduction

Not only is psychology one of the fastest-growing subjects to study at university worldwide, it is also one of the most exciting and relevant subjects. Over the past decade the scope, breadth and importance of psychology have developed considerably. Important research work from as far afield as the UK, Europe, USA and Australia has demonstrated the exacting research base of the topic and how this can be applied to all manner of everyday issues and concerns. Being a student of psychology is an exciting experience – the study of mind and behaviour is a fascinating journey of discovery. Studying psychology at degree level brings with it new experiences, new skills and knowledge. As the Quality Assurance Agency (QAA) has stressed:

> psychology is distinctive in the rich and diverse range of attributes it develops – skills which are associated with the humanities (e.g. critical thinking and essay writing) and the sciences (hypotheses-testing and numeracy). (QAA, 2010, p. 5)

Recent evidence suggests that employers appreciate the skills and knowledge of psychology graduates, but in order to reach this pinnacle you need to develop your skills, further your knowledge and most of all successfully complete your degree to your maximum ability. The skills, knowledge and opportunities that you gain during your psychology degree will give you an edge in the employment field. The QAA stresses the high level of employment skills developed during a psychology degree:

> due to the wide range of generic skills, and the rigour with which they are taught, training in psychology is widely accepted as providing an excellent preparation for many careers. In addition to subject skills and knowledge, graduates also develop skills in communication, numeracy, teamwork, critical thinking, computing, independent learning and many others, all of which are highly valued by employers. (QAA, 2010, p. 2)

This book is part of the comprehensive new series, Psychology Express, that helps you achieve these aspirations. It is not a replacement for every single text, journal article, presentation and abstract you will read and review during the course of your degree programme. It is in no way a replacement for your lectures, seminars or additional reading. A top-rated assessment answer is likely to include considerable additional information and wider reading – and you are directed to some of these in this text. This revision guide is a conductor: directing you through the maze of your degree by providing an overview of your course, helping you formulate your ideas, and directing your reading.

Each book within Psychology Express presents a summary coverage of the key concepts, theories and research in the field, within an explicit framework of revision. The focus throughout all of the books in the series will be on how you should approach and consider your topics in relation to assessment and exams. Various features have been included to help you build up your skills and knowledge, ready for your assessments. More detail of the features can be found in the guided tour for this book on page xii.

By reading and engaging with this book, you will develop your skills and knowledge base and in this way you should excel in your studies and your associated assessments.

Psychology Express: Cognitive Psychology is divided into 12 chapters and your course has probably been divided up into similar sections. However we, the series authors and editor, must stress a key point: do not let the purchase, reading and engagement with the material in this text restrict your reading or your thinking. In psychology, you need to be aware of the wider literature and how it interrelates and how authors and thinkers have criticised and developed the arguments of others. So even if an essay asks you about one particular topic, you need to draw on similar issues raised in other areas of psychology. There are, of course, some similar themes that run throughout the material covered in this text, but you can learn from the other areas of psychology covered in the other texts in this series as well as from material presented elsewhere.

We hope you enjoy this text and the others in the Psychology Express series, which cover the complete knowledge base of psychology:

- *Biological Psychology* (Emma Preece): covering the biological basis of behaviour, hormones and behaviour, sleeping and dreaming, and psychological abnormalities.

- *Cognitive Psychology* (Jonathan Ling and Jonathan Catling): including key material on perception, learning, memory, thinking and language.

- *Developmental Psychology* (Penney Upton): from pre-natal development through to old age, the development of individuals is considered. Childhood, adolescence and lifespan development are all covered.

- *Personality and Individual Differences* (Terry Butler): normal and abnormal personality, psychological testing, intelligence, emotion and motivation are all covered in this book.

- *Social Psychology* (Jenny Mercer and Debbie Clayton): covering all the key topics in Social Psychology including attributions, attitudes, group relations, close relationships and critical social psychology.

- *Statistics in Psychology* (Catherine Steele, Holly Andrews and Dominic Upton): an overview of data analysis related to psychology is presented along with why we need statistics in psychology. Descriptive and inferential statistics and both parametric and non-parametric analysis are included.

- *Research Methods for Psychology* (Steve Jones and Mark Forshaw): research design, experimental methods, discussion of qualitative and quantitative methods and ethics are all presented in this text.

- *Conceptual and Historical Issues in Psychology* (Brian M. Hughes): the foundations of psychology and its development from a mere interest into a scientific discipline. The key conceptual issues of current-day psychology are also presented.

This book, and the other companion volumes in this series, should cover all your study needs (there will also be further guidance on the website). It will, obviously, need to be supplemented with further reading and this text directs you towards suitable sources. Hopefully, quite a bit of what you read here you will already have come across and the text will act as a jolt to set your mind at rest – you do know the material in depth. Overall, we hope that you find this book useful and informative as a guide for both your study now and in your future as a successful psychology graduate.

Revision note

- *Use evidence based on your reading, not on anecdotes or your 'common sense'.*
- *Show the examiner you know your material in depth – use your additional reading wisely.*
- *Remember to draw on a number of different sources: there is rarely one 'correct' answer to any psychological problem.*
- *Base your conclusions on research-based evidence.*

Explore the accompanying website at **www.pearsoned.co.uk/psychologyexpress**
→ Prepare more effectively for exams and assignments using the answer guidelines for questions from this chapter.
→ Test your knowledge using multiple choice questions and flashcards.
→ Improve your essay skills by exploring the You be the marker exercises.

Guided tour

→ Understand key concepts quickly

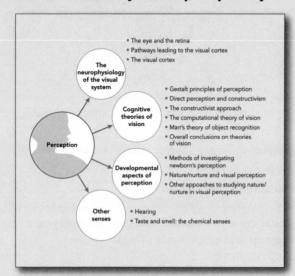

Start to plan your revision using the **Topic maps**.

Grasp **Key terms** quickly using the handy definitions. Use the flashcards online to test yourself.

In this way a problem space can be explored and hopefully the goal state will eventually be achieved. However, there are two main problems with the algorithm above – first, there is no mechanism for the algorithm to avoid getting into a loop where it either goes round in circles in the problem space, or simply

→ Revise effectively

How do schemas affect memory?

Scripts and schemas can lead to systematic biases in recall. Information congruent with a schema will be more likely to be recalled than incongruent information (Brewer & Treyens, 1981). However, highly distinctive information – like a skull in a shopping trolley – is more likely to be remembered than more commonplace items, the 'von Restorff' effect.

KEY STUDY

Remembering congruent and incongruent items

Brewer and Treyens (1981) asked participants to recall the contents of an office in which they waited. Congruent objects (e.g. chair) were better-remembered by participants than incongruent objects (e.g. skull). Many participants also reported seeing books – congruent objects – that had not been present in the room.

Schemas influence memory early on in life: Martin and Halverson (1983) found that children frequently changed the sex of the actor performing sex-inconsistent activities when recalling previously presented pictures.

Quickly remind yourself of the **Key studies** using the special boxes in the text.

viii

Test your knowledge

The nature of attention

3.1 What are the three functions of attention?

3.2 What is the attentional spotlight?

3.3 Outline the zoom lens approach to visual attention.

3.4 Describe feature integration theory.

Answers to these questions can be found on the companion website at:
www.pearsoned.co.uk/psychologyexpress

Prepare for upcoming exams and tests using the **Test your knowledge** and **Sample question** features.

Answer guidelines

⁕ *Sample question*   *Essay*

Is the multi-store model of memory the most appropriate way to view memory?

Approaching the question

This question requires a broad knowledge of memory theory. You'll need to give an overview of the model in question before going on to present limitations and alternatives.

Important points to include

Start with an overview of the multi-store model, specifying each element and briefly describing each. Next, evaluate the model, presenting some of the shortcomings. These include the type of information being presented, individual differences in recall ability and oversimplification. To do just this would only

Compare your responses with the **Answer guidelines** in the text and on the website.

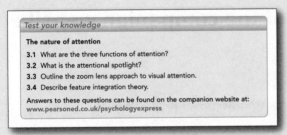

→ Make your answers stand out

Use the **Critical focus** boxes to impress your examiner with your deep and critical understanding.

CRITICAL FOCUS

Schema theory

Schemas allow us to take shortcuts in interpreting information. However, these shortcuts can mean that we may disregard relevant information in favour of information that confirms our pre-existing beliefs. This means that schemas can contribute to stereotypes and mislead by making it hard to retain new information not conforming to established schemas.

Although schema theories provide a comprehensive framework to explain the structure and organisation of knowledge in long-term memory, several problems exist. First is that there is no real consensus on the properties of schemas. This has led to a range of theories being proposed including Bartlett's schemata (1932), Schank and Abelson's

Make your answer stand out

In addition to doing all outlined above, the best answers will also examine what is meant by attention, drawing on Chun and Wolfe's (2000) work which has argued that attention is multifaceted, consisting of separate processes and loci of selection. Answers may also place the theories in their historical context – for example Broadbent's work was shaped by the information-processing approach prominent in cognitive psychology at the time, while later conceptualisations such as Chun and Wolfe's are influenced by computational theory.

Go into the exam with confidence using the handy tips to **make your answer stand out**.

Guided tour of the companion website

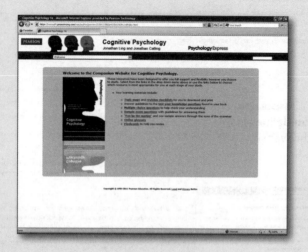

→ Understand key concepts quickly

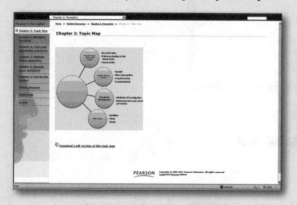

Printable versions of the **Topic maps** give an overview of the subject and help you plan your revision.

Test yourself on key definitions with the online **Flashcards**.

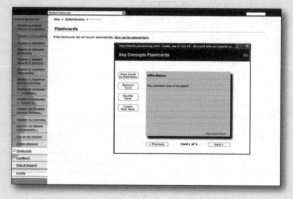

→ **Revise effectively**

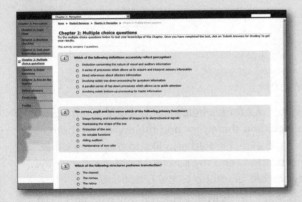

Check your understanding and practise for exams with the **Multiple choice questions**.

→ **Make your answers stand out**

Evaluate sample exam answers in the **You be the marker** exercises and understand how and why an examiner awards marks.

Put your skills into practice with the **Sample exam questions**, then check your answers with the guidelines.

**All this and more can be found at
www.pearsoned.co.uk/psychologyexpress**

Acknowledgements

Authors' acknowledgements

Jonathan Ling: I'm most grateful to J.C. for his help throughout this enterprise, and to the many other people, including the editor and the reviewers, both academic and student, for their guidance. I would also like to thank my other, better, half, for her patience and support, and my son for brightening my days. And finally, I wish to express my sincere gratitude to the proofreader.

Jonathan Catling: I would like to thank Jo, Isabel and Susie (my wife and kids) and also a big thank you to Lee Badham who was responsible for the artwork in Chapters 8–12.

Series editor's acknowledgements

I am grateful to Janey Webb and Jane Lawes at Pearson Education for their assistance with this series. I would also like to thank Penney, Francesca, Rosie and Gabriel for their dedication to psychology.

Dominic Upton

Publisher's acknowledgements

Our thanks go to all reviewers who contributed to the development of this text, including students who participated in research and focus groups which helped to shape the series format.

Dr Tina Byrom, Nottingham Trent University
Dr Derek Dorris, University College, Cork
Professor Alan Garnham, University of Sussex
Dr Kun Guo, University of Lincoln
Dr Lee Hadlington, De Montfort University
Mr Peter Karlsson, Lecturer at Halmstad University, Sweden
Dr James Stiller, Nottingham Trent University
Dr Richard Tunney, University of Nottingham

Student reviewers:
Steff Copestake, student at the University of Chester
Lindsay Pitcher, student at Anglia Ruskin University

1

A brief history of cognitive psychology

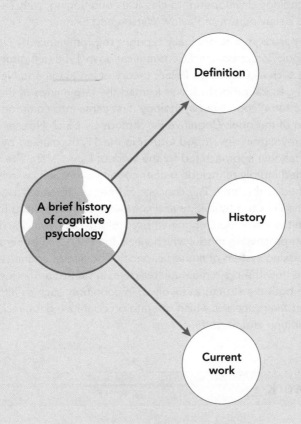

- Definition
- A brief history of cognitive psychology
- History
- Current work

A printable version of this topic map is available from:
www.pearsoned.co.uk/psychologyexpress

Definition

Cognitive psychology has been defined as the study of cognition; the mental processes that underlie human behaviour. This covers a wide range of subdisciplines including memory, learning, perception and problem solving.

History

Cognitive psychology has moved through several phases in its short history. From the work on introspection by Ebbinghaus at the end of the 19th century cognitive psychology developed into classical conditioning, with Thorndike and then on to the behaviourism of Pavlov, Watson and Skinner.

The cognitive paradigm was originally brought to prominence by Donald Broadbent's book *Perception and Communication* in 1958, although other developments such as Chomsky's (1956) theory of language and Newell and Simon's (1958) general problem solver formed the beginnings of the cognitive revolution. The term 'cognitive psychology' first came into common use with the publication of the book *Cognitive Psychology* by Ulrich Neisser in 1967. The cognitive revolution developed further in the 1970s, marked by a focus on the computational approach led by the work of David Marr. The subject matter expanded rapidly to include higher cognitive functions which were under-researched at the time. The concept of 'mental structures' became widely used and links to physiology and computer science started to be made. Since the cognitive revolution, cognitive psychology has been dominated by the information-processing model which views the mind as a general-purpose, symbolic processing system of limited capacity. The aim of cognitive psychology is to determine how the brain manipulates data. In particular the focus is on understanding both the structures involved in cognition, such as filters, lexicons and stores, and the processes which operate on cognitive data, including encoding, inhibition and forgetting.

Current work

Today the increasing sophistication of brain science, including the development of new technologies such as brain imaging, provides the possibility of the convergence of psychological and neurophysiological knowledge, and the emergence of new disciplines such as cognitive science and neuropsychology.

Overview of the book

Within this book we set out to highlight the key ideas, theories and debates within each of the key subdisciplines of cognitive psychology. However, we also highlight the potential applied nature of cognitive psychology, by looking at how people use basic cognitive skills in everyday environments, and how people use their knowledge to influence their behaviour in real-life situations. We also set out to highlight the interrelationships between each part of the cognitive system. The central areas are visual perception, attention, memory, language, thinking, decision making and human performance.

Further reading for Chapter 1

Bell, J. (2005). *Evaluating psychological information*. 4th ed. Harlow: Pearson.

Collins, S.C. & Kneale, P.E. (2000). *Study skills for psychology students*. London: Arnold.

Eysenck, M.W. (2010). *Cognitive psychology: A student's handbook*, 6th ed. Hove: Psychology Press.

Heffernan, T.M. (2005). *A student's guide to studying psychology*. 3rd ed. Hove: Psychology Press.

Scott, J.M., Koch, R., Scott, G.M. & Garrison, S.M. (2002). *The psychology student writer's manual*. 2nd ed. Harlow: Pearson.

Notes

Notes

2

Perception

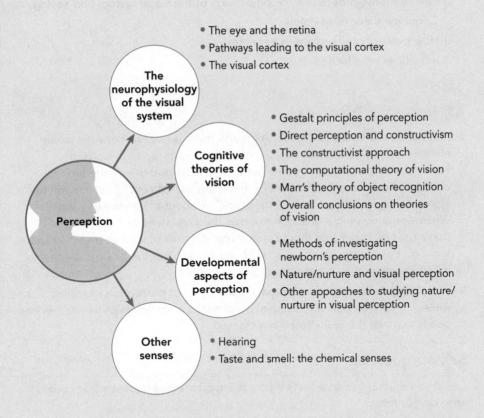

- The eye and the retina
- Pathways leading to the visual cortex
- The visual cortex

The neurophysiology of the visual system

Perception

Cognitive theories of vision

- Gestalt principles of perception
- Direct perception and constructivism
- The constructivist approach
- The computational theory of vision
- Marr's theory of object recognition
- Overall conclusions on theories of vision

Developmental aspects of perception

- Methods of investigating newborn's perception
- Nature/nurture and visual perception
- Other appoaches to studying nature/nurture in visual perception

Other senses

- Hearing
- Taste and smell: the chemical senses

A printable version of this topic map is available from:
www.pearsoned.co.uk/psychologyexpress

Introduction

Perception is a complicated series of processes through which we acquire and interpret sensory information. This interpretation allows us to perceive our environment in a meaningful way. Most perception courses focus mainly on the architecture of the visual system and theories of vision, and we've duplicated that emphasis in this chapter. You will also see briefer sections on audition and olfaction, though nothing on haptics (touch) as this topic is dealt with only rarely.

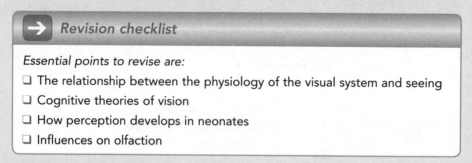

→ Revision checklist

Essential points to revise are:
☐ The relationship between the physiology of the visual system and seeing
☐ Cognitive theories of vision
☐ How perception develops in neonates
☐ Influences on olfaction

Assessment advice

- Perception is a broad discipline. Although there is overlap between some elements, most perception courses often teach sub-topics in isolation from each other: one week you'll get a lecture on gestalt and the next on perceptual constancies. This means that many assessment questions will be along the lines of 'What does X theory tell us about the nature of vision?' Whenever answering a question like this, if you're asked about a theory *don't* just talk about that theory – although the bulk of your answer may well focus on this theory, it's also crucial (if you want to get the highest grades) to introduce alternative perspectives.

- This chapter will adopt the approach used by most perception modules, where topics are dealt with in isolation of each other; however, where theories clearly contrast this will also be highlighted.

Sample question

Could you answer this question? Below is a typical essay question that could arise on this topic.

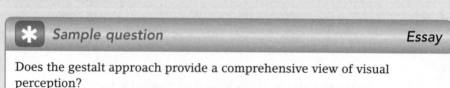

✳ Sample question   Essay

Does the gestalt approach provide a comprehensive view of visual perception?

Guidelines an answering this question are included at the end of this chapter, whilst guidance on tackling other exam questions can be found on the companion website at: **www.pearsoned.co.uk/psychlolgyexpress**

Further reading Perception

Key reading

Foley, H.J. & Matlin, M.W. (2010). *Sensation and perception*. 5th ed. Harlow: Pearson.

Schiffman, H.R. (2008). *Sensation and perception: An integrated approach*. 6th ed. Chichester: John Wiley.

Sekuler, R. & Blake, R. (2005). *Perception*. 5th ed. London: McGraw-Hill.

The neurophysiology of the visual system

Neurophysiology is the study of the responses of the nervous system to external stimulation. The focus is particularly on transduction – the conversion of energy (light, sound, etc.) into electrical signals – and visual perception provides a good example of this. The human visual system can be thought of as consisting of three separate segments – the eye, the visual pathways and the visual centres of the brain.

The eye and the retina

The structure of the eye

Our eyes serve two functions:

● forming an image of an object
● transducing images into electrochemical signals which are sent to the cortex via neural pathways.

We'll skip the non-visual parts which are primarily concerned with the protection, maintenance and shape of the eye and focus on those responsible for image formation.

The image-forming system

This consists of the cornea, pupil and lens (see Figure 2.1). Light enters through the cornea and is bent inward through the pupil to the lens, which focuses light on to the retina. The crystalline lens is most important for accommodation (focusing) to ensure clear images and can change shape to alter the eye's optical power. Problems like myopia and sclerosis occur when the lens loses flexibility.

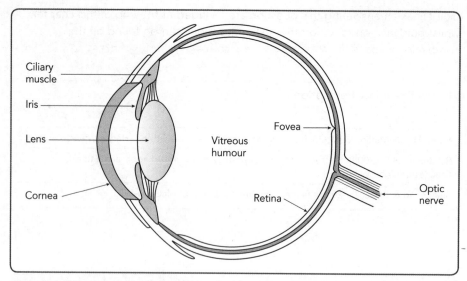

Figure 2.1 **The structure of the eye**

The transduction system: the retina

Located at the back of the eye, the retina is an outgrowth of the brain consisting of a thin and complex network of photoreceptor cells. The fovea (also called the macula) is a small depression in the retina densely packed with photoreceptors. The fovea has the best detail and the best colour sensation of anywhere in the eye, though it is less sensitive at low light levels. For the sharpest image, light is deflected onto the fovea.

There are three types of photoreceptor or retinal ganglion cells, the first two named for their appearance:

- *Rods*: operate at low light intensities, responsible for seeing at night, sensations are colourless. The human eye has about 120 million rods.
- *Cones*: operate at high light intensities, best during daylight, lead to colour sensations. Each eye has 8 million cones. Few cones are found around the periphery of the retina – where there is no colour vision.
- *Photosensitive ganglion cells*: help moderate circadian rhythms and pupil reaction, not involved directly with vision. Only discovered in humans by Zaidi et al. in 2007.

The optic disc (blind spot)

The optic disc is the point at which the axons of the retinal ganglion cells collect together and connect to the main body of the brain. There are no photoreceptor cells in this region, so this area of the retina is 'blind'.

Pathways leading to the visual cortex

Several pathways lead from the retina to the visual cortex (see Figure 2.2).

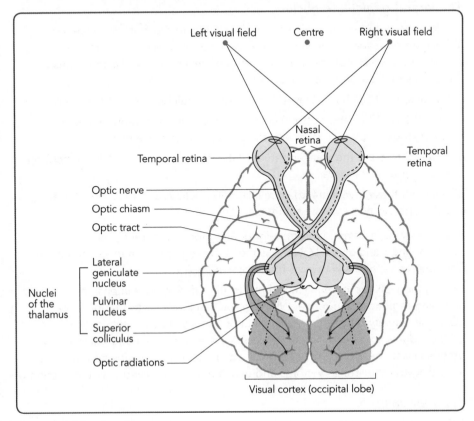

Figure 2.2 Visual pathways

The optic nerve

The optic nerve is the collection of axons leading to the visual centres of the brain from the eye. The optic nerve consists of retinal ganglion cells forming a cable of about a million axons. Axons are unmyelinated (that is, they have no outer cover) to reduce space. Fibres from different parts of the retina meet in the optic nerve in a very ordered fashion. The optic fibres transmit neural messages to the optic chiasm.

The optic chiasm

Optic neurons from each eye join at the optic chiasm. Some fibres within each optic nerve cross over and send impulses to the opposite side of the cerebral hemisphere. These are known as contralateral fibres; fibres that remain on the same side are the ipsilateral fibres. This means that messages dealing with any given region of the visual field arrive at a common destination in the visual cortex, regardless of the eye they came from. Both sets of fibres continue into the brain via the optic tracts. The optic tracts now contain fibres from both eyes.

The lateral geniculate nuclei

The left and right lateral geniculate nuclei (LGN) are the first relay station of fibres from the eyes on the way to the visual cortex. Here, axons from the retina terminate on the dendrites and cell bodies of new neurons. It is the axons of these cells that continue to the cortex.

In humans, the LGN has six layers which contain cell bodies and are stacked.

- Layers 1 and 2 (at the bottom) contain the largest cells, termed magnocellular layers; these are associated with the perception of movement.
- Layers 3 to 6 are the smaller parvocellular layers, associated with perception of colour and fine detail.
- Between these layers are koniocellular cells, believed to be connected to colour perception and the somatosensory system.

Axons carrying information from neighbouring regions of retina meet in neighbouring parts of the LGN. Thus the LGN recreates a 'map' of the image from the retina; this is known as retinotopic mapping.

Cells in the LGN are primarily concerned with differing light intensities between adjoining regions of the retina. Whilst this action is similar to that of retinal cells, LGN cells amplify differences in illumination detected by the retina. Whilst the LGN conducts some early visual processing, it also receives outputs from the other senses. Therefore it may be involved in filtering messages from the eyes according to other sensory inputs and hence may be involved in visual orienting.

Superior colliculus

This structure lies under the cerebrum and helps guide visual attention. If an object suddenly appears in the extremity of the visual field, it is the superior colliculus that guides eye movements so that the novel object can be observed optimally (i.e. using foveal vision).

The visual cortex

The visual cortex is located at the back of the cerebral hemispheres in the occipital lobes. Most visual processing takes place in the primary visual cortex (also known as the striate cortex or V1 area) and the extrastriate visual cortical areas (e.g. V2, V3, V4 and V5 regions).

The layout of cells in the primary visual cortex is highly ordered:

- cells are layered
- cells respond to stimulation of a restricted area of retina
- cells are highly organised and respond to particular stimulation producing a topographical map so each cerebral hemisphere deals with half of the visual field.

Mapping is spatially distorted so that the majority of the cortex is devoted to central (foveal) rather than peripheral vision – this is why we are better at picking out details from the centre of a scene rather than the periphery.

So far we have just considered what regions of the visual field cortical neurons are related to. We also need to think about what kind of information each cell is stimulated by.

Organisation within the visual cortex

Cells in the cortex are organised in columns (Hubel & Wiesel, 1977). Activation of these cells is dependent upon the input (e.g. length, width of stimulus), with different cells firing in response to specific inputs.

Cells in the visual cortex

Three main types of cell exist in the visual cortex:

1 Simple cells

- respond to particular stimuli (e.g. an edge or a line)
- only fire if an image falls exactly on a cell's receptive field (a region of the cell that responds to a specific stimulus)
- as responses are so specific, simple cells can signal the orientation of a stimulus falling within a particular region of the receptive field.

2 Complex cells

- also respond to particular orientations
- do not have such well-defined on and off areas; it is harder to predict what stimulus will cause activation
- respond most vigorously to a beam of light moving across the visual field.

3 Hypercomplex cells

- these cells detect lines of specific length
- recent research indicates these are subclasses of simple and complex cells.

Perceptual integration

One thing worth considering is how all this perceptual processing leads to a perception of the world that is so seamless. How does it become such a well-integrated whole if analysis is conducted across many regions of the brain, each of which has a separate analytical role? Current thought is that other, secondary, brain regions must be involved – in vision this blending of information is likely to be done in the visual association cortex, perhaps by guidance from the prefrontal cortex (Gazzaley & D'Esposito, 2007).

Further reading The biology of the visual system

Topic	Key reading
Visual cortex	Lennie, P. (1998). Single units and visual cortical organization. *Perception*, 27, 889–935.
Visual system	Nicholls, J.G., Martin, A.R. & Wallace, B.G. (1992). *From neuron to brain*. 3rd ed. Sunderland, MA: Sinauer.
Photosensitive retinal ganglion cells	Zaidi, F.H., Hull, J.T., Peirson, S.N., et al. (2007). Short-wavelength light sensitivity of circadian, pupillary, and visual awareness in humans lacking an outer retina. *Current Biology*, 17, 2122–8. Available from: http://www.ncbi.nlm.nih.gov/pmc/articles/PMC2151130/

Test your knowledge

The biology of the visual system

2.1 Name the image-forming structures of the eye.

2.2 What are the three types of retinal cells and what are their functions?

2.3 What does retinotopic mapping mean?

2.4 Describe the main types of cells in the V1 area.

Answers to these questions can be found on the companion website at: **www.pearsoned.co.uk/psychologyexpress**

 Sample question   Essay

Describe the organisation of the visual system from eye to cortex.

Cognitive theories of vision

Perceptual organisation is the process of organising components of a scene into separate objects. This segregation is crucial to object recognition. Several theories have attempted to explain how we do this.

Gestalt principles of perception

The gestalt approach focuses on form, arguing that it cannot be comprehended by merely looking at individual components. Form is dependent on the relationship *between* individual elements, rather than the elements themselves. The gestalt approach is holistic, in the sense that the whole is different from the sum of its parts.

Gestalt theory attempts to explain how the human perceptual system uses a range of principles to detect form, known as the *gestalt principles of organisation*. These principles are a series of factors believed to aid the perception of forms and promote their grouping. The gestaltists termed this detection of form (i.e. object shape) figure-ground segregation. These principles were, according to the gestaltists, innate.

Gestalt principles of organisation

These were developed principally by Wertheimer, though more recent work by Rock and Palmer (1990) has added further ones (connectedness and common region, see below). The fundamental gestalt principle of perceptual organisation is Prägnanz. In this law, the simplest and most stable interpretations are favoured: elements of this law can be seen in all of the laws outlined in the list below.

- Proximity: the tendency to group objects that are close to one another together as a perceptual unit or group.
- Similarity: alike items tend to be grouped.
- Closure: contours close to one another are likely to be united.
- Good continuation: two (or more) neighbouring components of a scene are grouped when they appear to be connected by say a straight or smooth line.
- Common fate: objects moving in the same direction will be perceived as related.
- Common region: elements will be grouped together when they are enclosed by a defined boundary.
- Uniform connectedness: elements that appear to be connected are more likely to be grouped.
- Meaningfulness or familiarity: objects are more likely to form groups when the elements appear meaningful.

CRITICAL FOCUS

The Gestalt approach

Problems with innate view

The gestaltists believed that perceptual organisation resulted from innate processes. Although some perceptual abilities do appear to have an innate component (see the section Developmental aspects of perception, p. 21), there is other evidence to support the idea that perception has a learnt component. For example, Segall, Campbell and Herskovits (1966) found that people from environments where straight lines are rare, such as rural South Africa, were less susceptible to the Müller–Lyer illusion than people from Western cultures. This influence of environmental knowledge is a problem for the gestalt approach which argues that perception is bottom-up – understanding a scene comes from application of the organisational principles – rather than being top-down, based on prior knowledge.

Difficulties applying laws

The fundamental principle of Prägnanz is not always easy to demonstrate in practice – people may view the same figure in very different ways (see e.g., Quinlan & Wilton, 1998) or perceptions of the same figure might change over time. This is hard to reconcile with the idea that we have an innate drive towards simplicity. The primacy of the laws has also been questioned by Julesz (1975) who found that participants also grouped forms according to their colour and brightness, rather than only using gestalt principles.

Descriptive rather than explanatory

The gestalt approach describes rather than explains. Although some gestaltists attempted to explain their theories by electrical field forces in the brain, empirical investigations have failed to support these. Where presented, explanations tend also to be post hoc: the description of form is always prior to the explanation of why the form is perceived. This makes it hard to generate predictions from this theory.

Other problems with the gestalt approach

Any theory of form perception must explain how form information is presented within the visual system, both initially and leading up to and including recognition. Gestaltists fail to say why these rules are necessary, and they have also been criticised for using vague language, with Bruce, Georgeson and Green (2003) arguing that it is difficult to understand clearly what is meant when gestaltists refer to a 'good' or 'simple' shape.

Conclusions

The gestalt approach is a plausible account of some of the processes of form perception. There is also evidence that some of the gestalt principles hold for other domains, such as music and haptics.

The focus on stimulus characteristics to understand the larger whole has had implications for more recent work which has continued this stimulus-based (bottom-up) interest. Some of the strategies (e.g. proximity) forwarded by the gestaltists were used by Marr (1982) as part of his computational approach to vision (see below). Gestalt principles have also been utilised in the work examining aesthetics in human–computer interaction.

Further reading Gestalt theory

Topic	Key reading
Discussion of the gestalt approach	Rock, I. (1995). *Perception*. New York: Scientific American.
Gestalt and neuropsychology	Herrmann, C.S. & Bosch, V. (2001). Gestalt perception modulates early visual processing. *Neuroreport, 12,* 901–4.

Test your knowledge

Gestalt theory

2.5 How did the gestaltists suggest form is extracted?

2.6 Describe the law of Prägnanz.

2.7 What is figure-ground segregation?

2.8 List four shortcomings of gestalt theory.

Answers to these questions can be found on the companion website at:
www.pearsoned.co.uk/psychologyexpress

 Sample question   *Essay*

Critically evaluate the gestalt approach to perception.

Direct perception and constructivism

The direct perception approach

Gibson (e.g. 1979) developed direct perception as an ecological approach to space perception. He argued attention should be on cues present in the environment rather than taking the retinal image as the starting point for perceptual processing.

According to Gibson, information is detected rather than processed: the visual environment provides sufficient information to allow interaction with the environment without the need for any further internal processing. Stimuli are not described in terms of passive images on the retina (cf. Marr's computational approach, below) but in terms of actively sampled information in the environment, termed the optic array.

Gibson argued that individuals perceive objects, not the planes, lightness discontinuities or primitive object shapes proposed by other theories. Because direct perception relies on information presented in the environment and rejects the idea of active processing it is a bottom-up theory.

Several cues exist that give an observer information about the environment. These include:

- *Optic flow pattern*: the apparent motion of objects in the environment caused by the relative motion between the observer and the scene.
- *Texture gradient*: this provides information about distance; elements become more densely packed, and decrease in size as distance increases.
- *Horizon ratio*: if two objects standing on the ground are the same size, their horizon ratios will be the same. This allows observers to judge the relative size of objects.

- *Direct perception* is an ecological approach: Gibson argued we should examine perception in the real world. His theory makes strong links between perception and action where the individual and the environment interact. For Gibson the end result of perception is not an internal representation of the visual environment but an awareness of possibilities to interact with the environment. These opportunities are termed affordances – a branch can be graspable, a fruit can be eaten.

CRITICAL FOCUS

The direct perception approach

Direct perception is both radical and controversial. Gibson emphasised the significance of environmental cues on perception which are neglected by other approaches. Although research on illusions (see the constructivist approach, below) does initially appear to contradict direct perception, Gibson stated that picture perception is indirect and so conclusions about real-world perception drawn from the use of pictures will be invalid: making inappropriate judgements is unsurprising, and unlikely to occur with more ecologically valid stimuli.

A strength of direct perception is in the way it focused later researchers on the interaction of individuals with their environments, away from the growing tendency to examine perception out of context with simple stimuli such as bars and grids.

Nonetheless, there are several limitations to Gibson's theory. Fodor and Pylyshyn (1981) argued that some of the terms used by Gibson, such as 'directly detected' and 'invariant', are so broadly defined as to be almost meaningless. In addition, the argument that anything we perceive is due to invariant properties of stimulation that require no further processing is difficult to accept because it implies we have invariants specifying friends' faces that do not require any stored memory that will enable us to recognise each of them appropriately.

Perceptual processes are also significantly more complicated than implied by Gibson. Marr (1982), Ullman (1980) and others have also pointed out that the detection of physical invariants such as image surfaces and optic flow is in itself an information-processing problem that requires significant effort.

The constructivist approach

Constructivist theory, or intelligent perception, proposes that the perceiver has an internal constructive (problem-solving) process which transforms an incoming stimulus into a percept. The constructivist approach is therefore active. Perception is an end product of a series of interactions between the initial stimulus, internal representations, memory and expectations. If these expectations are incorrect, misperceptions (e.g. visual illusions) occur.

Depth perception and constructivism: illusions

The retinal image is two-dimensional, and so the perceiver has to add depth to create a third dimension. This is accomplished by a range of cues including size constancy, perspective and stereopsis. Gregory (1997) investigated how such cues aid perception by examining the conditions in which they broke down to give perceptual errors.

Gregory (1997) argued that visual illusions, such as the Müller–Lyer and Poggendorff, occur when there is a conflict between cues in the scene and the retinal images (see Figure 2.3). The fact that children are less susceptible to some illusions gives further support to the constructivist approach because they will have had less experience of using cues to estimate alignment or length (e.g. Leibowitz & Gwozdecki, 1967).

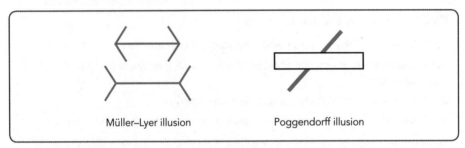

Müller–Lyer illusion   Poggendorff illusion

Figure 2.3 The Müller–Lyer and Poggendorff illusions

CRITICAL FOCUS

The constructivist approach

The constructivist approach has led to the discovery of a range of visual cues which influence perception. However, the strong view of this theory has been criticised. For example, the explanations forwarded for the operation of visual illusions are often unsatisfactory or contradictory – Gregory explains the Müller–Lyer illusion by reference to depth cues existing within the shapes, though Day (1972) argues it is the presence of conflicting cues rather than depth cues specifically that cause the illusion.

Others have criticised the artificial nature of the tasks used to produce perceptual errors, as well as the reliance on very brief presentations of stimuli. Recent work has tried to reconcile the constructivist and direct perception approaches (Norman, 2002), though fundamentally the constructivist view is that perception guides behaviour (Möller, 2000).

Further reading Direct perception and constructivism

Topic	Key reading
Constructivism	Gregory, R.L. (1997). *Eye and brain: The psychology of seeing.* Oxford: Oxford University Press.
Direct perception	Michaels, C.F. & Carello, C. (1981). *Direct perception.* Englewood Cliffs, NJ: Prentice-Hall.
Constructivism and direct perception	Norman, J. (2002). Two visual systems and two theories of perception: An attempt to reconcile the constructivist and ecological approaches. *Behavioral and Brain Sciences, 25,* 73–144.

Test your knowledge

Direct perception and constructivism

2.9 What did Gibson mean when he said perception was direct?

2.10 Outline two strengths and two weakness of the direct perception approach.

2.11 How do constructivists argue illusions operate?

2.12 Outline two criticisms of the constructivist approach to perception.

Answers to these questions can be found on the companion website at: www.pearsoned.co.uk/psychologyexpress

 Sample question   Essay

Critically evaluate the contribution of direct perception to our understanding of visual perception.

The computational theory of vision

The computational approach developed by Marr (1982) is based on the information-processing perspective which divides processes into a series of (definable) steps, part based on the information available from the environment (similar to direct perception theory) and part on calculation of these inputs.

Marr sought to avoid general theoretical debates to focus on understanding specific problems, the most fundamental being that of recognition: when we recognise things what is it that we are we doing? What is it that allows us to read very different types of handwriting and letters in different fonts and to recognise caricatures with apparent ease?

Marr's theory of object recognition

Marr's (1982) theory proceeds from the two-dimensional information presented on the retina through a series of stages to a three-dimensional perceptual representation (see Figure 2.4).

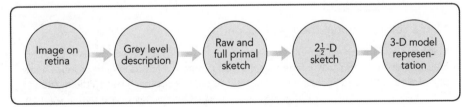

Figure 2.4 Stages in Marr's computational theory of vision.

1 **Grey level description**. The intensity of light at each point in the visual field is made explicit. Colour information is not processed.

2 **Raw primal sketch**. The representation of the image in terms of edges, which are computed by detecting differences in light intensity. The visual system applies rules – termed natural constraints – about the environment, such as the idea that gradual changes in shading are associated with shadows and sharp changes are usually edges. The visual system also identifies primitives such as blobs, bars and terminations that are combined with information about the location of edges as the raw primal sketch.

3 **Full primal sketch**. Raw elements are assembled to represent larger structures in the full primal sketch. Marr suggested we use simple grouping processes (analogous to those suggested by gestalt theorists) to link these features together to give a basic object outline. A problem here is that the visual system needs to decide what an edge is. For example, two similarly coloured objects which are illuminated similarly may be difficult to discriminate.

4 **2½-D sketch**. This describes the layout of structures in the world from a single perspective by integrating a variety of cues. In addition to the structures obtained from the primal sketch, perception of the scene is developed through analysis of depth and object motion. Reconstructing depth from flat retinal images is difficult. Numerous methods are used to accomplish depth perception, including stereopsis, shading and structure from motion. Through these, the 2½-D sketch can compute all necessary information about objects (outline, distance, size etc.). This representation is 2½-D because the sketch is viewer-centred and is superficial in that it does not draw any conclusions about three-dimensional structures.

5 **3-D model representation**. This aspect of Marr's theory is the least well-developed. In this stage, object recognition and computation of a three-dimensional image requires information about an object's identity and therefore stored knowledge. At this stage there will be a range of processes

that aid such categorisation, some of which Marr and Nishihara (1978) developed into a theory of object recognition. Marr argues that people recognise objects from their individual components – the process likely to underlie our ability to recognise people from their caricatures.

CRITICAL FOCUS

Marr's computational theory of vision

Marr's model is *relatively* simple, though each stage involves significant computation. Marr and Hildreth (1980) developed a computer program that was able to produce a raw primal sketch. Although plausible for machine vision, this approach bears little relation to human vision, especially on a physical level, so at best provides only a partial solution, particularly given its focus on bottom-up processing. Nonetheless, Marr stimulated much theoretical and empirical work, both in neuroscience (see, e.g., Deco & Rolls, 2007) and artificial intelligence, such as automatic face recognition (Bicego et al., 2008).

Further reading Computational theory of vision

Topic	Key reading
Detailed introduction to computational theory	Bruce, V., Georgeson, M.A. & Green, P.R. (2003). *Visual perception: Physiology, psychology and ecology.* Hove: Psychology Press.
Detailed discussion of computational approach	Frisby, J.P. & Stone, J.V. (2010). *Seeing: The computational approach to biological vision.* Cambridge, MA: MIT Press.
Application of computational theory	Sarkar, S. & Boyer, K.L. (1993). Perceptual organization in computer vision. *IEEE Transactions on Systems, Man & Cybernetics, 23,* 383–99.

Test your knowledge

Computational theory of vision

2.13 On which approach did Marr base his theory?

2.14 What are the stages of Marr's computational theory of vision?

2.15 What is the difference between a raw and a full primal sketch?

2.16 Describe top-down and bottom-up processing.

Answers to these questions can be found on the companion website at: **www.pearsoned.co.uk/psychologyexpress**

 Sample question   Essay

Critically evaluate the contribution of Marr's computational theory to the understanding of vision.

Overall conclusions on theories of vision

Several theories have attempted to explain the process of visual perception. These can be viewed as forming a continuum from those reliant entirely on information present in the environment, like direct perception, to those that adopt a bottom-up perspective, such as the computational approach. However, what must be understood is that all these theories are only partial explanations – vision works through cues in the optic array, but also operates through comparing differences in shading gradients and comparing percepts with memories. Other approaches also make useful contributions, such as the gestalt emphasis on stimulus configuration for object perception. Further theories like Biederman's recognition by components (RBC), which suggests objects are analysed into primitives to aid recognition, and Triesman's feature integration theory (FIT), which focuses on the attentional aspects of vision, both include aspects of top-down (knowledge-based) processing largely neglected by Marr.

Developmental aspects of perception

A fundamental question asked in perceptual development is 'What can a newborn infant perceive?' In trying to answer this, researchers have investigated the extent to which infants are born with perceptual capabilities or if they are acquired through experience (i.e. the nature/nurture debate). There are a range of views:

1 **Empiricists**: infants are a 'tabula rasa' (blank slate) upon which experiences are imprinted.
2 **Nativists**: many perceptual abilities are present at birth, e.g. for the gestalt school, the tendency to organise is innate.
3 **Current status**: combination of both approaches – babies are born with some abilities, but they also have a great capacity for learning (e.g. Mehler & Dupoux, 1994).

Researchers have attempted to pinpoint the contribution of each influence.

Methods of investigating newborns' perception

Habituation and the preferential looking technique

Infants spend less time looking at familiar stimuli. Therefore if the infant spends little time looking at a new stimulus, it means they cannot discriminate between this and the previous stimulus. This technique is effective for finding out the extent of the difference there needs to be between two stimuli for an infant to detect difference. Habituation is useful for testing ability to discriminate colour, brightness and shape (e.g. Fantz, 1961). Results show that by 1 month infants can distinguish between objects (i.e. they show a preference for a particular object) and by 3 months they can recognise their mothers' faces (and also show preference for all faces).

Conditioning

This is a more difficult method to employ, but is useful in determining whether children have perceptual constancies. For example, by giving them a 'peek-a-boo' response as a reward, Bower (1965) conditioned infants to turn to the left whenever they saw a 30 cm cube presented 1 m away. Infants responded to a 90 cm cube 3 m away, indicating that infants have size constancy.

Physiological responses

Heart rate increases in response to scary noises or sights. Thus if a child is held over a drop and her heart rate increases, she is able to see (and understand) distance.

None of the above methods can be used without difficulty as infants can easily become distracted and sometimes responses can be ambiguous. Nonetheless, if similar findings are obtained using different techniques then greater confidence can be placed in them.

Nature/nurture and visual perception

The infant visual system is functional, but tends to be inferior to that of an adult. For instance, Atkinson and Braddick (1981) found newborns had much poorer acuity, and only detected lines 30 times wider than those an adult could pick up.

Infant visual perception has been widely investigated, for example in pattern perception (especially human faces) and space perception (especially depth perception and size constancies). We'll focus on the latter topic.

Spatial perception in newborns

There has been a focus on 'constancies'. Shape constancy was investigated by Slater and Morison (1975), who habituated infants to a shape before showing them the same shape from a novel angle. The infants were uninterested, which shows they have shape constancy from birth. Distance constancy also appears to be innate (Bower, 1965).

KEY STUDY

Gibson and Walk (1960) investigated depth perception using a visual cliff. They argued that if depth perception is absent, a child would crawl off the edge of the cliff. Infants as young as 6 months would not crawl over the edge, which indicates binocular disparity is fully developed early on. Other research that monitored heart rates supports this conclusion.

Other approaches to studying nature/nurture in visual perception

What's the case for environmental influences on perception? Investigations into the effect of the environment have usually been conducted on animals for ethical reasons and have either deprived sensory experience or manipulated it.

Absence of stimulation

Animals are reared in dark conditions for several months from birth before being tested using lights or patterned stimuli. Such animals have difficulty discriminating between patterns. Although they can detect light, neurons in the retina and visual cortex show atrophy.

Hubel and Wiesel (e.g. 1962) concluded that light stimulation is needed to develop the visual system. In particular, there appears to be a 'critical period' during which external stimulation is needed. In kittens this is 4–6 weeks for vision. If deprived of visual stimulation during this critical period there will be a subsequent loss of perceptual ability.

Manipulation of experience

Where exposure is manipulated, there is a significant influence on later visual ability. For example, Leventhal and Hirsch (1977) found kittens raised without exposure to patterned stimuli could still detect orientation but this was only monocular. Similarly, restricting vision to horizontal lines leads to an inability to detect vertical ones (Stryker & Sherk, 1975).

Limited stimulation in humans

While it is unethical to deliberately deprive humans, naturally occurring deprivation can occur. Infants who have had to wear an eye patch after surgery for cataracts in their first year of life have reduced acuity in the deprived eye. This indicates that there is a critical period in infant development for visual perception, although recent work suggests that there are different critical periods for different aspects of perception (Lewis & Maurer, 2005).

Overall implications and summary

Extensive experience is not absolutely necessary for normal perception. However, certain types of stimulation are needed during critical periods. These critical periods are likely to occur in most modalities and for all species. Recent work indicates that there is some degree of hardwiring for facial processing that is qualitatively different from that present for other visual stimuli (Park, Newman & Polk, 2009), though work with monkeys shows these are also likely to require appropriate stimulation to function effectively (Sugita, 2008).

Perception is therefore shaped by a number of influences: sensory apparatus present at birth, basic sensory inputs (e.g. visual information) and subsequent experiences (e.g. knowledge can facilitate recognition – a farm scene would facilitate recognition of a cow).

Further reading Developmental aspects of perception

Topic	Key reading
Sensitive periods in child development	Lewis, T.L. & Maurer, D. (2005). Multiple sensitive periods in human visual development: Evidence from visually deprived children. *Developmental Psychobiology, 46,* 163–83.
Perceptual capacities of infants	Spelke, E.S. (1990). Principles of object perception. *Cognitive Science, 14,* 29–56.
Detailed discussion of perceptual development	Kellman, P.J. & Arterberry, M.E. (1998). *The cradle of knowledge: Development of perception in infancy.* Cambridge, MA: MIT Press.
Overview of perception	Smith, P.K., Cowie, H. & Blades, M. (2003). *Understanding children's development.* 4th ed. Oxford: Blackwell.

Test your knowledge

Development aspects of perception

2.17 Describe three methods of examining infant perceptual development.

2.18 What evidence is there to support the presence of depth perception in infants?

2.19 Define critical periods.

2.20 How might a newborn's perceptual development be influenced by experience?

Answers to these questions can be found on the companion website at:
www.pearsoned.co.uk/psychologyexpress

 Sample question   *Essay*

Evaluate the extent to which environmental factors influence perceptual development.

Other senses

Hearing

Hearing is the perceptual experience of sound, and is used both for signalling – to alert to danger – and for communication. Human hearing is very sensitive, able to detect sounds between 20 and 20,000 Hz and having a dynamic range of 150 dB.

The auditory system: structure and function

The auditory system must perform three functions before we can hear: deliver acoustic information to the receptors, transduce sounds into electrical signals and process the signals to indicate qualities of sounds such as location, volume and pitch.

Outer ear

Sound passes through the pinna (ears) into the auditory canal. Sound waves resonate along this to the tympanic membrane, or eardrum.

Middle ear

The middle ear is a cavity containing three small bones or ossicles – the malleus, incus and stapes – which transmit vibrations from the tympanic membrane to the membrane covering the oval window which leads to the inner ear. These ossicles increase the strength of sound-related vibrations from the air to allow them to transmit through the oval window to the fluid in the cochlea.

Inner ear

The fluid-filled cochlea contains the organ of Corti which contains inner and outer hair cells. These cells are covered in cilia which bend in response to movements by the organ of Corti, and the basilar and tectorial membranes. The motion of the cilia leads to the transduction of sounds. Early theorists such as Helmholtz (see also Braun, 1996) suggested that hearing worked via the vibration of these cilia; however, current theories propose that hearing works through detecting a wave of sound travelling through the structures of the ear.

Auditory pathways

The auditory nerve carries electrical signals from the cochlea to the cochlear nucleus and then to the olivary nucleus in the brainstem, the inferior colliculus of the midbrain and the medial geniculate nucleus of the thalamus. Neurons then connect with the primary auditory receiving area in the temporal lobe of the cortex, known as A1, which in turn links to other auditory regions in the temporal lobe.

Subjective dimensions of sound

Early theories of hearing assumed a direct relationship between environmental sounds and their mental representation, so that for instance the physical dimension of frequency corresponded with the subjective dimension of pitch. Research shows that the experience of sounds is both complex and subjective (von Békésy, 1960), and that perception of loudness and pitch are influenced by other variables including intensity, perceived location, auditory adaptation and auditory fatigue. Disorders including autism (Khalfa et al., 2004) and psychiatric illness (Iakovides et al., 2004) may also influence hearing.

Auditory scene perception

When we hear sounds they are rarely presented in isolation: sounds come from a range of sources at different amplitudes and frequencies. To make sense of this, we must analyse the information presented. Auditory scene analysis is a complicated process in which the sounds presented are compared to knowledge about the events that might have generated them (Bregman, 1990). Auditory scenes are interpreted in two ways – by auditory grouping using schemas derived from prior knowledge and by using grouping mechanisms similar to those proposed by the gestaltists for visual perception. Therefore, sounds are interpreted through the use of a combination of bottom-up and top-down processes.

Further reading Audition	
Topic	*Key reading*
Auditory scene analysis	Bregman, A.S. 1990. *Auditory scene analysis.* Cambridge, MA: MIT Press.
Speech understanding	Greenberg, S. (1996). Understanding speech understanding: Towards a unified theory of speech perception. *Proceedings of the ESCA Workshop on the Auditory Basis of Speech Perception,* Keele University, pp. 1–8.
Psychoacoustics	Moore, B.C.J. (2004). *An introduction to the psychology of hearing.* London: Academic Press.

Test your knowledge

Hearing

2.21 What are the structures and function of the inner ear?

2.22 Describe the auditory pathways in the brain.

2.23 What factors can influence subjective perception of sound?

Answers to these questions can be found on the companion website at: **www.pearsoned.co.uk/psychologyexpress**

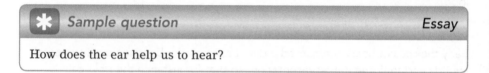

✳ Sample question

Essay

How does the ear help us to hear?

Taste and smell: the chemical senses

Although smell and taste are linked, smell is 10,000 times more sensitive than taste. Some animals are more sensitive than others to odours – rats are around 8 times more sensitive to odours than humans, dogs approximately 90 times.

Animals with high olfactory acuity are known as macrosmatic. They usually have a large olfactory epithelium compared to humans. Humans are microsmatic, having little olfactory sensitivity compared to other species (though some people may be macrosmatic compared to others).

Although in many animals odours play a significant role in attraction, in humans the link is more contentious. Research on the effects of odour on mood and on menstrual synchrony between women in close proximity (the 'McClintock effect') has also been criticised.

What are we smelling?

There are three characteristics of detectable odours:

- *Volatile* – must easily evaporate at normal temperatures so that molecules of the substance can be carried through the air
- *Water-soluble* – molecules must pass through mucus coating the inner surface of the nasal cavity to reach the olfactory cells
- *Lipid-soluble* – the olfactory hairs are composed primarily of lipids and the surface of the olfactory cells also contain lipids.

Anatomy of olfaction

Odours are detected by the olfactory mucosa located high in the nasal cavity. The olfactory mucosa is linked up to the olfactory bulb, an outcropping of the brain, where odour processing begins. Vertebrates' noses appear to connect to two sensory channels, olfaction and the vomeronasal system.

In the olfactory system, neurons' cilia contain olfactory receptor proteins that transport odorant molecules. Several types of proteins exist which allow sensation of a wide range of odours. In addition to these, free nerve endings enable responses to intense odours (e.g. ammonia).

The role of vomeronasal organs (VNO) is less clear. Although they generate electrical signals, they bypass the olfactory bulb but link to the limbic system, the area of the brain concerned with emotional responses. Damage to the VNO system in animals produces disturbances in sexual behaviour, so some have theorised this is the organ upon which pheromones act.

What determines what we smell?

Several variables impact on our ability to detect odours.

- *Pathology*. Olfaction degrades when we have a cold as the mucus in the nasal cavity becomes too thick for odour molecules to penetrate. Pathology can also lead to changes in sensitivity with Alzheimer's disease (Waldton, 1974), brain tumours and schizophrenia all associated with disturbances to smell.
- *Age*. In a study with 1.2 million participants, Wysocki and Gilbert (1989) found olfaction was best in people aged from mid-20s to late 40s. From 60, sense of smell tends to worsen, though there are large individual differences.

- *Sex.* Women are better than men at recognising most common odours; men tend to be better at detecting stronger odours (Cain, 1982). Brand and Millot (2001) argue this is for evolutionary reasons due to a sexual division of labour.
- *Smoking.* Higher levels of smoking leads to greater impairment. Smoking affects non-smokers, though it returns to normal on cessation. Air pollution also influences olfaction.
- *Visual impairment.* Blind people may have better olfaction than sighted.
- *Smell and memory.* Smell and memory are closely linked, with odour memory showing less decay than other sensory memory. The 'Proust effect' is where a memory associated with an odour can be invoked by that odour.

Research has shown that recall can be enhanced if learning was done in the presence of an odour and that same odour is presented at the time of recall – useful for exam revision!

Further reading Olfaction

Topic	Key reading
Mood and olfaction	Black, S.L. (2001). Does smelling granny relieve depressive mood? Commentary on 'Rapid mood change and human odors'. *Biological Psychology, 55*, 215–18.
Sex differences in ocular detection	Brand, G. & Millot, J-L. (2001). Sex differences in human olfaction: Between evidence and enigma. *Quarterly Journal of Experimental Psychology B, 54B*, 259–70.
Physiology of olfaction	Brewer, W.J., Castle, D. & Pantelis, C. (2006). *Olfaction and the brain.* Cambridge: Cambridge University Press.

Test your knowledge

Olfaction

2.24 Define macrosmatic, microsmatic and anosmia.

2.25 What are the three characteristics of detectable odours?

2.26 List four variables that could influence smell.

Answers to these questions can be found on the companion website at: **www.pearsoned.co.uk/psychologyexpress**

 Sample question   **Essay**

Review the research that has examined individual differences in olfaction.

Chapter summary – pulling it all together

→ Can you tick all of the points from the revision checklist at the beginning of this chapter?

→ Attempt all of the Test yourself questions.

→ Attempt the essay questions within the chapter using the guidelines below.

→ Go to the companion website at www.pearsoned.co.uk/psychologyexpress to access more revision support online, including interactive quizzes, flash cards, You be the marker exercises as well as answer guidance for the Test yourself and Sample questions from this chapter.

Answer guidelines

 Sample question **Essay**

Critically evaluate the gestalt approach to perception.

Approaching the question

This question is asking you to assess the value of the gestalt approach. Like many questions you'll be given at higher levels of study, you'll need to give both sides of the argument, before drawing some conclusions based on the balance of evidence. It's easy to get sidetracked into giving a very full account of gestalt theory, but the real marks are to be gained in addressing the *contribution* of the theory, not the fine detail.

Important points to include

To answer this question an overview of the gestalt approach is necessary. This overview will cover the key theorists, the concentration on form, and – briefly – the gestalt principles, the most important of which is Prägnanz. The next part of your answer should evaluate the contribution of the theory to visual perception: that it is generally a plausible account of some perceptual processes, and has made a significant contribution to research on visual perception in its focus on stimulus characteristics as part of a bottom-up approach to perception. There are several problems with the theory, and these include the innate perspective it takes and the often descriptive nature of the theory. When it comes to the conclusion, refer back to the question – is it a *comprehensive* view? Although the theory has made a significant contribution to theoretical approaches to visual perception, the gestalt approach does not give a comprehensive view of the different stages of visual perception, unlike other theories such as Marr's computational approach.

Make your answer stand out

Most people answering a question on gestalt will have a reasonable idea of some of the principles and perhaps one or two of the criticisms of the theory. Better answers will give more comprehensive coverage to both theory and shortcomings, the very best answers will make reference to specific researchers, and, in particular draw on more recent research that has used the gestalt approach, such as work on human–computer interaction (e.g. Tractinsky & Hassenzahl, 2005).

Explore the accompanying website at **www.pearsoned.co.uk/psychologyexpress**

→ Prepare more effectively for exams and assignments using the answer guidelines for questions from this chapter.

→ Test your knowledge using multiple choice questions and flashcards.

→ Improve your essay skills by exploring the You be the marker exercises.

Notes

3

Attention

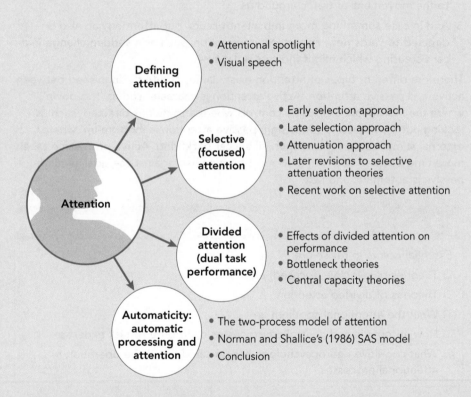

- Defining attention
  - Attentional spotlight
  - Visual speech

- Selective (focused) attention
  - Early selection approach
  - Late selection approach
  - Attenuation approach
  - Later revisions to selective attenuation theories
  - Recent work on selective attention

- Attention

- Divided attention (dual task performance)
  - Effects of divided attention on performance
  - Bottleneck theories
  - Central capacity theories

- Automaticity: automatic processing and attention
  - The two-process model of attention
  - Norman and Shallice's (1986) SAS model
  - Conclusion

A printable version of this topic map is available from:
www.pearsoned.co.uk/psychologyexpress

Introduction

Attention allows us to select the information that is most relevant for us at a particular point in time. We need to be able to attend to the important information while filtering out the irrelevant. This is accomplished in three ways:

1 Selectively attending to some information while filtering out other inputs, such as listening to a traffic update on the car radio while phasing out the noise of the engine.

2 Modulating or enhancing the attended-to information according to our needs. For example, we may apply a little of our attentional capacity to the noise the engine is making when we drive, and a great deal of our resources to the movement of traffic around us.

3 And in case something more important occurs, our attention can also be directed towards new, important, information, such as a sudden change in a car's steering which might indicate a flat tyre.

Therefore different types of attention exist: James (1890) distinguished between active and passive attention. Active attention is characterised as 'top-down', where the individual consciously controls where attention is directed, such as looking out for a specific street sign; passive attention is 'bottom-up' where external stimuli draw our attention, like a car backfiring. Active processing takes more time because each stimulus must be matched against the goal in mind; passive is automatic and fast.

> **➡ Revision checklist**
>
> *Essential points to revise are:*
> - ❏ Theories of selective (focused) attention
> - ❏ Theories of divided attention
> - ❏ What the attentional spotlight is
> - ❏ How automatic and controlled processes contribute to task expertise
> - ❏ What cognitive neuropsychology has revealed about the operation of attentional processes

Assessment advice

● Getting the basics of attention right isn't too difficult. With selective attention research in particular there's a clear historical sequence, backed up with an increasingly nuanced approach to the evaluation of the data. The best approach to understanding selective and divided attention is to sketch out a timeline of the research. Once you become familiar with this progression, and the central claims of each theory, develop your knowledge of the studies carried out to support (or reject) these claims.

- Appreciating the link between theory and research is crucial to getting the highest grades, as is citing evidence to support the points that you make. Widen your reading beyond the textbooks by getting a couple of recent papers on attention. There are some useful reviews (some of which we refer to below) which will help deepen your understanding.

- A word of caution: some of the research published on attention can be challenging, so before you pick up the latest cutting-edge journal paper, ensure you first understand the basics. Do this, and you'll get much more from the article.

- Attention assessments commonly focus on just one of the topics shown in the topic map – there's too much theory to deal with more than one of these in an exam question. However, it is important to consider theories and research from other perspectives; so you'll find the section on automaticity has implications for what we know about divided attention – performance on well-practised tasks will usually be better under dual task conditions than with less familiar tasks. Equally, understanding that the attentional spotlight can vary has connotations for selective attention.

Sample question

Could you answer this question? Below is a typical essay question that could arise on this topic.

 Sample question   *Essay*

Critically evaluate Broadbent's (1958) assumption that auditory attention is an early process.

Guidelines on answering this question are included at the end of this chapter, whilst guidance on tackling other exam questions can be found on the companion website at: **www.pearsoned.co.uk/psychologyexpress**

Defining attention

There is a lack of clarity over the precise definition of attention. Early definitions of attention referred to selective processing – directing our attention towards something, in other words a conscious process. The problem with this definition is that there are a number of other things that will also claim our attention, without any guidance from ourselves – think about a car backfiring and how we are automatically drawn to the source of this noise, or how a toothache can make it difficult to concentrate on a book. Therefore it's far better to see attention as referring to a range of psychological phenomena rather than a single one.

A working definition of attention is that it is the process that controls the information that enters consciousness; this process has a limited capacity and can be consciously controlled. Attention is therefore best conceptualised as a filter.

According to Posner (1993), there are three distinct phases of attentional research:

1 The 1950s and 1960s – humans as a single channel processor
2 The 1970s to mid-1980s – focus on internal automatic and controlled processes
3 Late 1980s on – cognitive neuroscience, focusing on patient data and computer modelling.

Each of these phases was shaped by the theories prevailing within cognitive psychology at the time; similarly the technology available also had a clear impact on the nature of the studies conducted.

Further reading Attention

Key reading

Styles, E.A. (2006). *The psychology of attention*. Hove: Psychology Press.

Pashler, H.E. (1999). *The psychology of attention*. Cambridge, MA: MIT Press.

Chun, M.M. & Wolfe, J.M. (2001). Visual attention. In B. Goldstein (Ed.), *Blackwell Handbook of Perception* (pp. 272–310). Oxford: Blackwell. Available from Marvin Chun's website, this chapter is an excellent overview of the field.

Attentional spotlight

Active selection has often been referred to as a spotlight (e.g. Posner, 1980), with the spotlight of attention focusing on a specific part of the visual field, and information outside this area more difficult to detect. Posner found that while we have some control over whether we pay attention to cues in the region we're focusing on (such as arrows), some peripheral cues (such as flashes of light) are more difficult to ignore. Eriksen and St. James (1986) argued that attention was more sophisticated than this and that we have control over the size of the focal area – in other words, more of a zoom lens than a spotlight.

Visual search

Our ability to direct our visual attention to search for information has been studied widely. The most influential approach to visual search was developed by

CRITICAL FOCUS

The attentional spotlight

Although Posner and Eriksen both presented data to support their models of control over attentional processes, the flexibility of the zoom lens is more plausible. However, both models assume that when we focus, we attend to a specific area of the visual field. Research with patients with visual neglect (such as by Marshall & Halligan, 1994, reported later), and by Neisser and Becklen (1975) with healthy participants indicates that we can direct our attention to whole objects rather than to a particular region of the visual field. Simon and Chabris (1999) showed very clearly how focused attention can lead to us missing out on potentially interesting information.

Treisman and Gelade (1980) with Feature Integration Theory (FIT). According to this, attention binds different features of an object (e.g. colour and shape) into consciously experienced wholes. This is useful to us as it allows us to find target objects in a background of other objects.

Central to FIT are the concepts of simple and conjoint searches:

- *Simple searches* are where the target object differs from the non-targets on all features. Simple searches are fast and are unaffected by the size of the set of targets – you'd be able to find your red-haired friend in a crowd of blonde-haired people regardless of whether there were 5 blondes or 100.

- *Conjoint searches* are where the target is only unique in the combination of its features. So if your red-haired friend had glasses, but the crowd contained people with red hair without glasses, as well as blonde-haired people wearing glasses, the search would take far longer as we would have to scan each person in the set. Conjoint search is therefore serial, rather than parallel, and slower when the set size is larger.

Although FIT theory has been revised (e.g. Wolfe's Guided Search Theory, 1994), and alternative theories have been proposed (e.g. Duncan & Humphrey's Attentional Engagement Theory, 1992 which proposed that speed of search is also related to similarity between non-targets), this is still widely accepted as a reasonable explanation of visual search processing.

Further reading The nature of attention

Topic	Key reading
Fate of unattended information	Chun, M.M. & Marois, R. (2002). The dark side of visual attention. *Current Opinion in Neurobiology*, *12*, 184–9. Available from: http://people.uncw.edu/tothj/PSY510/Chun-The%20Dark%20Side%20of%20Attention-CON-2002.pdf.
Review of visual search literature	Wolfe, J.M. (1994). Guided search 2.0: A revised model of visual search. *Psychonomic Bulletin & Review*, *1*, 202–38.

Test your knowledge

The nature of attention

3.1 What are the three functions of attention?

3.2 What is the attentional spotlight?

3.3 Outline the zoom lens approach to visual attention.

3.4 Describe feature integration theory.

Answers to these questions can be found on the companion website at:
www.pearsoned.co.uk/psychologyexpress

 Sample question   **Essay**

Are we able to control visual attention? Substantiate your views on the basis of existing theories of visual attention.

Selective (focused) attention

Selective attention is what we do when we focus on one source of information, while ignoring others. An important debate in selective attention is determining the point where information is filtered out of consciousness. There have been three approaches to this question – early selection, late selection and attenuation.

Early selection approach

Early work on attention used the dichotic listening approach to generate data. In dichotic listening tasks, participants are presented with different stimuli to each ear and instructed to follow only one. Participants are asked to 'shadow' the appropriate stimulus by repeating it aloud. This serves two functions: it shows that participants are following the instructions, and more importantly allows researchers to examine whether information intrudes from the unattended channel. On the basis of this early work by Cherry (1953) – investigating the cocktail party phenomenon – and Poulton (1956), Broadbent (1958) drew a number of conclusions about the type of information that could be selected, concluding that participants could separate messages on basis of physical characteristics (e.g. male vs. female voices) but not semantic ones (such as the content of different stories).

Broadbent (1958) attempted to interpret Cherry's findings in his theory (see Figure 3.1).

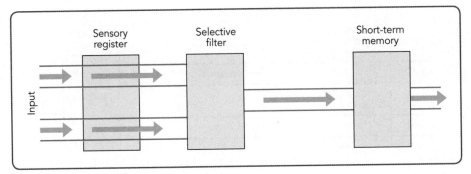

Figure 3.1 **Broadbent's filter theory (1958)**

Key ideas

1 Two inputs presented simultaneously gain access to sensory buffer.

2 One input is allowed through a filter based on its *physical* characteristics (why we can't filter on basis of meaning). This is a single (serial) channel known as the bottleneck in attentional processing.

3 The filter is necessary to prevent overloading of our limited attentional capacity.

This is an *early* selection model – i.e. information is filtered out before semantic processing occurs.

CRITICAL FOCUS

Broadbent's filter theory

Just because physical cues are useful at discriminating, it doesn't mean they are the only cues used. Later research also found that practice improves retention of information from non-shadowed messages (Underwood, 1974). Furthermore, some semantic processing or intrusion from the unattended channel does take place (Corteen & Wood, 1972; von Wright, Anderson & Stenman, 1975).

Late selection approach

The late selection approach was developed after studies conducted by Treisman (1964) indicated that some processing of unattended information does take place. For example, participants had more difficulty shadowing a message when the message in the unattended channel was similar than when it was different. These results showed semantic processing had taken place *after* selective filtering, at odds with early selection theory. Deutsch and Deutsch (1963) developed a theory to account for these results, proposing that information was processed much later in attention (see Figure 3.2).

Key ideas

1 All sensory inputs are analysed completely (i.e. parallel processing).

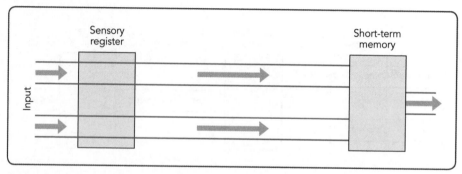

Figure 3.2 Deutsch and Deutsch's late selection theory (1963)

2 The most important signal is responded to if it is above the threshold of
   arousal (the tallest boy analogy), e.g. hearing your name vs. listening to the
   hum of air conditioning. In other words, the level of arousal is determined by
   the signals present.

CRITICAL FOCUS

Deutsch and Deutsch's late selection theory (1963)

Although breakthroughs occurred, they were only observed in 6 per cent of trials, so
it is unlikely that all incoming information is processed. This supports neither the early
nor late views of attention

Attenuation approach

Treisman (1960, 1964) found more evidence inconsistent with Broadbent's theory,
such as some 'breakthroughs' from the unattended message: participants could
pick up a story in the other ear. She found shadowing became more difficult if
the information presented to both ears was similar, i.e. it appears some semantic
information is being analysed (see Figure 3.3).

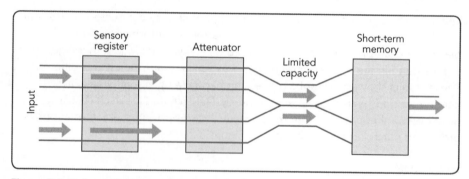

Figure 3.3 Treisman's attenuation theory (1964)

Key ideas

1 The location of the bottleneck is flexible.

2 Filter attenuates (reduces) the strength of the unattended message.

3 However, activation can also be raised above threshold, which Treisman argued is why we can still pick up relevant information from unattended sources, see e.g. Gray and Wedderburn's (1960) results on split span grouping, where participants combined jumbled information played into each ear into consistent information.

Later revisions to selective attention theories

Broadbent (1971) updated his theory to include Treisman's idea of attenuation, but still argued that attention was based on early selection. He also introduced the idea of pigeonholing (similar to the idea of priming), which changes the attentional threshold under certain circumstances.

Deutsch and Deutsch (1963) refined their theory to assert that only important inputs lead to responses. This refinement can be viewed as circular – what does 'important' mean? Johnston and Heinz (1978) proposed a less rigid model allowing processing to occur earlier.

Visual selective attention

Although this section has focused on auditory perception, some interesting work on visual selective attention has also been conducted, with broadly similar findings. Participants have difficulty noticing other information when they have been told to focus on a particular element of a scene, such as when two films are superimposed on each other (Neisser & Becklen, 1975), or even when this involves a man in a gorilla suit walking across the screen and waving at the viewer (Simon & Chabris, 1999).

Further reading

Topic	Key reading
Perceptual load	Lavie, N. (2005). Distracted and confused?: Selective attention under load. *TRENDS in Cognitive Sciences, 9*, 75–82.
Attentional blindness	Simons, D.J. & Chabris, C.F. (1999). Gorillas in our midst: Sustained inattentional blindness for dynamic events. *Perception, 28*, 1059–74. Available from: http://citeseerx.ist. psu.edu/viewdoc/download?doi=10.1.1.125.9246&rep=rep1& type=pdf.

Recent work on selective attention

Some theorists have tried to move away from the early/late debate altogether. For example, Chun and Wolfe (2000) argue that attention is not a solitary process with a single locus, early or late, but is rather a multifaceted term referring to a range of actions and foci. Lavie, Hirst, de Fockert and Viding (2004) also concluded that attentional performance is related to perceptual and working memory loads, as well as the amount of control needed to perform a task.

There have also been re-evaluations of earlier works. Conway, Cowan and Bunting (2001) replicated earlier work by Moray (1959) and others on the cocktail party phenomenon, finding that a third of participants could detect their own name in an unattended message. However, Conway et al. found participants were significantly more likely to detect their names if they had a relatively low working memory capacity, which suggests that they had difficulty inhibiting distracting information. This result is an important one, as it shows that attentional performance is related to memory. This suggests attention cannot be viewed in isolation, and also that a more nuanced approach can reveal some interesting issues.

Further reading **Selective attention**

Topic	Key reading
Working memory and selective attention	Conway, A.R., Cowan, N., Bunting, M.F. (2001). The cocktail party phenomenon revisited: The importance of working memory capacity. *Psychonomic Bulletin & Review*, 8, 331–5.
Review of selective attention research	Driver, J. (2001). A selective review of selective attention research from the past century. *British Journal of Psychology*, 92, 53–78.
Selection mechanisms	Lavie, N., Hirst, A., de Fockert, J. & Viding, E. (2004). Load theory of selective attention. *Journal of Experimental Psychology: General*, 133, 339–54.

Test your knowledge

Selective attention

3.5 Describe the dichotic listening paradigm.

3.6 What is the late selection approach to selective attention?

3.7 Explain what Treisman meant by attenuation.

3.8 What implications does Conway et al.'s (2001) research have for the understanding of attention processing?

Answers to these questions can be found on the companion website at: www.pearsoned.co.uk/psychologyexpress

---

 *Sample question*   **Essay**

Critically evaluate the evidence for visual selective attention.

Divided attention (dual task performance)

Multitasking – performing more than one activity at a time – has become the norm for many people. Psychologists have developed a range of explanations for how dividing attention across tasks impacts on our performance. In this section we'll examine these theories, but before we do this, an understanding of the differences between focused and divided attention paradigms is important. Some of the most important differences are shown in Table 4.1.

Table 4.1 Comparison of focused and divided attention paradigms

Selective (focused) attention	Divided attention
• 2+ inputs, participants instructed to follow only one input • Shows the types of information we can attend to, e.g. voice but not topic • Can show what happens to unattended information	• 2+ inputs but participants instructed to follow *all* inputs • Useful for examining capacity limits • Also used in other areas, e.g. memory

Effects of divided attention on performance

Dividing attention has a significant impact on performance. For example, Schouten, Kalsbeek and Leopold (1960) found low-capacity tasks (e.g. threading nuts on to bolts) caused little interference with the performance of the primary (pedal pressing) task. However, high-capacity tasks caused significantly more difficulty (e.g. IQ test performance went from adult level to that of an 8-year-old).

KEY STUDY

Combining compex tasks

Spelke, Hirst and Neisser (1976) found that participants could combine two complex tasks – reading and dictation – but only after extensive practice. Furthermore, although participants could combine these tasks, they still made errors and arguably the reading task allowed participants to switch their attention between tasks.

Therefore, there is general agreement that three factors have a significant influence on dual-task performance: task similarity (similar tasks cause more problems than different ones), task difficulty (harder tasks cause more interference than easier ones) and practice (more practice improves performance). There are two main theoretical explanations for improvements in dual-task performance: bottleneck theories and theories of central capacity.

Bottleneck theories

These theories argue that performance is limited by a structural limitation, for example Welford (1952) argued that there is a central bottleneck in processing which limits dual-task performance. There is also evidence from the psychological refractory period (PRP).

KEY CONCEPT

Psychological refractory period

The PRP is the delay in response which occurs when two signals requiring two responses are presented in rapid succession. When the second stimulus is presented before the response to the first is made, the second response is delayed, presumably because responses had been queued (Posner & Boies, 1971). The closer the onset of the two signals, the greater the delay in response to the second signal.

Further research on PRPs has weakened this view, for example changing the type of response required from a button press to a verbal response removed task interference completely (MacLeod, 1978). Similarly, warning participants about what to expect also improved performance (Pashler, 1990).

Central capacity theories

Central capacity theories contend that there is no structural limitation. Knowles (1963) argued we have a pool of processing resources with a limited capacity which is shared between tasks, so it is not the number of tasks that determines performance but their difficulty. Moray (1967) theorised that there is no bottleneck: interference is due to excess demands on capacity which can occur at any stage of processing.

From this work, Kahneman (1973) developed his theory of attention and effort in which resources can be flexibly allocated, and importantly that this allocation is related to motivation and arousal – an important consideration for *all* psychological tasks, not just those relating to attention. There are some shortcomings, such as the circular suggestion that performance is determined by interference on a concurrent task; this is problematic as task difficulty is measured by interference and interference is used as a measure of task difficulty. Individual differences in attention also exist, and no clear definition of arousal exists.

Limitations with the idea of resources

How do we measure resources (Norman & Bobrow, 1975); how many types of resources might exist? Is the resource general, as argued by Posner and Boies (1971), that is just divided up according to the tasks needed to be accomplished, or are there separate resources for each domain, such as for visual and auditory information (see e.g. McLeod, 1978)?

More recently, research has focused on the practical implications of dual-task performance, such as driving behaviour while using mobile phones. Similarly to other areas of attention, recent research has shown that divided attention is also influenced by working memory as well as cognitive state, with increased performance in some conditions after glucose administration.

Further reading Divided attention research

Topic	Key reading
Working memory	Gregory, J.H., Colflesh, G.J.H., Andrew, R.A. & Conway, A.R.A. (2007). Individual differences in working memory capacity and divided attention in dichotic listening. *Psychonomic Bulletin & Review, 14,* 699–703. Available from: http://pbr.psychonomic-journals.org/content/14/4/699.full.pdf.
Mobile phone use	Stavrinos, D., Byington, K.W. & Schwebel, D.C. (2009). Effect of cell phone distraction on pediatric pedestrian injury risk. *Pediatrics, 123,* 179–85. Available from: http://pediatrics.aappublications.org/cgi/reprint/123/2/e179.
Multitasking	Ophira, E., Nass, C. & Wagner, A.D. (2009). Cognitive control in media multitaskers. *Proceedings of the National Academy of Sciences, 106,* 15583–7. Available from: http://www.pnas.org/cgi/content/full/106/37/15583.

Test your knowledge

Divided attention

3.9 What factors affect dual task performance?

3.10 What is the psychological refractory period (PRP)?

3.11 Outline Kahneman's theory of attention and effort.

3.12 What are the main differences between the bottleneck and central capacity theories of dual task performance?

Answers to these questions can be found on the companion website at: www.pearsoned.co.uk/psychologyexpress

---

 Sample question   *Essay*

What do dual-task performance studies tell us about the nature of divided attention?

Sample question   *Problem-based learning*

Imagine that, as a practising cognitive psychologist, you have been asked to present data to a government committee on the safety of smoking while driving. Which side of the argument would you take? What empirical evidence is there to support your view?

Automaticity: automatic processing and attention

The development of any skill requires time before it can be executed without difficulty. Think of learning to drive a car. At first, great effort and control are required, but after much practice the task becomes automatic and can be performed without effort. Psychologists have tried to identify the processes and factors involved in these processes.

The two-process model of attention

Using a visual search paradigm, Shiffrin and Schneider (1977) found participants given an easy version of a task involving detecting previously learnt letters exhibited high levels of performance irrespective of the number of targets presented, showing automatic processing. However, when the search task was made more difficult by changing distracters from numbers to letters, performance was significantly slowed as participants needed to search serially (i.e. item by item), which Shiffrin and Schneider termed controlled processing. From these data they developed their two-process model of attention.

Fundamental point

Mental operations that are practised are performed more quickly and accurately also undergo qualitative changes – such as moving from serial to parallel performance to free capacity for other tasks.

- *Controlled* = limited capacity, requires attention, serial, flexible in changing situations, used for difficult or unfamiliar tasks, e.g. learning to drive a car.
- *Automatic* = unlimited capacity, no attention required, parallel, difficult to modify once learnt, easy tasks, highly familiar tasks.

Evaluation of the two-process model

Although a plausible model, there are some problems (see Neuman, 1984), including difficulties in demonstrating that no attention is required to perform a task. Neuman argues that attention is still required, but that this falls below the level of awareness. The theory is therefore perhaps more use as a descriptive tool, as there are clear weaknesses with defining processes as either controlled or automatic. Dissatisfaction with the two-process model led to the development of Norman and Shallice's (1986) SAS model.

Norman and Shallice's (1986) SAS model

In their SAS (Supervisory Attentional System), Norman and Shallice (1986) distinguished between fully and partially automatic processes. They had three levels of functioning: fully automatic, partially automatic and deliberate control by the supervisory attentional system (similar to the controlled aspect of Shiffrin and Schneider). A more natural explanation than the dichotomy proposed in the two-process theory, they proposed that automatic processes are beyond conscious control, but if we're performing a novel task, or when more attentional control is required, the SAS provides additional control over the task.

This model has been supported by performance on the Stroop task (Lovett, 2005). Several disorders have been linked with problems with automaticity, including Huntington's disease, affective disorders and dyslexia.

Attentional automaticity has also been widely implicated in memory (see e.g. Hasher & Zacks, 1979). For example, Baddeley (1990) has argued the SAS could perform a similar function to the central executive in working memory in the way it diverts resources. Other work has attempted to develop a procedural understanding of the processes underpinning attention and the development of skills, such as the adaptive control of thought – rational (ACT-R) approach (e.g. Anderson, 1996).

Conclusion

Several theories have attempted to explain the phenomenon of automaticity in attention. Of these, the SAS is probably the most successful. But does it make sense to talk of a dichotomy or a typology of processes? Some argue that such an approach is theoretically sterile and that it is far better to look at processes as points on a continuum. Automaticity may seem fairly theoretical, but knowing what kind of information people are likely to recall has implications for, among other things, recall of colour in eyewitness situations (e.g. Patel, Blades & Andrade, 2002).

Further reading **Automaticity**	
To extend your understanding, look up the following passages:	
Topic	*Key reading*
Dyslexia	Savage, R. (2004). Motor skills, automaticity and developmental dyslexia: A review of the research literature. *Reading and Writing*, *17*, 301–24. Available from: http://www.springerlink.com/index/V4351G3137328500.pdf.
Huntington's disease	Thompson, J.C., Poliakoff, E., Sollom, A.C., Howard, E., Craufurd, D. & Snowden, J.S. (2010). Automaticity and attention in Huntington's disease: When two hands are not better than one. *Neuropsychologia*, *48*, 171–8. Available from: http://linkinghub.elsevier.com/retrieve/pii/S0028393209003443.

Test your knowledge

Automaticity

3.13 How do automatic and controlled process differ?

3.14 What are the weaknesses of the two-process model?

3.15 Outline the SAS model.

3.16 What does automatisation mean?

Answers to these questions can be found on the companion website at:
www.pearsoned.co.uk/psychologyexpress

 Sample question **Essay**

Is Shiffrin and Schneider's two-process model of attention a satisfactory explanation of automatic processing? Answer with reference to other processing models.

Chapter summary – pulling it all together

→ Can you tick all of the points from the revision checklist at the beginning of this chapter?

→ Attempt all of the Test yourself questions.

→ Attempt the essay questions within the chapter using the guidelines below.

→ Go to the companion website at www.pearsoned.co.uk/psychologyexpress to access more revision support online, including interactive quizzes, flash cards, You be the marker exercises as well as answer guidance for the Test yourself and Sample questions from this chapter.

Answer guidelines

 Sample question **Essay**

Critically evaluate Broadbent's (1958) assumption that auditory attention is an early process.

Approaching the question

This question requires a good understanding of the major theories of selective (focused) attention, as you'll need to be able to contrast other theories with Broadbent's approach.

Important points to include

Like most questions which require evaluating an issue, you'll need to present an overview of the topic before presenting contrasting research and theory. So, for this question you'd begin with an overview of Broadbent's work. This will include key ideas including the sensory buffer, filtering on the basis of physical characteristics and, importantly, the emphasis on early selection. The remainder of the essay will first introduce empirical evidence indicating shortcomings with Broadbent's theory, such as Underwood's finding that practice improved performance. The answer should then contrast the early selection approach with the late selection approach of Deutsch and Deutsch, and the attenuation theory of Treisman, providing evidence supportive of these theories that argue attentional selectivity occurs at other points in information processing. A conclusion weighing up these theories and the evidence, probably coming down against Broadbent, should complete the essay.

> ### Make your answer stand out
>
> *In addition to doing all outlined above, the best answers will also examine what is meant by attention, drawing on Chun and Wolfe's (2000) work which has argued that attention is multifaceted, consisting of separate processes and loci of selection. Answers may also place the theories in their historical context – for example Broadbent's work was shaped by the information-processing approach prominent in cognitive psychology at the time, while later conceptualisations such as Chun and Wolfe's are influenced by computational theory.*

> Explore the accompanying website at **www.pearsoned.co.uk/psychologyexpress**
> → Prepare more effectively for exams and assignments using the answer guidelines for questions from this chapter.
> → Test your knowledge using multiple choice questions and flashcards.
> → Improve your essay skills by exploring the You be the marker exercises.

Notes

Notes

4

Theories of memory

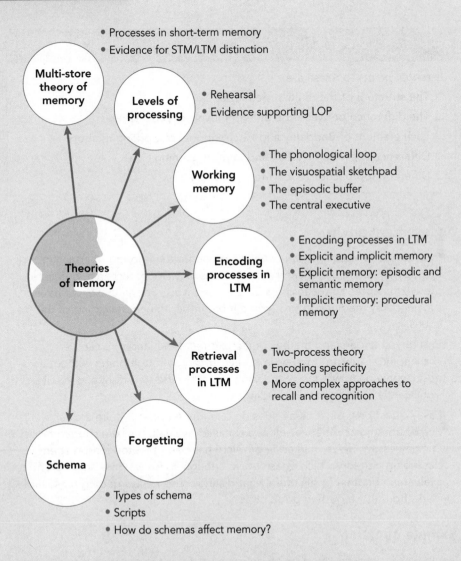

- Processes in short-term memory
- Evidence for STM/LTM distinction

Multi-store theory of memory

Levels of processing
- Rehearsal
- Evidence supporting LOP

Working memory
- The phonological loop
- The visuospatial sketchpad
- The episodic buffer
- The central executive

Theories of memory

Encoding processes in LTM
- Encoding processes in LTM
- Explicit and implicit memory
- Explicit memory: episodic and semantic memory
- Implicit memory: procedural memory

Retrieval processes in LTM
- Two-process theory
- Encoding specificity
- More complex approaches to recall and recognition

Forgetting

Schema
- Types of schema
- Scripts
- How do schemas affect memory?

A printable version of this topic map is available from:
www.pearsoned.co.uk/psychologyexpress

Introduction

The memory process can be divided into three main stages: encoding, where new information is perceived, storage, where information is held for future application, and retrieval, where information is retrieved from storage for use. Several approaches have attempted to explain these processes operate. We'll review three of these – the multi-store, levels of processing and working memory theories. Given the increasing prominence of the latter approach, we will devote most space in this section to working memory.

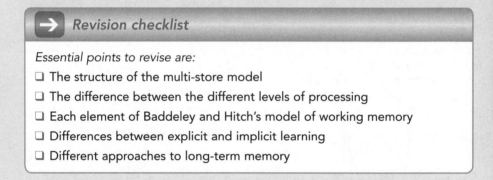

→ *Revision checklist*

Essential points to revise are:
- ❏ The structure of the multi-store model
- ❏ The difference between the different levels of processing
- ❏ Each element of Baddeley and Hitch's model of working memory
- ❏ Differences between explicit and implicit learning
- ❏ Different approaches to long-term memory

Assessment advice

- In this chapter we supply an overview of the more important theories of memory, outlining some central distinctions in memory research, before, in the next chapter, summarising some applied work. For all these, we have provided key readings to give you a more in-depth understanding of the issues.

- Ensure you understand the basics first. Some of the literature can be challenging – Tulving's papers in particular can be tough going without a good working knowledge of the topic. Get this first step right and you'll get significantly more from your reading.

- **Essay questions:** most essay titles on memory theories require a clear description of each theory before a detailed evaluation of the shortcomings. In many essays we've marked, a problem has been that too long is spent describing a theory which doesn't give enough space (or time, in an exam) to evaluate in depth – this is often what distinguishes essays getting reasonable marks from those getting good ones.

Sample question

Could you answer this question? Below is a typical essay question that could arise on this topic.

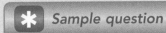 **Sample question** *Essay*

Is the multi-store model of memory the most appropriate way to view memory?

Guidelines on answering this question are included at the end of this chapter, whilst guidance on tackling other exam questions can be found on the companion website at: **www.pearsoned.co.uk/psychologyexpress**

Further reading Memory

Key reading

Baddeley, A., Eysenck, M.W. & Anderson, M.C. (2009). *Memory*. Hove: Psychology Press.

Eysenck, M.W. & Keane, M.T. (2010). *Cognitive psychology: A student's handbook*. 6th ed. Hove: Psychology Press.

Quinlan, P. & Dyson, B. (2008). *Cognitive psychology*. Harlow: Pearson.

Multi-store theory of memory

Atkinson and Shiffrin (1968) proposed that memory consists of three separate stores: the sensory register, short-term store and long-term memory (see Figure 4.1). The sensory register has a large capacity, but information in this store decays rapidly and is easily overwritten by similar new information (Sperling, 1960). This register represents information iconically which allows briefly presented visual data to be retained in memory for later processing. Other representations exist, such as echoic memory for hearing, though these have been less studied.

The short-term store has a limited capacity – determined by Miller (1956) to be seven items ±2, although other research has suggested it is lower – four items – for visual information (Cowan, 2001).

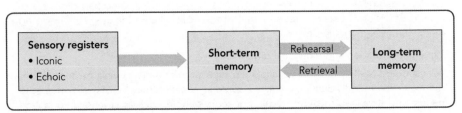

Figure 4.1 Overview of the multi-store model (Atkinson & Shiffrin, 1968)

Processes in short-term memory

Several researchers have examined the serial position curve, in which participants see or hear a series of stimuli and are asked to recall them. Glanzer and Cunitz (1966) observed a typical pattern where earlier-presented items are likely to be well-remembered (the primacy effect) as are the last-presented items (the recency effect).

Atkinson and Shiffrin argued that short-term memory (STM) was where processing such as mental arithmetic took place (cf. working memory, below). If information persists in STM for long enough, it enters long-term memory (LTM). LTM has a large capacity and duration, storing information for later retrieval. Research has focused on the reliability of LTM in the lab using word lists to examine interference in memory (e.g. Keppel & Underwood, 1962) as well more applied work focusing on eyewitness reliability (reviewed in the next chapter).

Evidence for STM/LTM distinction

Cognitive neuropsychological studies support the distinction between STM and LTM through double dissociation. Scoville and Milner (1957) reported their patient 'HM' had normal STM but impaired LTM. In contrast, patient 'KF' reported by Shallice and Warrington (1970) had poor STM, but normal LTM. This double dissociation indicates that short- and long-term memory may involve different processing mechanisms.

Primacy and recency effects in free recall are also evidence for a qualitative difference in processing between STM and LTM. The Brown–Peterson paradigm, where rehearsal of items is prevented by a distracter task, also leads to reductions in recall.

CRITICAL FOCUS

The multi-store theory

The multi-store model is a plausible theory of memory, and provided a testable framework for later work. However, there are several shortcomings, related principally to the emphasis placed on the structural aspects of memory, rather than the processes involved in it. For example, researchers have found it difficult to separate the short- and long-term stores based on different coding, retrieval or brain structures. One way this has been dealt with is by viewing STM as simply a well-activated part of LTM (e.g. Cowan, 2001) or as part of a revised multi-store model like Baddeley's (2000) working memory model, outlined below.

Type of information and individual differences

Atkinson and Shiffrin did not consider the type of information being presented, nor did they explore individual differences – some information may be of more interest to people and thus lead to better recall. For some people, such as savants, information can be stored without the need for rehearsal and without evidence of decay.

Oversimplification

The model assumes that both STM and LTM are unitary, with the stores always operating in the same way. This is not borne out by the evidence – KF's STM difficulties were restricted to verbal information, with non-verbal processing unaffected. LTM is also unlikely to store all information, factual, skill-related, etc. in a single unvariegated store.

Linearity

According to the multi-store model, information passes sequentially through the stores. This does not fit with the requirement of information from the long-term store – such as pronunciation – before it can be processed in STM.

Further reading Multi-store model of memory

Topic	Key reading
Distinction between STM and LTM	Nee, D.E., Berman, M.G., Moore, K.S. & Jonides, J. (2008). Neuroscientific evidence about the distinction between short- and long-term memory. *Current Directions in Psychological Science, 17*, 102–6.

Levels of processing

Craik and Lockhart's (1972) levels-of-processing (LOP) framework proposed that memory does not consist of separate stores, but is a continuum along which depth of encoding varies. The likelihood of an item of information being remembered is related directly to the depth of the processing occurring at encoding. Processing may range from superficial or physical analysis (e.g. whether a word is written in capitals) to phonemic (whether it rhymes with another word) and to deep or semantic analysis (e.g. whether the word is a type of plant; see Figure 4.2). Deeper processing leads to stronger memory traces that are more likely to be remembered.

Rehearsal

LOP distinguishes between maintenance and elaborative rehearsal. Maintenance rehearsal occurs when item information is repeated, while elaborative rehearsal involves deeper, semantic, analysis. Only elaborative analysis improves long-term memory, in contrast to the multi-store model which views *any* rehearsal as improving memory. Although simple repetition of material (e.g. reading the same words repeatedly) does help storage (Tulving, 1966), a slightly more effective strategy is that of maintenance rehearsal where the information to be remembered is maintained in consciousness (e.g. by rehearsing the same words). This distinction between repetition and rehearsal is a subtle but important one.

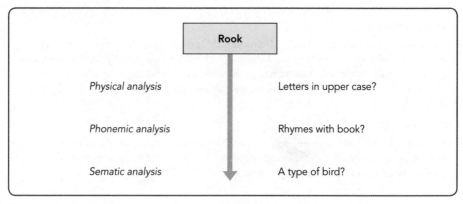

Figure 4.2 Levels of processing framework (Craik & Lockhart, 1972)

In contrast, elaborative rehearsal, where the material to be remembered is associated with other information already stored in memory, is far more effective than either technique (Hyde & Jenkins, 1969).

Evidence supporting LOP

Craik and Tulving (1975) observed a direct relationship between depth of processing and cued recall and found elaboration led to significantly higher retention. Slamecka and Graf (1978) observed that recall was also better when participants generated their own retrieval cues for words – the generation effect – which supports the idea of a strong link between the way in which information is encoded and how it is retrieved.

Distinctiveness also influences recall, with more distinctive traces better recalled (Eysenck & Eysenck, 1980), as does asking participants to relate words to themselves – the self-reference effect (Rogers, Kuiper & Kirker, 1977).

CRITICAL FOCUS

The LOP approach

The LOP framework was the first to highlight the association between processes at encoding and later retrieval, and the link between depth of processing and recall is useful as a general idea. It also emphasised the importance of elaboration and distinctiveness in memory. However, there are several shortcomings of this approach:

Circularity

The LOP framework has been criticised for its circularity: if an item is remembered it must have been processed more deeply, but then this deeper level of processing is used to explain recall performance (there is a reciprocal relationship between greater depth and better memory). Without an independent measure of 'depth' it is difficult to see how this criticism can be countered.

Deeper is not always better

Participants tested with rhymes when they had been asked to use rhyming at encoding (i.e. shallow encoding) performed better than when given a standard recognition test (Morris, Bransford & Franks, 1977). This indicates that compatibility between encoding and retrieval – which Morris et al. referred to as transfer-appropriate processing (TAP) – may be more important than depth of processing.

Other problematic data

Maintenance rehearsal can lead to better retention (Nelson, 1977). Amnesic patients are able to perform semantic (deep) processing tasks but still have poor memory (e.g. Knowlton & Squire, 1995).

Update

In a later reformulation, Lockhart and Craik (1990) argued that the LOP had been presented as a framework, rather than a theory, and they accepted that shallow processing did not always lead to rapid forgetting and that processing did not always proceed from shallow to deep.

Further reading **Levels of processing**

Topic	Key reading
Overview	Craik, F.I.M. & Tulving, E. (1975). Depth of processing and the retention of words in episodic memory. *Journal of Experimental Psychology: General, 104,* 268–94.
TAP	Morris, C.D., Bransford, J.D. & Franks, J.J. (1977). Levels of processing versus transfer appropriate processing. *Journal of Verbal Learning and Verbal Behavior, 16,* 519–33.

Working memory

The working memory (WM) model developed by Baddeley and Hitch (1974) was an attempt to model the processes operating in STM. As such, it is an alternative to the short-term store proposed by Atkinson and Shiffrin. There are three principal components in the WM model: two slave systems, the phonological loop and visuospatial sketchpad which are controlled by the master system, and the central executive. In 2000, Baddeley added a further slave system, the episodic buffer (see Figure 4.3). A number of brain imaging studies have indicated that at least some of these functions may be anatomically separate (e.g. Della Sala & Logie, 1993; Prabhakaran, Narayanan, Zhao & Gabrieli, 2000).

The phonological loop

The phonological (or articulatory) loop stores a limited number of speech sounds for a short period of time. It consists of two components, the passive

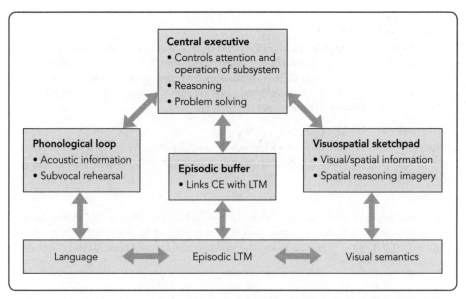

Figure 4.3 Overview of the working memory model (adapted from Baddeley, 2000)

phonological store and an articulatory or subvocal control process supporting mental rehearsal. A range of experimental evidence supports the phonological loop.

- *Phonological similarity effect*: recall is impaired when items are similar in sound but not in meaning (e.g. lark, dark) which implies that verbal information is initially encoded in memory phonologically (Conrad & Hull, 1964).

- *Irrelevant speech effect*: irrelevant speech – even if in a foreign language – will impair recall performance on a verbal memory task as this has direct access to the phonological store. In contrast; non-verbal sound such as white noise will not reduce performance (e.g. Salamé & Baddeley, 1989). However, later researchers found that speech is not a critical element of this phenomenon and that other sounds such as sequences of different tones can interrupt recall (e.g. Jones, Beaman & Macken, 1996).

- *Word length effect*: Baddeley, Thomson and Buchanan (1975) showed that recall was relative to word length, with recall for lists of words worse when the words had more syllables. This may be due to longer words taking more time to articulate and therefore increasing the chance of forgetting, either through the memory trace decaying or from interference from other information.

- *Articulatory suppression*: articulating irrelevant material during a memory task leads to impaired recall. Baddeley et al. (1975) reasoned this is because the articulatory rehearsal process is disrupted causing the memory traces in the phonological loop to decay.

The visuospatial sketchpad

The visuospatial sketchpad (or visuospatial working memory) is the visual version of the phonological loop, temporarily holding and manipulating visual and spatial information in similar ways to the phonological loop with speech. According to Baddeley (1997), the spatial system is important for geographical orientation and the planning of spatial tasks.

Logie (1995) argued that the visuospatial sketchpad should be subdivided into the *visual cache* which stores information about form and colour, and the *inner scribe* which is responsible for rehearsal, information related to movement and the transferring of information back to the central executive. Although less research has examined the visuospatial sketch pad, a range of evidence supports its existence:

- *Independence of phonological loop and visuospatial sketch pad*: tasks involving visual or spatial coding do not interfere with those having articulatory coding (e.g. Brooks, 1967). However, when participants are asked to perform two tasks both having a spatial component, performance drops (Quinn & McConnell, 1996).
- *Irrelevant visual material*: concurrent viewing of irrelevant visual material impaired retention of visual information (Logie, 1991).
- *Visual similarity effect*: Hitch, Halliday, Schaafstal and Schraagen (1988) found that young children showed more errors in recognising a series of pictures that were similar to each other (brush, rake) than when they were different (pen, pig).
- *Mental rotation*: Shepard and Metzler (1971) showed people can accurately manipulate images of complex shapes, with longer times taken to mentally rotate images with greater displacement from a comparison picture than those having less.

The episodic buffer

Baddeley (2000) introduced the episodic buffer as a third slave system controlled by the central executive. The episodic buffer acts as an interface between the other slave systems and LTM and as a temporary store in which information from a number of sources is bound together into a coherent whole which can be retrieved and used as a modelling space to assist learning. The buffer may also process information not dealt with by the other slave systems, such as music and semantic information.

The central executive

The central executive directs attentional resources to the other subsystems of WM, as well as being responsible for higher-level thought processes involved in reasoning and language comprehension. The central executive has only a limited attentional capacity and no capacity for storage (storage resides in the subsidiary slave systems and LTM); if a task is too demanding the central executive's resources will be drained leading to a reduction in task performance. The central executive is therefore an intermediary between the slave systems and LTM, focusing and switching attention within tasks as well as activating representations within LTM (Logie & Duff, 1996).

Research has demonstrated that memory loads do not decrease central executive performance (such as performing verbal reasoning tasks), which indicates memory capacity and reasoning are independent of each other. However there are several issues that have yet to be determined, including whether the central executive has a single pool of attentional resources that can be selectively allocated, whether there are a number of different control processes, and whether these control processes are hierarchically organised.

CRITICAL FOCUS

Working memory

The working memory framework is a significant improvement on Atkinson and Shiffrin's (1968) model in describing the processes operating in STM. Baddeley and Hitch's work formed the basis for research showing that STM is more than just a pathway through to LTM, but also a place where information is used dynamically to perform a wide range of everyday cognitive tasks. Recent research has considered WM capacity as an indicator of more complex abilities (Engle, 2001). Applied research has increasingly focused on WM capacity and task performance, such as in human–computer interaction (e.g. Ziefle & Bay, 2006). There are, however, limitations to this model.

Imprecision

One criticism has been that the model is imprecise, for example the exact role played by the central executive has not been clarified – a wide range of capabilities and responsibilities have been attributed to it, almost as a 'catch all' process.

Replication

There have been difficulties replicating key phenomena, for example Jones and Macken (1993) concluded that the phonological store was not necessarily a store, nor was it entirely phonological, and difficulties in explaining all the findings of studies (such as why Baddeley et al., 1975, had a word length effect that was larger for visually presented items).

More recent developments

Dissatisfaction with Baddeley and Hitch's model of WM led to the development of other models of WM by Cowan (2005) and Ericsson and Kintsch (1995) which view WM as a part of LTM.

Future models of WM need to provide a clearer, more testable specification of the functions and interrelationships of the subcomponents (Andrade, 2001) as well as develop knowledge regarding the biological implementation of the framework and the role of WM in other cognitive tasks.

Further reading Working memory

Topic	Key reading
Description of WM model	Baddeley, A. (1992). Working memory. *Science, 255*, 556–9.
Neural basis of WM	D'Esposito, M. (2007). From cognitive to neural models of working memory. *Philosophical Transactions of the Royal Society B, 362*, 761–72. Available from: http://rstb.royalsocietypublishing.org/content/362/1481/761.full.pdf+html.
Phonological loop	Hanley, J.R. & Bakopoulou, E. (2003). Irrelevant speech, articulatory suppression, and phonological similarity: A test of the phonological loop model and the feature model. *Psychonomic Bulletin & Review, 10*, 435–44.

Test your knowledge

Theories of memory

4.1 Outline three criticisms of the multi-store model of memory.

4.2 What is the difference between maintenance and elaborative rehearsal?

4.3 Describe the role of the central executive in memory.

4.4 How does Cowan's approach to working memory differ from Baddeley and Hitch's?

Answers to these questions can be found on the companion website at: **www.pearsoned.co.uk/psychologyexpress**

 Sample question   *Essay*

What contribution has the working memory model made to our understanding of memory?

Encoding processes in long-term memory

Information stored in LTM is used in a variety of ways – for example, to recognise friends, solve crosswords, or remember the content of a lecture. In this section we will outline the processes and theories focusing on the storage and retrieval of information in LTM.

Encoding processes in LTM

Several processes are responsible for storing information in LTM. These include attention, repetition and rehearsal. Without attention, information cannot be consciously processed, so it would be logical to expect that in order to store information we would need to consciously attend to it; however, as we'll see with implicit learning, this attention need not always be obvious.

Explicit and implicit memory

LTM can be divided into two broad categories, explicit and implicit memory. Explicit or declarative memory is further divided into episodic and semantic components which are consciously recalled. Implicit memory is automatic or unconscious and incorporates procedural memory. A division between declarative and procedural knowledge has much empirical support and has formed the basis for Anderson's ACT-R (1996), an attempt to define the cognitive and perceptual processes in human learning and memory.

Explicit memory: episodic and semantic memory

Tulving (1983) suggested there are two types of LTM, semantic and episodic, which differ in the type of information retained, though the encoding process is the same:

- *Episodic memory*: the storage and retrieval of specific events. This requires contextual knowledge like the time and place the event occurred, such as what you had for breakfast, or what you did on your last holiday.
- *Semantic memory*: knowledge that does not have contextual elements like time or place. These memories do not include contextual knowledge and can be viewed as general knowledge – capital cities, verb endings in French, etc.

Updating this theory, Wheeler, Stuss and Tulving (1997) stated that the main distinction was not the type of content, but the subjective experience associated with the memory at encoding and retrieval. They drew on evidence from brain-damaged patients which showed different blood flow in semantic and episodic memory tasks.

Semantic and episodic memory are both aspects of declarative or explicit memory where performance on a task requires conscious recollection of previous experience.

Implicit memory: procedural memory

Implicit memory is where performance on a task is facilitated in the absence of conscious recollection. One form of implicit memory is procedural memory in which we perform actions, such as driving a car or writing, without having to consciously think about them. Implicit memory tasks differ from traditional explicit tasks in that participants will not be instructed to remember information but will still be tested on it. Data supporting implicit memory comes from normal participants, such as Tulving, Schacter and Stark's (1982) word-fragment completion task, as well as from brain-damaged patients who have impaired explicit memory but intact implicit memory (Squire, 1987).

CRITICAL FOCUS

Explicit and implicit memory

The terms 'implicit' and 'explicit' tell us nothing about memory structure because they are descriptive concepts that are primarily concerned with a person's psychological experience at the time of retrieval (Schacter, 1987). Although the two processes do appear to be independent of each other, it is also unclear whether there is just one type of implicit memory or whether there are several.

Further reading Encoding processes in LTM

Topic	Key reading
Implicit memory	Roediger, H.L. (1990). Implicit memory retention without remembering. *Scientific American*, 45, 1043–56.
Encoding processes in implicit and false memories	Schacter D.L., Gallo D.A., & Kensinger E.A. (2007). The cognitive neuroscience of implicit and false memories: Perspectives on processing specificity. In J.S. Naime (Ed.), *The foundations of remembering: Essays honoring Henry L. Roediger III* (pp. 353–77). New York: Psychology Press.
Overview of memory processes	Tulving, E. (2000). Introduction to memory. In M.S. Gazzaniga (Ed.), *The new cognitive neurosciences*, 2nd ed. (pp. 727–32). Cambridge, MA: MIT Press. Available from: http://alicekim.ca/IntroMem00.pdf. (Almost all of Endel Tulving's papers can be found on Alice Kim's site http://alicekim.ca/tulving/.)

Retrieval processes in LTM

Failure to retrieve a memory is not necessarily evidence that the memory has gone forever, or that it was never encoded in the first place. Several attempts have been made to describe the retrieval process, in particular the general superiority of recognition over recall.

Two-process theory

Two-process theory states that recall consists of two stages: the first is search and retrieval; the second, recognition. As recall involves an additional process, the assumption is that recall will be more prone to errors or retrieval failures than recognition which only has a single stage where errors can occur. Although much research has supported this, there is also work that has shown a superiority for recall over recognition (e.g. Tulving & Thompson, 1973). Further work has also indicated that recognition memory may also involve more than one kind of retrieval process.

Encoding specificity

Tulving and Thompson (1973) demonstrated that a simple 'generate and recognise' account of recall – where participants retrieve potential items from memory and see if they match the sought-after cue – did not take account of all the data. In response to this, Tulving (1982) proposed the encoding specificity hypothesis. This states that successful retrieval of information is more likely when the overlap between the context at encoding and the context at retrieval is high. Tulving argued this applies equally to both recall and recognition.

KEY STUDY

Encoding cues and recall

Tulving and Osler (1968) presented participants with a list of 24 weakly associated cue-target pairs (e.g. CITY-dirty), and then tested for immediate recall with either the same cue as at encoding (CITY-), another weakly but equally associated cue (VILLAGE-), or no cue at all (free recall). They found the encoding cue improved recall performance relative to free recall, but the equally associated cue did not.

Further evidence of the importance of context at encoding and retrieval was obtained by Godden and Baddeley (1975) who gave word lists to deep-sea divers either on the beach or underwater. They found recall was significantly better when conditions at encoding and retrieval matched (i.e. the external context was the same).

CRITICAL FOCUS

Encoding specificity

Although Godden and Baddeley (1975) found some support for encoding specificity, they also found that recognition was unaffected by context, which indicates that context has differential effects on recall and recognition, in contrast to Tulving's belief. Similar findings on the effect of internal context (e.g. mood, intoxication) have also been observed.

There are other problems with encoding specificity, such as the lack of an independent measure of information overlap. Nonetheless, the account of memory provided by the encoding specificity hypothesis is central to most connectionist models of human memory (e.g. McClelland & Rumelhart, 1985), and the idea of replicating the encoding context at retrieval has been important for work in eyewitness testimony (see next chapter).

More complex approaches to recall and recognition

The models presented so far have met with criticism, particularly for viewing recall and recognition as unitary concepts. Research now shows that memory consists of multiple systems operating using different processes and which are to some degree anatomically separate (see e.g. Squire, 2009 for a review). Theories to support this more complex view of memory have been put forward for recognition by Gardiner (1988) with the remember-know paradigm, and for recall by Jones (1982) who suggested information can be retrieved by both direct and indirect cues.

Further reading Retrieval processes in LTM	
Topic	*Key reading*
Recognition in amnesia	Brandt, K.R., Gardiner, J., Vargha-Khadem, F., Baddeley, A.D. & Mishkin, M. (2008). Impairment of recollection but not familiarity in a case of developmental amnesia. *Neurocase*, *15*, 60–5. Available from: http://www.ncbi.nlm.nih.gov/pmc/articles/PMC2919061/.
Research and theory on retrieval processing	Squire, L.S. (2009). Memory and brain systems: 1969–2009. *Journal of Neuroscience, 29*, 12711–16.
Encoding specificity	Zeelenberg, R. (2005). Encoding specificity manipulations do affect *retrieval* from memory. *Acta Psychologica, 119*, 107–21.

Forgetting

Forgetting is the loss of information already stored in long-term memory. There are several theories of forgetting, though a distinction can be made between availability theories and accessibility theories.

- *Availability theories* propose memories are forgotten because they have been permanently lost from the brain through the fading of memory traces.

- *Accessibility theories* argue that memories still exist but are difficult to retrieve, for example through lacking the appropriate cues to access a memory.

There are four principal explanations for why forgetting occurs: trace decay, consolidation, interference and retrieval failure.

1 *Trace decay*. The spontaneous decay of information over time due to decay in the memory pathways from a lack of use of the information. Peterson and Peterson (1959) found the longer the delay between encoding and retrieval the greater the decay.

2 *Consolidation*: Forgetting occurs through physiological damage or deterioration (i.e. organic causes) such as amnesia, Alzheimer's disease or old age.

3 *Interference*. Interference theory proposes that new information and stored memories compete to cause forgetting. There are three forms of interference, retroactive, proactive and output. Retroactive interference occurs when

new information interferes with older knowledge, such as leading questions changing the memories of an eyewitness. Proactive interference is when older information impacts on retention of new information, such as having difficulty remembering your new PIN number because of knowledge of your old one. Output interference happens when the act of trying to retrieve information interferes with the recall of other information, as memory retrieval uses up space in short-term memory.

4 *Retrieval (cue-dependent) failure.* Tulving and Wiseman (1975) argued that recall fails when we do not have appropriate cues to retrieve it. They proposed two types of cues exist, state-dependent where there is a relationship between internal physiological state at encoding and retrieval, and context-dependent where recall is cued by external cues, such as visual information.

CRITICAL FOCUS

Theories of forgetting

Trace decay is difficult to test objectively because it is hard to rule out other factors in forgetting such as interference or lack of cues. Jenkins and Dallenbach (1924) found forgetting may be due to events that happen between learning and recall interfering with ability to recall rather than decay.

Although much evidence supports cue-dependence theory (e.g. Godden & Baddeley, 1975), as interference theory has often used nonsense syllables as stimuli and so is also prone to criticisms of ecological validity. Furthermore, motivated forgetting for traumatic memories might also occur, which may be resistant to cuing.

The theory also has yet to explain how participants can retrieve information on tests that they failed to recall in earlier ones.

Test your knowledge

Encoding and retrieval processes in LTM

4.5 What is the difference between implicit and explicit memory?

4.6 How do episodic and semantic memory differ?

4.7 Describe how the two-process model of recall might account for differences in performance between recall and recognition.

4.8 What is the difference between proactive and retroactive interference?

Answers to these questions can be found on the companion website at:
www.pearsoned.co.uk/psychologyexpress

 Sample question   *Essay*

Critically evaluate Tulving's encoding specificity model.

Schema theory

Schemas (or schemata) are mental models or representations used to assimilate, organise and simplify knowledge. They develop through experience and are unique to each individual. As our interpretation and memories of events are related to these schemas people will often have different recollections of the same event.

Bartlett's 'War of the Ghosts'

Bartlett (1932) conducted one of the first systematic examinations of the relationship between schemata and memory by asking participants to recall the story 'War of the Ghosts'. Bartlett found that participants systematically reconstructed the story based on their own knowledge, rather than having an exact memory of the story. This indicates memory is an active construction rather than a direct representation of events.

Types of schema

There are three main categories of schemas: person schema, self-schema and scripts.

Person schemas and self-schemas

Person schemas consist of general knowledge and beliefs about other people's consistent traits and characteristics. Information is more likely to be remembered if it is congruent with a schema. For example Cohen (1981) found participants more frequently recalled that a video of a librarian showed her wearing glasses than that she owned a bowling ball. Self-schemas are general knowledge that we believe to be true about our own personality traits, abilities, goals etc. Person and self-schemas influence behaviour. For example if we see ourselves as health conscious then we would be more likely to eat healthy food and take exercise (Kendzierski & Costello, 2004). Having negative self-schemas has also been found to be associated with depression (Evans, Heron, Lewis, Araya & Wolke, 2005).

Scripts

Scripts contain generic information about frequently occurring events. They allow us to anticipate what is going to happen as well as (sometimes inappropriately) fill in missing details. Schank and Abelson (1977) developed script theory to explain how we are able to make inferences about events, such as having a restaurant script which would include the actors involved, such as a waiter, and information about the event, such as paying the bill at the end of meal. Bower, Black and Turner (1979) found participants had considerable overlap in the lists of restaurant events they produced.

How do schemas affect memory?

Scripts and schemas can lead to systematic biases in recall. Information congruent with a schema will be more likely to be recalled than incongruent information (Brewer & Treyens, 1981). However, highly distinctive information – like a skull in a shopping trolley – is more likely to be remembered than more commonplace items, the 'von Restorff' effect.

KEY STUDY

Remembering congruent and incongruent items

Brewer and Treyens (1981) asked participants to recall the contents of an office in which they waited. Congruent objects (e.g. chair) were better-remembered by participants than incongruent objects (e.g. skull). Many participants also reported seeing books – congruent objects – that had not been present in the room.

Schemas influence memory early on in life: Martin and Halverson (1983) found that children frequently changed the sex of the actor performing sex-inconsistent activities when recalling previously presented pictures.

The distorting effects of schemas can be constructive changes, occurring during the encoding stage, or reconstructive, occurring at retrieval stage. However, it is difficult to determine exactly when these changes occur – they may even occur at both stages.

CRITICAL FOCUS

Schema theory

Schemas allow us to take shortcuts in interpreting information. However, these shortcuts can mean that we may disregard relevant information in favour of information that confirms our pre-existing beliefs. This means that schemas can contribute to stereotypes and mislead by making it hard to retain new information not conforming to established schemas.

Although schema theories provide a comprehensive framework to explain the structure and organisation of knowledge in long-term memory, several problems exist. First is that there is no real consensus on the properties of schemas. This has led to a range of theories being proposed including Bartlett's schemata (1932), Schank and Abelson's scripts (1977), Eysenck and Keane's dynamic memory theory (1995) and Caroll's (1994) story grammars. It is also difficult to use schema predictively in order to say what is likely to be remembered in specific situations, or to avoid circularity in the definition of specific schemas.

As schema theory focuses on an aggregation of experiences, the theory has difficulties in explaining instances where very detailed and accurate recall occurs of unique events. There has also been criticism of the failure to tackle the processes involved in the selection and retrieval of the most appropriate schema for a given situation.

Further reading Schema theory

Topic	Key reading
Schema and emotion	Mather, M. & Johnson, M.K. (2003). Affective review and schema reliance in memory in older and younger adults. *American Journal of Psychology, 116*, 169–90. Available from: http://www.jstor.org/stable/1423576.
Recall of inconsistent terms	Pezdek, K., Whetstone, T., Reynolds, K., Askari, N. & Dougherty, T. (1989). Memory for real-world scenes: The role of consistency with schema expectation. *Journal of Experimental Psychology: Learning, Memory, and Cognition, 15*, 587–95.
Reconstruction of episodic memory	Schacter, D.L. & Rose, D. (2007). The cognitive neuroscience of constructive memory: remembering the past and imagining the future. *Philosophical Transactions of the Royal Society B, 362*, 773–86. Available from: http://rstb. royalsocietypublishing.org/content/362/1481/773.full.

Test your knowledge

Schema theory

4.9 What is a schema?

4.10 What are the four ways in which a schema is thought to affect the encoding process?

4.11 Describe the differences between person schemas and scripts.

Answers to these questions can be found on the companion website at: www.pearsoned.co.uk/psychologyexpress

---

 Sample question   *Essay*

Critically evaluate the contribution of schema theory to our understanding of memory processes.

Chapter summary – pulling it all together

→ Can you tick all of the points from the revision checklist at the beginning of this chapter?

→ Attempt all of the Test yourself questions.

→ Attempt the essay questions within the chapter using the guidelines below.

→ Go to the companion website at www.pearsoned.co.uk/psychologyexpress to access more revision support online, including interactive quizzes, flash cards, You be the marker exercises as well as answer guidance for the Test yourself and Sample questions from this chapter.

Answer guidelines

 Sample question   *Essay*

Is the multi-store model of memory the most appropriate way to view memory?

Approaching the question

This question requires a broad knowledge of memory theory. You'll need to give an overview of the model in question before going on to present limitations and alternatives.

Important points to include

Start with an overview of the multi-store model, specifying each element and briefly describing each. Next, evaluate the model, presenting some of the shortcomings. These include the type of information being presented, individual differences in recall ability and oversimplification. To do just this would only answer half of the question – you're asked not only to evaluate the multi-store model, but to also present alternatives. The most obvious improvement is Baddeley and Hitch's (1974) working memory model, which developed partly in response to concerns about the ability of the multi-store model to explain a wide range of empirical data. You could also reference other theories, such as Craik and Lockhart's (1972) levels-of-processing framework. It would be easy to get carried away with referring to a wide range of theories and supporting data. This is less of a problem in an essay, but in a timed exam, you'd need to keep well focused. Ultimately, you would probably conclude that the multi-store model has been superseded by more robust theories, though they themselves also have their weaknesses.

Make your answer stand out

Markers are always pleased to see new material referred to in answers that has not been taken from lecture notes or the set text. Referring to more recent, but less well-known theories, such as those of Cowan (2005) and Ericsson and Kintsch (1995), will catch the eye of the marker and are likely to have a positive impact on your grade.

Explore the accompanying website at **www.pearsoned.co.uk/psychologyexpress**
→ Prepare more effectively for exams and assignments using the answer guidelines for questions from this chapter.
→ Test your knowledge using multiple choice questions and flashcards.
→ Improve your essay skills by exploring the You be the marker exercises.

Notes

Notes

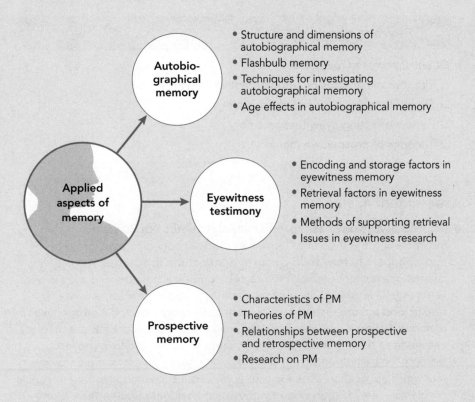

5

Applied aspects of memory

- Structure and dimensions of autobiographical memory
- Flashbulb memory
- Techniques for investigating autobiographical memory
- Age effects in autobiographical memory

Autobiographical memory

Applied aspects of memory

Eyewitness testimony

- Encoding and storage factors in eyewitness memory
- Retrieval factors in eyewitness memory
- Methods of supporting retrieval
- Issues in eyewitness research

Prospective memory

- Characteristics of PM
- Theories of PM
- Relationships between prospective and retrospective memory
- Research on PM

A printable version of this topic map is available from:
www.pearsoned.co.uk/psychologyexpress

Introduction

As we saw in the last chapter, researchers have examined a wide range of cognitive processes related to memory in the laboratory. In recent years there has been growing interest in applying this knowledge to real world issues. Such applied research has as its central aim a focus on realism, or ecological validity. The main proponent of this approach was Neisser (e.g. 1967) who argued that the theoretical findings obtained from the lab needed to be put to the test in more realistic situations, though this has been criticised because of a lack of control over extraneous variables (Banaji & Crowder, 1989). One solution to this dispute is to combine the findings of applied and lab-based research on the same topic. Where there is overlap in the findings, greater confidence can be placed on their conclusions.

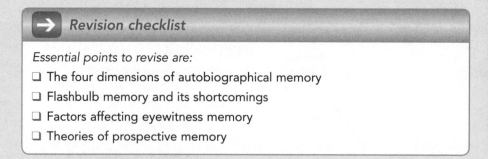

Revision checklist

Essential points to revise are:
- ❏ The four dimensions of autobiographical memory
- ❏ Flashbulb memory and its shortcomings
- ❏ Factors affecting eyewitness memory
- ❏ Theories of prospective memory

Assessment advice

- Applied psychology has expanded rapidly over the last 20 years, incorporating the theoretical advances made in cognitive psychology and applying them to real-world contexts. Some of the topics explored in this chapter are related – as we'll see, autobiographical memory and eyewitness testimony have several areas of overlap. We'll also review some of the research on a more recent development in memory research – prospective memory. As you might expect, questions on these applied areas are different in tone from those in more theoretical areas (though note that applied research isn't atheoretical, it just focuses on issues that are of more obvious real-world application). The focus of applied questions tends to be on real-life problems – 'are children poorer witnesses than adults?', rather than asking you to evaluate a given theory.
- **Essay questions**: one of the most common topics covered in applied cognitive psychology modules is eyewitness testimony. Because of the wide range of issues explored in this field, we have given it extensive coverage; in particular highlighting comparisons between the performance of children and adults – a frequent topic in eyewitness work. In addition, we've focused on

some of the applications (and hence likely questions) of both autobiographical and prospective memory.

Sample question

Could you answer this question? Below is a typical essay question that could arise on this topic.

 Sample question *Essay*

Critically evaluate the claim that children are unreliable witnesses.

Guidelines on answering this question are included at the end of this chapter, whilst guidance on tackling other exam questions can be found on the companion website at: **www.pearsoned.co.uk/psychologyexpress**

Further reading Applied aspects of memory

Key reading

Esgate, A., Groome, D. et al. (2004). *An introduction to applied cognitive psychology*. Hove: Psychology Press.

Herrmann, D.J., Yoder, C.Y. & Gruneberg, M. (2006). *Applied cognitive psychology: A textbook*. Mahwah, NJ: Lawrence Erlbaum Associates.

Robinson-Riegler, G. & Robinson-Riegler, B. (2008). *Cognitive psychology: Applying the science of the mind*. Boston, MA: Pearson.

Autobiographical memory

Autobiographical memory is recall for information related to the self. There are two components to autobiographical memory, episodic and semantic.

Episodic memories are events personally experienced at a particular time and place, such as your last holiday or your first kiss. Schroots, van Dijkum and Assink (2004) argue that the episodic component of autobiographical memory should be further subdivided into prospective (expectation-related) and retrospective (memory) components.

Semantic memories are not specifically related to location or time; these include personal facts such as your favourite meal, or the name of a childhood friend.

Structure and dimensions of autobiographical memory

There are four dimensions to autobiographical memory:

1 Biographical and personal facts – this includes place and date of birth, the names of family members and schools attended (Tulving, 1972). This incorporates information that can not be strictly remembered (such as being born in a specific hospital).

2 Copies or reconstructions of the original event – autobiographical memories can be either direct copies of the original event, which are very vivid and include sensory and emotional information, or reconstructions of the event reinterpreted in the light of later information. Older memories are more likely to be reconstructed than newer ones (Robinson & Swanson, 1993).

3 Specific or generic recollections – generic autobiographical memories are memories of repeated events which are not fixed to a specific instance, such as recollections of walking to school (Neisser, 1986). These contrast with specific memories which are related to novel events, which may form flashbulb memories (see below).

4 Observer perspective or field perspective – autobiographical memories can be seen from different perspectives. The observer perspective is where the memory is pictured from another person's viewpoint; the field perspective is where the memory is seen from the viewpoint of the individual whose memory it is.

Conway (1996) divides autobiographical memory into three categories: lifetime periods, general events and event-specific knowledge. Lifetime periods are significant ongoing periods, such as attending a particular school, or living with someone. General events are repeated or extended events associated with shorter periods of time, such as weeks or months, for example specific holidays. The final level consists of event-specific knowledge consisting of rich event-related details such as images and feelings. Event-specific knowledge relates to events over short time spans, from seconds to hours. Each of these levels is likely to be linked to the others – we can recall specific details of our time at school, for example.

In a later elaboration of this theory, Conway and Pleydell-Pearce (2000) proposed the self-memory system (SMS), a model of autobiographical memory formulation where autobiographical knowledge and episodic memories are combined, a process controlled by the working self which contains goals, knowledge about the self and other information that facilitates access to autobiographical knowledge.

Flashbulb memory

Flashbulb memories are vivid snapshots of the circumstances in which we heard consequential or traumatic information.

Brown and Kulik (1977) argued flashbulb memories are more accurate, detailed and resistant to forgetting than other memories. They proposed there was a unique neural mechanism for flashbulb memories that was different from the formulation of ordinary autobiographical memories. Several researchers examined memories for a range of high-profile events including the assassination of John F. Kennedy (Schacter, 1996) and the Challenger Space Shuttle disaster (Terr et al., 1997).

There is some basis for viewing flashbulb memories as different from other autobiographical memories. Terr et al. (1997) found that children were more likely to have vivid and accurate recall of the Challenger disaster when they had experienced higher levels of emotion and had stronger personal interest in the events. Schacter (1996) also reported his own recollection of the assassination of JFK had not deteriorated in the 30 years since the event. Although some evidence supports this phenomenon, it remains controversial.

EVALUATION

The flashbulb memory phenomenon

There are potential problems with the special mechanism hypothesis. Flashbulb memories may only be better-remembered because they are rehearsed more frequently, rather than resulting from a different neural process, though some work has shown that brain regions associated with emotion react differently in response to recalling emotionally neutral events than emotionally charged flashbulb events (Davidson & Gilsky, 2002).

Flashbulb memories can occur for events even when they are not surprising or shocking – we often have very vivid memories of specific moments on holiday when we're very relaxed, in contrast to Brown and Kulik's theory.

One of the defining features of flashbulb memories is accuracy. Several researchers have disputed that flashbulb memories are more memorable than everyday memories, arguing that flashbulb memories principally differ from other memories in having greater vividness, rather than necessarily being more memorable (e.g. Talarico & Rubin, 2003).

Other research has also questioned whether flashbulb memories are stable over time, finding few children had such memories less than a year after the Challenger disaster (Bohannon, 1988), though this may have been due to the age of participants.

Techniques for investigating autobiographical memory

Several methods have been used to examine autobiographical memory (see Roediger & Marsh, 2003). These include Galton's (1879) cue word or memory probe method in which participants have to recall autobiographical events in response to cue words, priming paradigms where speed of retrieval is measured in response to cues and simulated biographical events where autobiographical events are created in the lab for later recall. The Autobiographical Memory Test (AMT), Crovitz Test and Rubin Paradigm are based on Galton's technique and have been used widely to examine recall of personal events.

Such tests have several limitations, including their open-ended nature which does not allow probing of specific time periods. There is also no standard scheme for converting episodic recollections into standard quantitative scores to allow comparisons across studies. A further issue has been over-reliance on this technique to explore autobiographical memory, though other techniques exist such as diary studies.

Diary studies of autobiographical memory

There have been several instances of individuals recording events that happened to them in a diary and later testing themselves on this information.

KEY STUDY

Linton's diary studies

Linton (e.g. 1986) recorded at least two events on index cards each day for six years. Each month she randomly tested herself on these memories as well as trying to recall the date of the events and the emotional salience. After 3–4 years she remembered 65 per cent of incidents, but surprisingly found no relationship between the salience or emotionality of the events and their memorability, in contrast to Wagenaar (e.g. 1986). Note that these findings are based on single case studies of people who decided to test their own memories repeatedly over several years, and so may not be representative of how memory works.

Diary and cue-word studies both show a tendency to forget less pleasant events (the Pollyanna Principle) and for repeated events to lose their episodic qualities. There are exceptions to this positive focus, notably that people with depression are more likely to recall negative events, perhaps because they are rehearsed more (Lemogne et al., 2006).

As a technique, the diary approach is very demanding so impractical for widespread use. Constant testing of these memories is also likely to involve some kind of rehearsal and hence lead to enhanced recall.

Age effects in autobiographical memory

Autobiographical memory is not equal over the years – certain periods of life appear to be relatively well-remembered, while others are not remembered at all. Researchers have attempted to explain this lack of a clear trend. In this section we'll examine three age-related patterns in autobiographical memory, infantile amnesia, recency effect and bump effects.

Infantile amnesia

Infantile or childhood amnesia is the inaccessibility of memories for events occurring in infancy and early childhood. Although children can remember events, these memories do not persist into adulthood. There have been several explanations for infantile amnesia, including interference or memory decay (Wetzler & Sweeney, 1986, based on forgetting rates in adults), incomplete language development preventing encoding of memories in a way that can be extracted by language-based adults (Schachtel, 1947) or, most likely, lack of neurological development in the hippocampus preventing the formation of memories (see e.g. Newcombe, Drummey, Fox, Lie & Ottinger-Alberts, 2000).

Recency and bump effects and autobiographical memory

Two correlated effects of ageing exist on memory. These are the bump effect, which is the disproportionably higher likelihood that individuals will recall memories from between the ages of 10 and 30 in individuals aged over 35 (Rubin, Wetzler & Nebes, 1986). This is strongly correlated to the recency effect, of which individuals remember more recent memories from this age range than earlier ones.

There are three explanations for these effects. The cognitive account emphasises the novelty and distinctiveness of events in this period – leaving school, starting work, having a family, that occur prior to the stability of later life. The identity explanation proposes that memories are better retained from this period because they are related to the establishment of the self. The final explanation is maturational – that cognitive abilities are better in this period and so encoding of information is likely to be better.

Further reading Autobiographical memory	
Topic	Key reading
Childhood amnesia	Bauer, P. (2004). Oh where, oh where have those early memories gone? A developmental perspective on childhood amnesia. *Psychological Science Agenda, 18* (12). Available from: http://www.apa.org/science/about/psa/2004/12/bauer.aspx.
Autobiographical memory and ageing	Rubin, D.C. (2000). Autobiographical memory and aging. In D. Park and N. Schwarz (Eds), *Cognitive aging: A primer* (pp. 131–49). Philadelphia, PA: Psychology Press.
Positive bias in autobiographical memory	Rubin, D.C. & Berntsen, D. (2003). Life scripts help to maintain autobiographical memories of highly positive, but not highly negative, events. *Memory & Cognition, 31*, 1–14. Available from: http://www.springerlink.com/content/5308051858205647/fulltext.pdf
Comparison of episodic and autobiographical memory	Roediger, H.L. & Marsh, E.J. (2003). Episodic and autobiographical memory. In A.F. Healy & R.W. Proctor, *Experimental psychology, Vol. 4, The handbook of psychology* (pp. 475–97). New York: Wiley.
Overview of memory	Schacter, D.L. (1996). *Searching for memory: The brain, the mind, and the past.* New York: Basic Books.

Test your knowledge

Autobiographical memory

5.1 What are the four dimensions of autobiographical memory?

5.2 Define flashbulb memory.

5.3 List three explanations for infantile amnesia.

5.4 What is the bump effect in autobiographical memory?

Answers to these questions can be found on the companion website at: **www.pearsoned.co.uk/psychologyexpress**

 Sample question   *Essay*

What has research told us about the structure of autobiographical memory?

Eyewitness testimony

Eyewitness research focuses on issues relevant to criminal investigations, although this is broadly defined – much eyewitness research focuses on general event memory rather than issues that are strictly forensically applicable.

Witnesses are often unreliable (Loftus & Palmer, 1974), to the extent that mistaken eyewitness identification has been identified as the most important factor leading to false convictions (Rattner, 1988). Nonetheless, eyewitness research has a significant impact on changing legal assumptions about the reliability of eyewitness evidence, especially on the role played by children in the criminal justice system (Dent & Flin, 1992).

The factors influencing eyewitness performance can be divided into issues related to encoding and storage and to retrieval.

Encoding and storage factors in eyewitness memory

Stress

For ethical reasons, researchers cannot engineer stressful events themselves, however they used naturally occurring stressful events such as inoculations (Peters, 1988), interrogations (Morgan et al., 2004) or visits to dungeons (Valentine & Mesout, 2009).

Heightened stress has a negative effect on identification of a target person and on recall of crime-related details. Deffenbacher (1994) proposed that the negative effect on recall of high levels of anxiety was related to high levels of

KEY STUDY

Robbery eyewitness accounts

Christianson and Hübinette (1993) interviewed witnesses of robberies to compare their emotional experiences of the robbery with the amount they recalled of various aspects of the situation, including the time and date of the crime and characteristics of the robbers. They questioned three groups of people, victims (bank tellers) and bystanders who were either other bank employees or customers. The effect of witness group was significant, with tellers recalling more than other employees who recalled more than customers.

physiological activation (e.g. increased heart rate). Conscious awareness of this activation would lead to less focus on information related to the crime and hence lower recall. Bystanders would have less elevated physiological activation and thus better recall.

Weapon focus

Weapon focus is the tendency for witnesses to violent crime to focus their attention on the weapon used at the expense of other information. Maass and Kohnken (1989) found participants were better able to recall details of a woman who had held a pen than when she held a syringe. Weapon focus remains controversial, with some research reporting no correlation between self-reported affect and recall accuracy (Mitchell, Livosky & Mather, 1998).

Central versus peripheral information

Type of information is an important determinant of what is recalled. Memon and Vartoukian (1996) observed that 'central' information – important parts of an event, such as actions or the people involved – were remembered better than peripheral information, such as the colour of a confederate's shoes.

Retrieval factors in eyewitness memory

Post-event information and false memories

The misinformation or false memory effect occurs where recall of an event is influenced by information received after the event has been widely established. For example, in perhaps the most well-known study of eyewitness recall, Loftus and Palmer (1974) showed that different phrasing of questions led to significantly different estimates of speed in a film of a car accident. Repeated interviews incorporating fallacious information can even create entirely new, false memories, especially in small children (Hyman & Loftus, 2002).

The mechanism behind the misinformation effect is believed to be retrieval-induced forgetting. This is where retrieval of the misleading post-event information strengthens over time, causing an inhibition of the memory trace of the initial event (MacLeod, 2002).

Creating false memories is especially effective when using techniques such as guided imagery, a technique often used in therapy to try to recover memories of sexual abuse (Loftus, 2003). Memories created in the lab may be so convincing that the participant cannot believe that the memories are not real once debriefed (Lindsay, Hagen, Read, Wade & Garry, 2004).

Although it is difficult to distinguish between implanted and real memories, slight differences exist that can be found when already knowing which memories are fake. Lindsay et al. (2004) reported that when participants are asked to guess which memory is false; they can correctly identify the false memory despite feeling that it really happened.

CRITICAL FOCUS

The Deese–Roediger–McDermott (DRM) effect

One of the most common ways that false memories have been studied is by the Deese–Roediger–McDermott (DRM) effect. Participants are given lists of words that are all associated with a prototype but the prototype itself is not presented. For example, if the prototype is 'cold', the list would consist of the 15 words most highly associated with cold, presented in order from the most highly associated (hot) to the least highly associated (frost). The DRM effect is the high-confidence false recall or recognition of the prototypes. This false retrieval often exceeds that of other highly associated distracters and even the correct recall or recognition of low-associate targets (Deese, 1959; Roediger & McDermott, 1995). Type of encoding affects recall of the prototype with the highest recall evoked from elaborative encoding, and serial learning evoking the least recall.

The DRM task is a useful way to study false memories. However, it is unable to isolate the different processes that contribute to false memories, and does not inform about the basis of individual differences to the DRM effect (Gallo, 2010).

Age

Age differences in recall have been widely investigated. Although free recall typically produces very accurate responses regardless of age (e.g. Marin, Holmes, Guth & Kovac, 1979), adults tend to recall a greater amount of information than older children, and older children usually recall more information than younger ones (Cole & Loftus, 1987). Young children's free recall of events, while less comprehensive, is at least as accurate as that of older individuals.

When direct questions are asked, age differences usually diminish (Zaragoza, 1987).

Therefore age, per se, does not appear to prevent an accurate description of events. Rather than young children having difficulty in the recollection of information, it is likely that the interaction between age and other environmental factors such as interviewer effects (Moston, 1992) or shyness (Ceci, Toglia & Ross, 1987) disproportionately affect young children.

Delay

The longer the delay before questioning, the greater the deficits in recall (see e.g. MacLin, MacLin & Malpass, 2001). However, witness age interacts with delay. Poole and White (1993) observed no differences in recall between the recall of children and adults after an immediate interview but, after a delay of two years, adults made less than half the errors of children.

Typicality effects

In the last chapter, we discussed the influence of prior knowledge, or schema, on recall. Schema theory also has implications for eyewitness testimony (Zaragoza, 1987), with recall affected by ideas (or schema) about what happens during typical crimes (Holst & Pezdek, 1992), or their stereotypes about the characteristics of particular individuals (Leichtman & Ceci, 1995).

Methods of supporting retrieval

Researchers have examined verbal and non-verbal methods of enhancing recall and recognition. Verbal methods include different approaches to interviewing, while non-verbal methods include props and environmental or context reinstatement.

Verbal methods: interviewing

Better interviewing techniques lead to more information being recollected and more accurate memory. Eyewitnesses are more accurate when they are asked open questions (e.g. 'Tell me what happened') rather than closed questions (e.g. 'Was the bank robber wearing a Richard Nixon mask?').

There are a range of approaches to interviewing, the best known probably being the Cognitive Interview (CI), developed by Fisher and Geiselman (1992). The CI incorporates a range of memory retrieval techniques including context reinstatement to increase the quantity of information obtained into an organised interviewing structure. The CI elicits significantly more correct information from witnesses than either a standard interview or the techniques police officers typically use.

Later work has identified problems with this technique. For example, the CI does not always facilitate recall when compared to a structured interview (Memon, Cronin, Eaves & Bull, 1993). While CI and control groups may not differ in accuracy, CI increases the number of errors (Bekerian & Dennett, 1993).

Non-verbal methods of enhancing recall

Researchers assessing non-verbal memory aids can generally be divided into two distinct groups, those who have examined the effect of props on recall and the rest who have focused on other non-verbal memory cues like environmental reinstatement.

Props

Props are physical cues which mimic some aspect of a situation; they may be specific to a particular environment, such as a model of a particular scene of crime, or be more general in nature, such as anatomically correct dolls. Most research into the effectiveness of props has been conducted with children as they are more linguistically limited, which may act as a barrier to reliable testimony (Saywitz, Nathanson & Snyder, 1993).

Reinstatement

In context or environmental reinstatement, witnesses are returned to the location where they originally experienced a particular event. This reinstatement may occur physically (Smith & Vela, 1992) or mentally, by the use of projective memory techniques similar to those suggested by Fisher and Geiselman (1992) for use in interviews.

Context reinstatement has a facilitative effect on memory both with adults (Smith & Vela, 1992) and, especially, children. Wilkinson (1988) found context reinstatement led to recall almost twice that of children out of context. However, other studies using different methods have failed to replicate these effects (e.g. Pipe & Wilson, 1994).

Other methods of supporting eyewitness performance

Several provisions have been made to help child witnesses give statements (reviewed in Perry & Wrightsman, 1991), including the use of video evidence, giving testimony via live TV links, in special closed, in camera, court sessions, or from behind barriers which shield them from the accused.

Issues in eyewitness research

Stimuli and ecological validity

Various stimuli have been used to examine eyewitness recall, including stories, cartoons, slides and films. This led Battermanfaunce and Goodman (1993) to criticise some stimuli as being so trivial in nature that they can have little relevance to the kinds of things that witnesses will be asked about in the courtroom.

In naturalistic studies witnesses tend to perform better in recall of everyday activities than on laboratory-based memory tasks. There is strong support for testing under naturalistic conditions. Cornell and Hay (1984) tested two large groups of 5- and 8-year-olds under one of three encoding conditions. In one condition the children went on a guided walk along a route, in another condition children saw a videotape of the same route, in the final condition children saw a sequence of slides which were taken along the route. Cornell and Hay found that both younger and older children made significantly fewer navigational errors when retracing the route if they had walked along it than in either of the other conditions.

Relevance of stimuli

The relevance of stimuli or events to an individual will affect memory accuracy. For example, Baker-Ward, Hess and Flannagan (1990) observed that children had better memory for actions that they had themselves performed than those they had only observed.

Activities, especially those that relate to goals and are interesting to participants, are also recalled better than other types of event information by both children (Goodman, Rudy, Bottoms & Aman, 1990) and adults (Bäckman, Nilsson & Chalom, 1986).

CRITICAL FOCUS

The naturalistic approach

A disadvantage of naturalistic research is the problem of extraneous, uncontrolled, variables (Seelau & Wells, 1995). Where one lab-based study found that high stress led to lower eyewitness accuracy (Deffenbacher, 1983), another study, based on recall of an actual shooting, showed the reverse pattern: those who reported the highest levels of stress were actually the most accurate (Yuille & Cutshall, 1986). Seelau and Wells presumed that this positive correlation resulted from a natural confound: eyewitnesses who had the best view were closest to the shooting, and therefore more stressed than those further away.

The realism of the events used in eyewitness experiments is directly relevant to the conclusions that can be drawn: ecological validity does not refer solely to the form of the stimulus (e.g. a story as opposed to a live event), but also to the content of the stimulus (e.g. a bag-snatching incident compared to a fairy-tale).

Further reading Eyewitness testimony

Topic	Key reading
Stress and eyewitness recall	Deffenbacher, K.A., Bornstein, B.H., Penrod, S.D. & McGorty, E.K. (2004). A meta-analytic review of the effects of high stress on eyewitness memory. *Law and Human Behavior, 28,* 687–706.
Cognitive interview	Geiselman, R.E., Fisher, R.P., Mackinnon, D.P. & Holland, H.L. (1986). Enhancement of eyewitness memory with the cognitive interview. *American Journal of Psychology, 99,* 385–401.
Scripts and eyewitness recall	Holst, V.F. & Pezdek, K. (1992). Scripts for typical crimes and their effects on memory for eyewitness testimony. *Applied Cognitive Psychology, 6,* 573–87.
Suggestibility	Lindsay, D.S. & Johnson, M.K. (1989). The eyewitness suggestibility effect and memory for source. *Memory & Cognition, 17,* 349–58.
Eyewitness identification	Wells, G.L. & Olson, E.A. (2003). Eyewitness testimony. *Annual Review of Psychology, 54,* 277–95.

Test your knowledge

Eyewitness testimony

5.5 What is 'weapon focus' and why might it influence memory?

5.6 Why might typicality effects influence eyewitness recall?

5.7 Outline the cognitive interview procedure.

5.8 What are the potential shortcomings of adopting a naturalistic research methodology?

Answers to these questions can be found on the companion website at:
www.pearsoned.co.uk/psychologyexpress

 Sample question   *Essay*

To what extent does stress influence the performance of eyewitnesses?

Prospective memory

Prospective memory (PM) is the process of remembering to do things at some future point in time, like remembering to attend a party, or to carry out a specific task like remembering to pay a bill on time. PM is a frequent type of forgetting failure. PM has only recently been subjected to systematic empirical research, ranging from laboratory studies to self-rated assessments (Kliegel, McDaniel & Einstein, 2008).

Characteristics of PM

The PM is often viewed as a unitary construct, though this is unlikely (Einstein, Holland, McDaniel & Guynn, 1992) given that a range of attributes impact on PM performance (see Marsh & Hicks, 1998). A fundamental distinction in PM is between time-based (e.g. being somewhere at a specific time) and event-based PM (e.g. buying a specific item when you go into a shop), as well as whether the task is habitually or infrequently performed (Harris, 1980), and whether the action is to be performed in the near future or in the long-term future (Meacham & Leiman, 1982).

Several other variables also affect PM, such as the importance of the intention and its perceived benefits (Ellis, 1996), retrieval context (Harris, 1983) and the strategies used to aid recall (Harris, 1980).

Theories of PM

According to Einstein and McDaniel (1996), models of PM can be divided into automatic (effortless) retrieval and strategic retrieval. They combined these models into a multi-process framework which proposes that the attentional or strategic demands of retrieval vary according to the characteristics of the PM task, including issues like the importance of the intention and delay. Current work is attempting to develop an understanding of the role of attentional processes in PM. The preparatory and attentional memory (PAM) theory (Smith, 2003) proposes that some attentional resources are always required to successfully perform a PM task. Smith further proposes that task performance is related to working memory capacity, with PM supported by both prospective and retrospective components. Working memory use draws capacity away from any ongoing activity, resulting in a decrease in response accuracy and/or an increase in response time relative to when the ongoing activity is performed; this is known as the prospective interference effect (Marsh, Hicks, Cook, Hansen & Callos, 2003).

Smith and Bayen (2004) found a relationship between PM and the size of the prospective interference effect, with decreases in PM performance resulting from a reduction in preparatory processing, reducing the effect. Smith (2003) found evidence to support this, with a positive correlation between the size of the prospective interference effect and the accuracy of PM.

Relationship between prospective and retrospective memory

PM has similar processes to retrospective memory in terms of encoding, storage and retrieval. Retrospective and prospective memory are difficult to separate because any prospective task requires information to be held in memory until the appropriate time. Nonetheless, the two forms of memory are separate entities: Crowder (1996) argued that performance of intended actions is not an accurate reflection of memory for those actions. For example Kvavilashvili (1987) found that participants who demonstrated good PM by remembering to pass on a message were no more likely to remember the content of the message than those with poorer PM, indicating no differences in retrospective memory.

Research on PM

Developmental aspects

Studies of PM in older adults indicate that they do more poorly on time-based but not event-based tasks than younger adults (Henry et al., 2004). Older adults also show a greater sensitivity to increased cognitive load but tend to perform better in real-world tasks than lab tasks (Kvavilashvili & Ellis, 2004).

Studies of PM in children are relatively uncommon but tend to show that even children as young as two have reliable PM for simple tasks (Somerville, Wellman & Cultice, 1983).

Clinical neuropsychology of PM

Most clinical neuropsychological work on PM has been conducted with individuals with brain damage. This research has shown that damage to the prefrontal cortex causes PM problems because of the relationship this region has with executive function (e.g. Guynn, McDaniel & Einstein, 2001). Patients with

Alzheimer's disease have impairments to time- and event-based PM (e.g. Kazui et al., 2005), although patients with Parkinson's disease only show impairment in event-based tasks. Further research also shows impairments in patients with chronic pain (Ling, Campbell, Heffernan & Greenough, 2007) and with heavy alcohol use (Heffernan, Moss & Ling, 2002).

CRITICAL FOCUS

Prospective memory

PM is a useful term, but it implies that memory processes are the main factor in determining task performance. This is unlikely to be entirely the case as many other variables influence outcome such as planning, attention and action control (Ellis, 1996). Also, many of the PM tasks given to participants are somewhat arbitrary in nature (e.g. 'press the space bar every five minutes'), so the factors determining success in such tasks are likely to be very different from those used in everyday PM tasks. Conclusions based on tasks limited in ecological validity thus require replication using more realistic measures.

Further reading Prospective memory

Topics	Key reading
PM in schizophrenia	Elvevåg, B., Maylor, E.A. & Gilbert, A.L. (2003). Habitual prospective memory in schizophrenia. *BMC Psychiatry, 3*(9) Available from: http://www.biomedcentral.com/1471-244x/3/9.
Comparison of prospective and episodic memory	Roediger, H.L. (1996). Prospective memory and episodic memory. In M. Brandimonte, G.O. Einstein & M.A. McDaniel (Eds.), *Prospective memory: Theory and applications* (pp.149–55). Hillsdale, NJ: Lawrence Erlbaum Associates.
Overview of PM	Kliegel, M., McDaniel, M.A. & Einstein, G.O. (2008). *Prospective memory: Cognitive, neuroscience, developmental, and applied perspectives.* Mahwah, NJ: Lawrence Erlbaum Associates.
Overview of PM	McDaniel, M.A. & Einstein, G.O. (2007). *Prospective memory: An overview and synthesis of an emerging field.* London: Sage.

Test your knowledge

Prospective memory

5.9 Define prospective memory.

5.10 What is the prospective interference effect?

5.11 What are the main differences between retrospective and prospective memory?

5.12 Outline a shortcoming of prospective memory research.

Answers to these questions can be found on the companion website at:
www.pearsoned.co.uk/psychologyexpress

Sample question   Essay

What is prospective memory and is it distinct from retrospective memory?

Chapter summary – pulling it all together

→ Can you tick all of the points from the revision checklist at the beginning of this chapter?

→ Attempt all of the Test yourself questions.

→ Attempt the essay questions within the chapter using the guidelines below.

→ Go to the companion website at www.pearsoned.co.uk/psychologyexpress to access more revision support online, including interactive quizzes, flash cards, You be the marker exercises as well as answer guidance for the Test yourself and Sample questions from this chapter.

Answer guidelines

 Sample question   Essay

Critically evaluate the claim that children are unreliable witnesses.

Approaching the question

To answer this question you will need a core of knowledge relating to the eyewitness abilities of children, as well as an understanding of some of the methodological issues in eyewitness research.

Important points to include

The answer should consist of three parts – the main section on research investigating children as witnesses, a comparison with adults and an evaluation of the methodological issues that may influence the ability of all eyewitnesses – though focusing specifically on the abilities of children. To conclude, you would disagree with a strong claim that children are always unreliable witnesses while acknowledging that their performance is usually worse than that of adults. However, given appropriate support such as props their performance can be significantly improved.

Make your answer stand out

Good answers will not be expected to cite all the information outlined in this chapter, but to show evidence of understanding why children might be poor witnesses. This will involve discussion of the circumstances in which children are tested or interviewed, as well as discussion of their cognitive abilities. It's also worth making the point that it isn't just children that make unreliable witnesses – adults don't do too well either, and in some studies have been found to be no better or even worse than child witnesses.

Explore the accompanying website at **www.pearsoned.co.uk/psychologyexpress**

→ Prepare more effectively for exams and assignments using the answer guidelines for questions from this chapter.

→ Test your knowledge using multiple choice questions and flashcards.

→ Improve your essay skills by exploring the You be the marker exercises.

Notes

Cognition and emotion

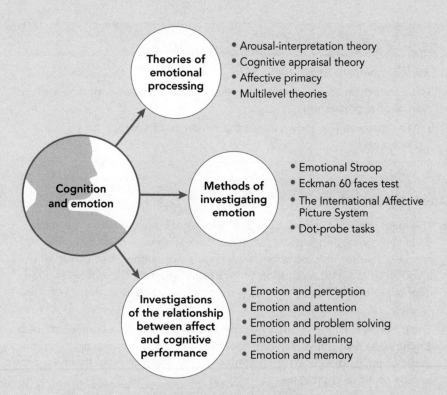

Theories of emotional processing
- Arousal-interpretation theory
- Cognitive appraisal theory
- Affective primacy
- Multilevel theories

Cognition and emotion

Methods of investigating emotion
- Emotional Stroop
- Eckman 60 faces test
- The International Affective Picture System
- Dot-probe tasks

Investigations of the relationship between affect and cognitive performance
- Emotion and perception
- Emotion and attention
- Emotion and problem solving
- Emotion and learning
- Emotion and memory

A printable version of this topic map is available from:
www.pearsoned.co.uk/psychologyexpress

Introduction

The influence of emotion has been neglected in much cognitive research. Eysenck (1997) argues this is due to the dominance of information-processing models that allow little scope for examining the influence of affective state on cognition. This misses out on an important element of our processing of information. In the previous chapter, we examined the impact of emotion on the formation of flashbulb memories, on recall of events where a weapon was present and the increased likelihood of depressed individuals remembering negative information.

In this section, we'll explore some of the work that has sought to explain the relationship between emotion and cognition. While the main focus will be on memory, we will also draw on examples from other areas of cognition.

 Revision checklist

Essential points to revise are:

❑ The four main approaches to the relationship between cognition and emotional processing

❑ What research has shown about the influence of emotion on cognitive processes

Assessment advice

● The main debate involving cognition and emotion is the extent to which cognitive processing is necessary for emotional experience. Unlike the previous chapter, the focus tends to be on theory rather than empirical work. If you were to tackle a question on this topic, you would probably include brief overviews of all the theories presented in this chapter as part of your answer.

● The theories we'll focus on can be viewed as existing on a continuum, with Zajonc's affective primacy at one end, and Lazarus's cognitive appraisal theory at the other, with arousal interpretation theory and multilevel theories in the middle of these approaches.

● **Essay questions**: Although there is significantly less work on cognition and emotion than some of the other areas we cover in this book, there is still a great deal of theory to understand. The earlier theories are fairly straightforward, but the wide range of multilevel theories require a little more effort to understand. Essay questions on this topic tend to be restricted to variations on the following 'To what extent does emotion need cognition?'. Helpfully, we've provided an outline answer to this at the end of the chapter.

Sample question

Could you answer this question? Below is a typical essay question that could arise on this topic.

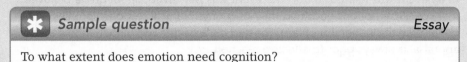

✳ *Sample question*	*Essay*

To what extent does emotion need cognition?

Guidelines on anwering this question are included at the end of this chapter, whilst guidance on tackling other exam questions can be found on the companion website at: **www.pearsoned.co.uk/psychologyexpress**

Theories of emotional processing

Several theories have been forwarded to explain the relationship between cognition and emotion. One issue that divides the various theories is the degree to which they see emotion as requiring cognitive processing.

Arousal-interpretation theory

Schacter and Singer (1962) proposed that the experience of emotion requires both physiological arousal and a label for that arousal, which comes from cognitive appraisal of the situation. This theory considers arousal to be non-specific, with it only taking on a particular form (e.g. fear) after interpreting the stimuli that caused the arousal on the basis of memories related to it. Schacter and Singer tested this prediction by injecting participants with adrenalin and then putting them in the same room as someone acting either euphorically or angrily. Participants who were misinformed (told the effects of the injection would be mild) or uninformed about the effects of the adrenalin were most likely to experience high emotion in the predicted direction.

CRITICAL FOCUS

Arousal-interpretation theory

The theory was one of the first to focus on the role of cognition in emotional events. However, different emotions are associated with different patterns of arousal, which contradicts this approach. The ecological validity of the tasks used to support the theory is low as they tended to focus only on high levels of arousal, so the theory may not apply to everyday emotions.

Cognitive appraisal theory

Arousal interpretation theory was further developed by Lazarus (1982) into his transactional account of emotional processing. For Lazarus, the emotional impact of an event was related to how the event was perceived, although he believed that specific emotions each had their own physiological response profiles, rather than the general profile suggested by Schacter and Singer. In this theory, appraisal is always prior to affective reaction.

Lazarus proposed three stages of appraisal – primary, where a situation is evaluated in terms of whether it is positive, negative or irrelevant to well-being, secondary, where the coping resources the individual has are examined, and reappraisal, where the stimulus and coping resources are reviewed and the appraisals changed if required.

KEY STUDY

Cognitive appraisal and emotional experience

In a study that demonstrated the effect of cognitive appraisal on emotional experience, Speisman, Lazarus, Mordkoff and Davidson. (1964) showed participants anxiety-provoking films including genital mutilation and a fatal workshop accident. Cognitive appraisal of the situation was manipulated by varying the soundtracks, such as by saying that the mutilation did not hurt or that the person in the workshop was an actor, which led to denial in the participants. Intellectualisation was produced by a voice-over that focused on the anthropological aspects of the mutilation film. Both denial and intellectualisation significantly reduced the level of stress reported by participants.

In an update to cognitive appraisal theory, Smith and Lazarus (1993) proposed that appraisal consisted of six components, two primary and four secondary, which were differentially activated by different emotional states.

CRITICAL FOCUS

Cognitive appraisal theory

Appraisal does appear to influence how we react to emotional stimuli. However, Lazarus's approach has been criticised for ignoring the social context as well as focusing on all emotional events as survival-threatening (Parkinson and Manstead, 1992). Similarly, because of the imprecision of the idea of appraisal it is hard to clearly characterise individuals' appraisals to given stimuli.

Affective primacy

In an alternative approach to Lazarus's contention that emotion always follows cognitive appraisal, Zajonc (1980) proposed that we can make affective judgements after very little processing of information, such as when information is presented below the level of conscious awareness. Murphy and Zajonc (1993) also found processing of emotion-related information could take place more quickly than cognitive information. In a later paper, Zajonc (2000) lists ten ways in which cognition and emotion differ, which he claimed shows that they arise from separate neuropsychological systems.

CRITICAL FOCUS

Affective primacy

Zajonc's theory that emotion can occur in the absence of cognition has been supported by a number of studies. Although there is an apparent difference between the theories of Zajonc and Lazarus, the issue is really in their views of cognition, with Zajonc viewing cognition as mental effort, and Lazarus seeing it as primitive perceptual evaluation (LeDoux, 1987). Other researchers have argued that cognition and emotion are related processes that are impossible to separate (Moors & De Houwer, 2006). At the least, it seems that the emotion-only route proposed by Zajonc is unable to process the kind of complex stimuli often used in social and emotional research.

Multilevel theories

More recent models have been proposed which attempt to explain some of the complexity of emotional behaviour that the other theories are not able to account for. Several multilevel theories exist (e.g. Power & Dalgleish, 1997; Scherer, 2001; Smith & Kirby, 2001; Teasdale & Barnard, 1993).

For example, Smith and Kirby (2001) developed a process model of emotion which divided appraisal into cognitive and associative modes, with the associative mode (which may contain information about phobias) activated at a lower threshold than the cognitive mode. Such a distinction helps to reconcile the differences in the data reported by the affective primacy and cognitive appraisal theories. Scherer (2001) extended appraisal theory to characterise individual emotions in terms of 18 dimensions. This approach suggests that emotions can be conceptualised as multidimensional.

There is some neuropsychological evidence that we do have two separate streams for emotion. For example, based on animal research, LeDoux (1996) argued that there are two hardwired emotional circuits in the amygdala, one operating quickly in response to threatening situations and the other reacting slowly after having determined the emotional significance of events.

In contrast, others have argued (e.g. Storbeck & Clore, 2007) that the study of emotion and cognition should be integrated because the phenomena themselves are integrated. They argue that rather than discrete emotions having separate and distinct areas in the brain, emotions emerge from a combination of affective and cognitive processes.

> ### CRITICAL FOCUS
>
> **Multi level theories**
>
> Multi level theories are more attractive than earlier theories as they are able to account for the range of evidence coming from studies of affect. The approach of these studies is also intuitively plausible – in some emotional situations we may act quickly or automatically (such as jumping up if a spider lands on us, despite the fact we know it's actually harmless), in others we may act in a more considered way.
>
> However, research is still at an early stage with these theories. This is partly related to the range of theories that have been put forward, but also because some of them are so complicated and break down the process so much that it's difficult to see what more they have to offer than just describing the data in the first place. Nonetheless, data does indicate that there probably are two processes operating at different speeds, which means that future theories are more likely to be multi- rather than single level.

Methods of investigating emotion

Several methods have been used to explore the relationship between cognition and emotion, including the Emotional Stroop Test and Ekman 60 Faces Test.

Emotional Stroop

In this modification of the original Stroop (1935) task, participants are shown emotional or neutral words. Interference effects exist for affective words relative to neutral words, especially when the affective words correspond with the self-schema assumed to be underlying any disorder. For example, in depressed but not in non-depressed individuals, 'failure' and 'sad' will take longer to name than neutral words. This difference is likely due to be due to interference effects arising from an attentional bias for emotionally relevant affective stimuli (Williams, Matthews & MacLeod, 1996).

Ekman 60 faces test

The Ekman 60 faces test uses a range of faces to test the recognition of six basic emotions (anger, disgust, fear, happiness, sadness and surprise). The test is used to detect impairments of emotion. Several disorders have been shown to be associated with impairment including frontotemporal and semantic dementia (e.g. Calabaria, Cotelli, Adenzato, Zanelti & Miniussi, 2009).

The International Affective Picture System

The International Affective Picture System (IAPS) is a database of photographs varying in emotion and arousal (Lang, Öhman & Vaitl, 1988). The pictures ranged from accidents and mutilations, to pleasant images of puppies and babies.

Non-clinical participants show high correlations in their ratings of these pictures and that people scoring high on a psychopathy scale show no difference in response times to positive images or neutral images while those scoring lower on the scale take longer to respond to positive images (Mitchell, Richell, Leonard & Blair, 2006).

Dot-probe tasks

The dot-probe task is a measure of selective attention (MacLeod, Mathews & Tata, 1986) used to examine attention to threatening stimuli in individuals diagnosed with anxiety disorders such as depression and post-traumatic stress disorder. In this paradigm, participants are briefly shown two stimuli, one of which is neutral and the other threatening, before a dot is presented in the location of one stimulus. Participants indicate the location of this dot as quickly as possible. Quicker reaction times in response to threatening stimuli are seen in clinically anxious individuals and has been interpreted as an elevated attention to threat. However, in a review Schultz and Heimberg (2008) found that the dot-probe paradigm produced inconsistent results and more recent work using faces instead of pictures has also shown poor reliability.

Investigations of the relationship between affect and cognitive performance

In his 2003 paper, Davidson claimed that one of the seven deadly sins of cognitive neuroscience was to assume that emotion and cognition are independent of each other. In this section, we'll examine research that has investigated the influence of affect on cognition.

Emotion and perception

Several studies have found a link between emotion and perception. For example, Riener, Stefanucci, Proffitt and Clore (2003) found that participants who had listened to sad music as they stood at the bottom of a hill were more likely to overestimate the steepness of the hill. Pain perception also appears related to mood – patients report lower levels of pain after being given antidepressants (Blumer, Zorick, Heilbronn & Roth, 1982). It is likely that pain and depression are associated – Weisenberg, Raz and Hener (1998) found participants who had just watched a humorous film had increased tolerance to cold.

Emotion and attention

Difficulties with concentration among people with depression have been widely documented (e.g. Weingartner, Cohen, Murphy, Martello & Gerdt, 1981). For example, as people become more depressed, they engage in fewer processes that require attention (Hartlage, Alloy, Vazquez & Dykman, 1993). Farrin, Hull, Unwin, Wykes and David (2003) found depressed participants made more errors than non-depressed in a test of sustained attention as well as showing increased reaction times following errors, which Farrin et al. interpreted as a form of catastrophic reaction to failure.

Öhman's visual search

Several visual search studies have observed that emotional stimuli are detected more rapidly than neutral ones. Öhman and Mineka (2001) argued this is due to the presence of a fear pathway in the brain evolved specifically to draw attention to potentially life-threatening situations by facilitating perception of threatening stimuli. This effect is stronger for negative stimuli, such as angry faces, than for positive ones (e.g. Eastwood, Smilek & Merikle, 2001).

Emotion and problem solving

In one of the few studies to have examined the influence of positive and negative emotions on problem solving, Gasper (2003) asked participants to form 4- or 5-letter words from strings of letters. She found that participants who had been asked to write about a happy event were more flexible in their reasoning than those who had written about a sad event. However, the 'sad' group were more likely to change their responses to adopt new strategies when there was evidence showing their current strategy was not working, while the happy group were more likely to change strategy spontaneously. Similarly, Isen, Daubman and Nowicki (1987) found that sad moods promoted greater attention to the data than happy ones.

Emotion and learning

Learning shows significant mood effects. For example, Norman, Tröster, Fields and Brooks (2002) found that patients with Parkinson's disease who were depressed performed significantly worse on a battery of tests, including learning lists, when compared to non-depressed patients. Poorer performance by the depressed patients could be interpreted as them having a greater level of cognitive impairment, and hence a different kind of treatment could be recommended.

Depressed individuals also appear to perform worse in tests of implicit learning (Naismith, Hickie, Ward, Scott & Little, 2006), however recent work by Pretz, Totz and Kaufman (2010) indicates that although there is a general trend for depressed people to perform worse on such tasks, individual differences may account for more of the difference between participants than the effects of mood.

Emotion and memory

As we saw in the section on eyewitness testimony, emotion can lead to a range of biases in recall. Emotion modulates and mediates cognitive processes in sometimes predictable ways. The relationship between the form of affect experienced (fear, joy, etc.) and memory has been the subject of much research.

General memory

Many common memory phenomena appear to be mediated by affect (see Storbeck & Clore, 2007 for a review). For example, schema effects in memory, semantic priming and reasoning all appear to be more pronounced in participants with positive moods, while negative mood appears to reduce the likelihood of false memory effects.

Mood reinstatement and congruence

Similarly to environmental reinstatement, recreating the mood present at encoding has been found to influence the retrieval of information. Kenealy (1997) found that free recall was significantly better when similar moods were created at encoding and retrieval by playing happy or sad music. Cued recall was unaffected by mood, which implies that although mood can influence retrieval, stronger cues surpass its influence.

In the mood-congruence effect, individuals find it easier to retrieve information that matches their current mood state. This relationship between mood and performance is believed to be caused by the activation of a semantic network of negative (or positive) memories, which enhance accessibility and the probability of retrieval of similar memories as part of semantic networks (see Bower, 1981). However, McFarland and Buehler (1998) discuss the mood-incongruent effect where people with low mood will retrieve more positive memories as a coping strategy.

Autobiographical memory

Memories for emotional autobiographical information vary with mood. Positive memories tend to be more vivid than either neutral or negative ones (D'Argembeau, Comblain & van der Linden, 2002), as well as being more resistant to forgetting which may be related to coping mechanisms by reducing the impact of negative events (Walker, Vogl & Thompson, 1997).

Depression has a significant influence on the retrieval of autobiographical memories. Most notably, this is displayed in the ease of retrieval of negative events. While in most individuals, recall of positive autobiographical memories is more detailed, in people who are depressed negative events are more vividly remembered (D'Argembeau et al., 2002). Williams and Broadbent (1986) also found that suicide attempters were able to retrieve fewer specific autobiographical memories of any kind than controls. Instead, they found that individuals with depression recalled more generalised events (repeated or recurring events). These results can be accounted for in two ways; first in terms of mood congruence, as depressed individuals remember negative events during frequent negative moods, and second, depressed individuals will often rehearse negative memories, which increases their salience and vividness.

Further reading Cognition and emotion	
Topic	*Key reading*
Relationship between cognition and emotion	Storbeck, J. & Clore, G.L. (2007). On the interdependence of cognition and emotion. *Cognition & Emotion, 21*, 1212–37. Available from: http://www.ncbi.nlm.nih.gov/pmc/articles/PMC2366118/pdf/nihms40350.pdf.
Appraisal of everyday emotion	Scherer, K.R., Wranik, T., Sangsue, J., Tran, V. & Scherer, U. (2004). Emotions in everyday life: Probability of occurrence, risk factors, appraisal and reaction pattern. *Social Science Information, 43*, 499–570. Available from: http://www.affective-sciences.org/system/files/2004_Scherer_SSI_Emosante.pdf.
Anxiety and cognition	Eysenck, M.W. (1997). *Anxiety and cognition: A unified theory.* Hove: Psychology Press.
Overview of cognition and emotions	Power, M. & Dalgleish, T. (2008). *Cognition and emotion: From order to disorder.* Hove: Psychology Press.

Test your knowledge

Cognition and emotion

6.1 What is the main shortcoming of Schacter and Singer's (1962) arousal-interpretation theory?

6.2 Outline Zajonc's (1980) theory of affective primacy.

6.3 How does mood influence learning?

6.4 List four ways that emotion influences cognition.

Answers to these questions can be found on the companion website at: **www.pearsoned.co.uk/psychologyexpress**

? Sample question   Essay

Evaluate the contribution of cognitive appraisal theory to our understanding of the relationship between cognition and emotion.

Chapter summary – pulling it all together

→ Can you tick all of the points from the revision checklist at the beginning of this chapter?

→ Attempt all of the Test yourself questions.

→ Attempt the essay questions within the chapter using the guidelines below.

→ Go to the companion website at www.pearsoned.co.uk/psychologyexpress to access more revision support online, including interactive quizzes, flash cards, You be the marker exercises as well as answer guidance for the Test yourself and Sample questions from this chapter.

Answer guidelines

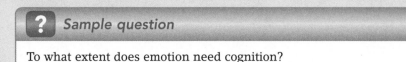

? *Sample question* **Essay**

To what extent does emotion need cognition?

Approaching the question

To answer this question it's important to focus on the precise wording – you aren't being asked whether cognition is necessary for emotion, but *how much* cognitive processing is required.

Important points to include

This question requires a brief review of the theories of cognition and emotion, with the focus on viewing them as being placed on a continuum: from the small amount of processing required by Zajonc's affective primacy theory to the greater need for cognition of Schacter and Singer's arousal interpretation theory through to the more intensive appraisal of Lazarus's theory. This approach will allow you to structure your answer more clearly, though remember to link back to the essay question after discussing each theory. Multilevel theories sit in the middle of this continuum as, like the two-process accounts of cognition and affect, they borrow from affective primacy (rapid processing) and cognitive appraisal (more considered responses). In conclusion you would want to state that cognition is a central part of emotional processing, but that the relationship between the two processes is likely to differ depending on the circumstances – quick in some situations, slower in others.

Make your answer stand out

Implicit in the question is the idea that all emotion requires at least some cognitive processing. While this is undoubtedly true (it's difficult to conceive of emotion occurring without at least some level of perception of affective information), Zajonc argued that emotion required very little cognitive effort. In addition to this, more recent multilevel theories have proposed that there are two separate processes present in the perception of emotional situations. Although multilevel theories are still in an early stage of development with some shortcomings such as over specification of emotion, this approach appears to be more representative of the range of emotional experiences we encounter.

Explore the accompanying website at **www.pearsoned.co.uk/psychologyexpress**
→ Prepare more effectively for exams and assignments using the answer guidelines for questions from this chapter.
→ Test your knowledge using multiple choice questions and flashcards.
→ Improve your essay skills by exploring the You be the marker exercises.

Notes

7

Cognitive neuropsychology

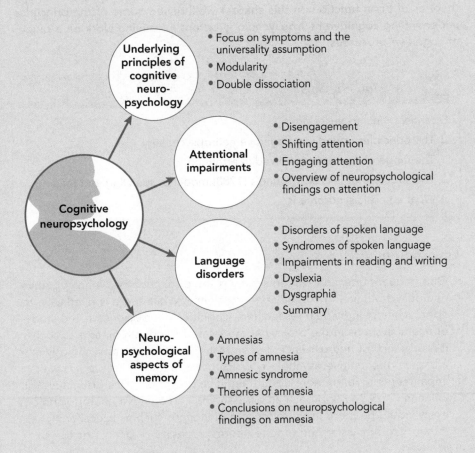

- **Underlying principles of cognitive neuro-psychology**
  - Focus on symptoms and the universality assumption
  - Modularity
  - Double dissociation

- **Attentional impairments**
  - Disengagement
  - Shifting attention
  - Engaging attention
  - Overview of neuropsychological findings on attention

- **Cognitive neuropsychology**

- **Language disorders**
  - Disorders of spoken language
  - Syndromes of spoken language
  - Impairments in reading and writing
  - Dyslexia
  - Dysgraphia
  - Summary

- **Neuro-psychological aspects of memory**
  - Amnesias
  - Types of amnesia
  - Amnesic syndrome
  - Theories of amnesia
  - Conclusions on neuropsychological findings on amnesia

A printable version of this topic map is available from:
www.pearsoned.co.uk/psychologyexpress

Introduction

Cognitive neuropsychology has had a significant impact on our understanding of a range of brain processes as well as the functional architecture of cognition. The cognitive neuropsychological approach is a non-experimental method based on the idea that one of the best ways to understand how a system works is to observe what happens when it goes wrong. By recording the errors that occur in a system a picture can be developed of how its components are organised and how they operate. Initially this approach relied almost entirely on data from patients with brain injuries; however the development of advanced imaging techniques has allowed data from non-brain-injured participants to be used to develop theories of brain function. In this chapter we'll review some of the principles underpinning cognitive neuropsychology before examining work on a range of cognitive processes.

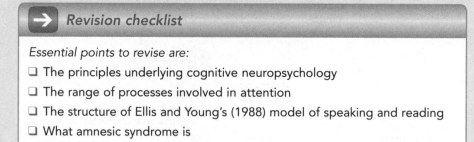

→ *Revision checklist*

Essential points to revise are:
❑ The principles underlying cognitive neuropsychology
❑ The range of processes involved in attention
❑ The structure of Ellis and Young's (1988) model of speaking and reading
❑ What amnesic syndrome is

Assessment advice

● One frequent question students have is the distinction between cognitive neuropsychology and cognitive neuroscience. While there is overlap in the approaches of individual researchers, cognitive neuroscience is the study of neural systems in the brain that are related to cognition, and as such it is a branch of neuroscience. In contrast, cognitive neuropsychology is a branch of cognitive psychology which uses data from individuals with impairments to learn more about cognitive processes. This distinction will influence how you approach an assessment – a cognitive neuropsychology essay would be more likely to focus on functions such as lexical analysis, rather than discussing the precise neural processes or brain structures involved.

● **Essay questions:** assessments on cognitive neuropsychology commonly focus on a specific area (such as attentional impairments); an understanding of the principles underlying cognitive neuropsychology will help you understand the claims made in the literature.

Sample question

Could you answer this question? Below is a typical essay question that could arise on this topic.

 Sample question   *Essay*

Critically evaluate the usefulness of the amnesic syndrome to understanding amnesia.

Guidelines on answering this question are included at the end of this chapter, whilst guidance on tackling other exam questions can be found on the companion website at: **www.pearsoned.co.uk/psychologyexpress**

Underlying principles of cognitive neuropsychology

Focus on symptoms and the universality assumption

Cognitive neuropsychological research studies symptoms rather than syndromes. This is because even within what appear to be well-defined disorders there are often clear differences between individuals who have been given the same diagnosis – for example some people with dyslexia have difficulty reading non-words, while others do not (e.g. Coltheart, 2006). As we will see below with the case of patient HM, cognitive neuropsychologists adopt a single case study approach rather than group studies; given the number of potential differences between individuals in terms of the extent and type of brain damage that has occurred, focusing on groups may mean that interesting differences are 'averaged out' between participants and so be missed by researchers.

Universality assumption

If every patient is different, how can we draw generalisable inferences about cognitive processing? This requires the 'universality assumption' (Caramazza, 1986), which is the assumption that there is no difference in cognitive processing or related processes between individuals prior to brain damage. Any difference between patients is therefore presumed to be due to their brain damage.

Modularity

Marr (1982) argued that any large computation can be split into independent and specialised subprocesses. Fodor (1983) extended this idea and suggested

The Universality assumption

This is an important concept in all branches of neuropsychology. However, individual differences do exist in 'normal' cognition (i.e. in the absence of morbidity) and so assumptions of average performance may sometimes be inappropriate. Also, patients rarely have exactly the same brain damage – without precise information about the type of brain damage present, drawing comparisons between patients can be problematic. Advances in brain scanning have the potential to address this issue.

that there are numerous cognitive processes or modules in the brain. According to Marr, modules are:

- autonomous, operating relatively independently, so that damage to one module does not directly affect other modules
- neurally distinct
- domain-specific, so that each module processes only one kind of information
- informationally encapsulated, processing in isolation from other modules
- innate
- fast
- mandatory; after activation processes proceed outside of conscious control.

Modularity

Though much data support the idea of neurological specificity, research on synaesthesia (where people might see a specific colour on hearing a particular musical note) poses a minor challenge to a strict model of modularity. Uttal (2003) has also argued against modularity in favour of domain-general processing where cognitive functions are distributed across the brain and cannot be localised into independent units.

Despite these criticisms, it is generally accepted that cognitive systems consist of relatively autonomous processing elements that can be disrupted by local brain damage, though most cognitive neuropsychologists adhere to a weaker form of modularity than that proposed by Fodor, with general agreement on domain specificity and informational encapsulation, but less agreement on his other propositions (e.g. reading is not innate!).

Subtractivity

Subtractivity is the idea that brain damage removes modules, or connections between them, but cannot add new modules or connections. The organisation of the remaining modules is also assumed to stay the same. This assumption is a good general rule, but work on brain plasticity indicates that the brain does have some ability to rebuild modules or make new or repair old connections (e.g. Mercado, 2008).

Isomorphism

Isomorphism is similar to phrenology – the idea that there is a relationship between the structure of the brain and the mind. This view is generally held to be valid, although it should be noted that cognitive functions can have functional modularity but not necessarily have anatomical modularity in that they may be distributed over several brain regions.

Transparency

Transparency is the view that deficits and normal function should indicate which module is damaged. Neuro psychological tests are assumed to allow valid conclusions to be drawn – poor performance on a digit span test will be presumed to indicate that there are problems with the cognitive module related to short-term memory function. However, given the complexity of the brain it may be possible that other processes could compensate for poor performance and so not reveal this during testing. There may also be deficits resulting from a different module from the presumed one – for example patients recalling only a few words from a list might do so because they have language problems rather than memory deficits.

Double dissociation

By observing patterns of dissociation – where two related mental processes are shown to operate independently of each other – it is possible to develop an understanding of the modular organisation of a specific cognitive ability. For example, patients with damage to Broca's area have difficulty understanding language but can still speak fluently. Other patients having damage to Wernicke's area are able to speak fluently but can't understand language. This indicates there are separate regions of the brain for language and speech.

Although determining such dissociations is important in developing an understanding of the modular architecture of cognition, Roediger (1990) argues that uncovering these relationships is not sufficient and that theorists should develop a theoretical framework to evaluate these modular accounts.

> **?** *Sample question* **Essay**
>
> Evaluate the assumptions underlying clinical neuropsychology.

Further reading Cognitive neuropsychology

Key reading

Coltheart, M. & Caramazza, A. (Eds) (2006). *Cognitive neuropsychology twenty years on.* Hove: Psychology Press.

Ellis, A.W. & Young, A.W. (1998). *Human cognitive neuropsychology: A textbook with readings.* Hove: Psychology Press.

Martin, G. (2006). *Human neuropsychology.* 2nd ed. Harlow: Pearson.

Parkin, A. (1999). *Explorations in cognitive neuropsychology.* Hove: Psychology Press.

Attentional impairments

Damage to the attention-related regions of the brain can lead to significant shifts in behaviour and experience. Cognitive neuropsychological research on visual attention has focused on the parietal cortex and thalamus. Posner and Petersen (1990) investigated disorders of visual attention and suggested that there are three separate abilities involved in visual attention: disengagement of attention, shifting of attention and engaging attention.

Disengagement

Disengagement is the ability to disengage attention from a given visual stimulus. This causes problems in patients with simultanagnosia. In this condition patients can only see one item when two or more are within their visual fields, even when the items are close together. The item they are attending to exerts a hold on attention which makes disengagement of attention difficult.

Patients with such visual neglect may only eat food on the right-hand side of their plate, or only draw one side of a picture they have been asked to copy. Note, however, that they are not blind – they are just not conscious of one side of visual space. Research with patients with neglect shows that it is possible to have no conscious perception of visual information, but still be able to make correct decisions based on this data (e.g. Marshall & Halligan, 1988; see also Blindsight, below).

KEY STUDY

Marshall and Halligan's burning house study

Marshall and Halligan (1988) presented a patient having left-sided neglect with two drawings of a house. The pictures were identical except that one had flames coming out of one of the windows. The patient reported no conscious awareness of the pictures when they were presented to the left visual field, though when asked to choose between them, she chose the one without the flames, indicating information can be accessed at a pre-conscious level.

Blindsight

Patients with blindsight (Weiskrantz, 1986) have damage to the primary occipital cortex but remain able to discriminate between stimuli that they have no conscious awareness of. Patients can determine the location, direction of movement, speed and size and some colour (Cowey & Stoerig, 2001), though they have little ability to determine object shape.

The basis for blindsight is uncertain. Barbur, Ruddock and Waterfield (1980) argue that information is detected through the superior colliculus, which is able to pick up object location and movement. However, Weiskrantz and others have pointed to the ability to detect more complex information such as object contours and colour which indicates that some cortical processing must be occurring – perhaps through links between subcortical structures and other (non-primary) regions of the visual cortex.

Shifting attention

Posner, Rafal, Choate and Vaughn (1985) studied patients with progressive supranuclear palsy. These patients have damage to the midbrain and consequently have difficulty making voluntary eye movements. Visual cueing studies show they also have difficulty shifting their attention vertically. Problems with shifting attention are also found in patients with Balint's syndrome who usually have severe difficulty with spatial tasks, such as orienting to visual stimuli, reaching for objects and grasping them. When stimuli are spaced far apart, patients with Balint's have more difficulty making judgements about whether, for example, the shapes are all the same colour, than when the shapes are closer together, due to their inability to shift their attention from one stimulus to another. This orientation problem also occurs in other modalities.

Engaging attention

Rafal and Posner (1987) examined patients with damage to the pulvinar nucleus of the thalamus. Visual cueing showed that responses were faster when valid cues were given (i.e. cue and following target were on the same side of the screen), and this was the case whether the target presented was to the damaged or undamaged side. However, responses were much slower when the target was presented to the side of visual field opposite to that of the brain damage. This suggests participants had a problem engaging their attention to the stimulus.

LaBerge and Buchsbaum (1990) found increased blood flow in the pulvinar nucleus when participants were told to ignore a certain stimulus. Therefore this region appears to be involved in preventing attention from being focused on an unwanted stimulus and in directing attention to significant stimuli.

Overview of neuropsychological findings on attention

According to Posner and Petersen (1990) these findings suggest that the parietal lobe first disengages attention from its present focus, then the midbrain area acts to move the index of attention to the area of the target, and the pulvinar nucleus is involved in reading out data from the indexed locations. Such division of attentional operations provides good support for the modularity hypothesis.

Further reading Cognitive neuropsychology of attention

Topic	Key reading
Attentional deficits due to lesions	Arend, I., Rafal, R. & Ward, R. (2008). Spatial and temporal deficits are regionally dissociable in patients with pulvinar lesions. *Brain*, *131*, 2140–52. Available from: http://brain. oxfordjournals.org/cgi/content/full/131/8/2140.
Simultanagnosia	Dalrymple K.A., Kingstone, A. & Barton, J.J.S. (2007). Seeing trees or seeing forests in simultanagnosia: Attentional capture can be local or global. *Neuropsychologia*, *45*, 871–5.
Blindsight	Danckert, J. & Rossetti, Y. (2005). Blindsight in action: What can the different sub-types of blindsight tell us about the control of visually guided actions? *Neuroscience & Biobehavioral Reviews*, *29*, 1035–46.
Supranuclear palsy	Williams, D.R., de Silva, R., Paviour, D.C. et al. (2005). Characteristics of two distinct clinical phenotypes in pathologically proven progressive supranuclear palsy. *Brain*, *128*, 1247–58. Available from: http://brain.oxfordjournals.org/ content/128/6/1247.full.

Test your knowledge

Cognitive neuropsychology of attention

7.1 What assumptions does cognitive neuropsychology make about the brain?

7.2 Describe simultanagnosia.

7.3 Which processes did Posner and Petersen argue contributed to attention?

7.4 Describe the deficits associated with Balint's syndrome.

Answers to these questions can be found on the companion website at: **www.pearsoned.co.uk/psychologyexpress**

 Sample question   *Essay*

Discuss how studies of visual neglect contribute to our understanding of the processes involved in attention.

Language disorders

Disorders of language are generally divided into problems with spoken language, and problems with written language; we'll do the same here.

Disorders of spoken language

Disorders of spoken language provide an excellent example of the modularity principle. Data from patients and healthy individuals have revealed a range of modules involved in language comprehension and production and led to the development of a functional architecture for hearing and speaking words (see Ellis & Young, 1988, and Figure 7.1).

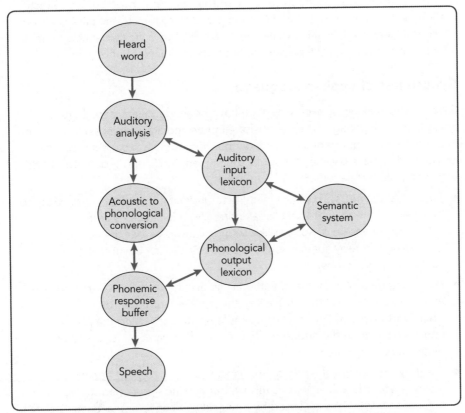

Figure 7.1 Ellis and Young's (1988) model for the recognition, comprehension and repetition of spoken words

Adapted from Parkin, A. (1999). *Explorations in cognitive neuropsychology*. Hove: Psychology Press, page 133, Figure 7.2

According to Ellis and Young, the modules have the following functions:

- *Auditory (acoustic) analysis*: converts speech into a phonemic code (e.g. 'ch', 'ee').
- *Auditory input lexicon*: the phonemic code accesses the lexicon to find a match for the code (i.e. a match with a stored word).
- *Semantic system*: the meaning of the activated word is extracted.
- *Phonological output lexicon*: this contains information about how to pronounce words.
- *Phonemic response buffer*: responsible for speech generation.
- *Acoustic to phonological conversion*: a direct route from acoustic analysis to the phonemic response buffer enables reproduction of non-words which lack lexical entries.

The modular account has been reasonably well specified, and it is possible to see how problems in specific modules will lead to predictable problems in speech comprehension and production. For example, disturbance to the auditory input lexicon will lead to difficulties with object naming, but if the semantic system is intact then patients will still be able to describe the function of objects.

Syndromes of spoken language

Several syndromes in spoken language have been identified, based on assessment of language comprehension (understanding utterances), production (making meaningful utterances, for example describing a picture such as the cookie theft picture used by Goodglass & Kaplan, 1972) and repetition of both familiar and unfamiliar words and non-words.

- *Pure word deafness.* This is an inability to understand spoken words, despite being able to read, write and speak normally. This indicates a problem with comprehension of speech-like sounds caused by deficits in phonemic processing whereby speech sounds cannot be broken down into their constituent phonemes.
- *Pure word meaning deafness.* Patients can accurately repeat words but are unable to understand their meaning, though the words can be understood when written down. This implies a problem with converting the phonemes into information in the auditory input lexicon that can be processed effectively by the semantic system.
- *Auditory phonological agnosia.* This is an inability to repeat non-words or novel new words (e.g. scientific terms), but with no impairment to repetition of familiar words. This is caused by a difficulty in converting acoustic inputs to phonological information.
- *Anomia.* Patients with anomia have an impaired ability to name objects. This could be due to problems either at the semantic level (semantic anomia) with selecting the correct abstract form of the word (the lemma) from the lexicon – such as saying 'celery' instead of 'lettuce'. Difficulties could also exist at the phonological level in producing the correct phonological form of the word,

despite the word being present in the lexicon – an extreme version of the 'tip of the tongue' phenomenon.

- *Anomia for proper versus common nouns.* Some patients cannot recall names of people but have otherwise excellent memory; this indicates that proper and common nouns are represented differently in the brain (Kripke, 1980).

- *Neologistic jargon aphasia.* Patients with jargon aphasia can speak grammatically but have difficulty finding the correct words to the extent that they make up new words, such as using 'cherching' for 'chasing' or 'stringt' for 'stream' (Ellis, Miller & Sin, 1983). Jargon aphasia is also known as fluent or Wernicke's aphasia after the researcher who described patients with good comprehension and fluency but poor meaning to speech.

- *Agrammatism.* This is the opposite of jargon aphasia, where patients can find the correct words but can't order them grammatically. Agrammatism is also known as non-fluent or Broca's aphasia. The double dissociation of the symptoms of agrammatism and jargon aphasia is an indication that there are separate stages for the planning of syntax (agrammatism) and content (jargon aphasia).

- *Dysphasia.* A less severe version of aphasia, though the term is often used more broadly to refer to problems with spoken and written communication.

Impairments in reading and writing

Difficulties with reading and writing have been examined extensively in patients with brain damage. Ellis and Young (1988) extended their model of spoken word recognition to incorporate these problems (see Figure 7.2).

Ellis and Young's extended model contains three visual modules corresponding to their auditory equivalents. These consist of:

1 *Visual analysis*: analyses the written word to determine its constituent graphemes – individual letters or specific combinations of letters (e.g. 'ck').

2 *Visual input lexicon*: receives inputs from visual analysis and matches these to stored representations of words.

3 *Grapheme to phoneme conversion (GPC)*: uses knowledge about pronunciation to determine how both familiar and unfamiliar words should sound.

As we saw with spoken language, disturbance to any of the modules in this model will lead to predictable problems with reading. For example, people with surface dyslexia who over-rely on rules of pronunciation for grapheme to phoneme conversion will be likely to make mistakes when words are pronounced irregularly, such as corps and sword.

Dyslexia

Dyslexia is an umbrella term for a range of difficulties in reading. As we're focusing on cognitive neuropsychology in this chapter, we'll examine acquired dyslexias – those which occur after brain damage, rather than developmental

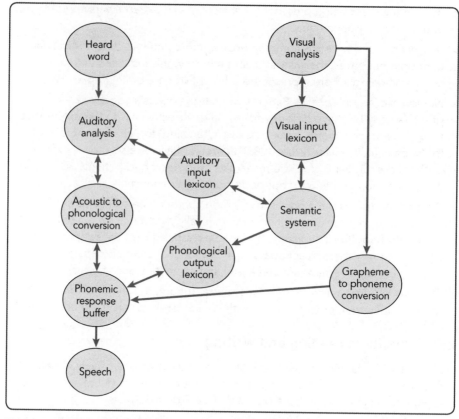

Figure 7.2 Ellis and Young's (1988) spoken word model extended to include a modular account of reading.

Adapted from Parkin, A. (1999). *Explorations in cognitive neuropsychology.* Hove: Psychology Press, page 155, Figure 8.1

dyslexias (for further details on developmental dyslexias, see the Ramus et al. paper in the Further reading section below). Dyslexias can be divided into two categories, peripheral and central.

Central dyslexia

Central dyslexias affect the ability to understand and read aloud written words. Three forms of central dyslexia have been identified – surface, phonological and deep. The range of deficits observed in each of these can be related back to problems with the modules identified in Ellis and Young's model.

- *Surface dyslexia.* This causes problems with reading irregular words due to over-reliance on grapheme–phoneme conversion rules (e.g. pronouncing 'pint' to rhyme with 'hint'). Impairment is not total, which implies that some ability to use other modules remains. As surface dyslexics display a wide range of abilities, the usefulness of the term is disputed.

- *Phonological dyslexia.* individuals with phonological dyslexia have problems with reading unfamiliar words and non-words (Beauvois & Dérousené, 1979). In phonological dyslexia, visual errors occur, but not semantic errors.

- *Deep dyslexia.* In deep dyslexia there are difficulties with reading unfamiliar words as well as both semantic errors (e.g. reading 'duel' as 'sword') and visual errors (e.g. reading 'polite' for 'politics'). Problems are particularly apparent for function words (e.g. 'the', 'it') which are often missed out (Marshall & Newcombe, 1973).

Peripheral dyslexias

Peripheral dyslexias are related to disruptions in the early stages of word recognition reducing the ability to process the visual forms of written words.

Three types of peripheral dyslexia have been identified: neglect dyslexia, attentional dyslexia and pure alexia.

- *Attentional dyslexia.* Although reading is still possible through recognising whole words, individual letters can be detected but not combined with their neighbours (e.g. identifying the letter 'h' in 'chop' but the attentional system suppresses the remaining letters). The cause of this is uncertain and perhaps relates to problems controlling the attentional spotlight. Shallice (1988) argued it took place early in processing; Warrington, Cipolotti and McNeil (1993) argued it was later.

- *Neglect dyslexia.* Neglect dyslexia affects the processing of letters at one end of a word, or whole words on one side of text, usually the left. For example, 'huge' would be misread as 'hug' (Hillis et al., 2005).

- *Pure alexia (or letter-by-letter reading).* Complete written words cannot be recognised. Each letter has to be identified separately before the word can be established and so reading proceeds slowly, with short words read faster than long ones. Pure alexia is likely to be due to an impairment in ability to parallel process letters in a word.

The dual-route cascaded model

The dual-route cascaded model (DRC) (Coltheart, Rastle, Perry, Langdon & Ziegler, 2001) is probably the best explanation for the deficits observed in the dyslexias outlined in the preceding sections. DRC is a computational model of reading, based on the modules and processes shown in Figure 7.2. DRC has two main assumptions. First, processing throughout the model is cascaded, with activation in earlier modules immediately flowing to later modules. Second, there are three* routes for translating written words into sound: a lexical semantic route, a lexical non-semantic route using word-specific knowledge, and a non-lexical grapheme-to-phoneme conversion (GPC; see Figure 7.2). The DRC is a useful framework to describe problems patients have reading aloud.

---

* As the two lexical routes are contrasted with the phonological route, the model is referred to as dual route.

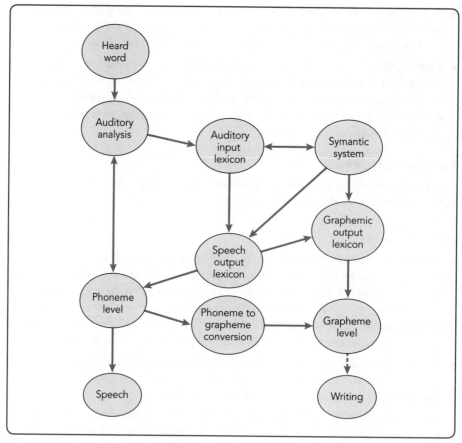

Figure 7.3 Ellis and Young's (1988) model for the recognition, comprehension and repetition of spelling of heard words

Adapted from Ellis, A.W. and Young, A.W. (1998). *Human cognitive neuropsychology: A textbook with readings.* Hove: Psychology Press. Page 175, Figure 7.1.

The DRC model

Assumption of independence

The DRC model assumes that the phonological and lexical routes are separate, however Glushko (1979) found non-words that were similar to irregular words (e.g. 'sint' and 'pint') took longer to name than when they were similar to regular names (e.g. 'sint' and 'hint') which implies that the lexical route can affect the non-lexical route.

Naming and word regularity

DRC also predicts that the naming of familiar words should not be related to their spelling. However, irregularly spelt words are usually named more slowly (Harley, 1995).

The summation hypothesis

Some patients have impaired semantics but intact reading of irregular words. Hillis and Caramazza (1991) proposed that there is only a lexical semantic and a non-lexical route, and that when the semantic route is partially impaired, information from the non-lexical route, even for an irregular word, summed with semantically approximate information from the impaired semantic route, is sufficient to support correct reading of irregular words.

Connectionist attractor model

Plaut, McClelland, Seidenberg and Patterson (1996) argued severe impairment of semantic memory cannot leave reading of irregular words intact. Instead, patients with semantic impairment will show surface dyslexia, as a degraded semantic system will impair the ability to know what a real word is.

Dysgraphia

Dysgraphia is an impairment of spelling or writing and follows a similar modular pattern to both spoken language and reading. Extending the model presented in Figure 7.2, Ellis and Young (1988) proposed (Figure 7.3) the following modules:

- *Graphemic output lexicon*: a memory store containing the spellings of familiar words. It is probable that there are different graphemic and phonological output lexicons.
- *Phonological output lexicon*: provides information about the spoken form of words.
- *Phoneme–grapheme conversion*: when words are unknown or non-words, spellings are constructed from the spoken form of the word.

Dysgraphias that affect spelling are central and those that affect writing are peripheral. As with dyslexia, we will examine acquired disorders following brain damage rather than developmental difficulties.

Central dysgraphias

- *Surface dysgraphia.* Reliance on phoneme–grapheme conversion rather than the graphemic output lexicon will lead to good performance on spelling non-words but predictable regularisation errors for irregular words (e.g. 'cassel' for 'castle').
- *Phonological dysgraphia.* This occurs with damage to the phoneme–grapheme module and results in deficits in spelling of non-words. There has been debate about whether there are separate lexicons for the spelling of words (i.e. orthographic lexicons) for reading and for writing (see e.g. Miceli & Capasso, 2006). Research with patients who have significantly better reading than spelling or vice versa appears to support this idea. However, other work has found that some patients could not detect the correct version of a word in

comparison to their own misspelt versions. Brain imaging data should help to clarify this debate.

- *Deep dysgraphia.* Deep dysgraphia causes problems at the semantic level (e.g. writing 'time' when the heard word is 'clock') but suggests that the route from semantics to the graphemic output lexicon remain operative (Bub & Kertesz, 1982).

- *Non-semantic spelling.* Patterson (1986) reported a patient who could not speak, repeat, read aloud, name objects, write the names of objects or write spontaneously, but performed dictation well. The absence of semantic knowledge but with intact spelling of even irregular words indicates spelling can operate via a non-semantic route.

Peripheral dysgraphias

- *Grapheme level impairment.* Patients make frequent spelling errors orally and in writing. These include additions, deletions, transpositions and letter substitutions in writing to dictation (e.g 'b' for 'p'). Patients are able to copy and form letters, which indicates the problem is at grapheme level where abstract letter identity forms are stored.

- *Allograph level impairment.* This is characterised by problems with writing the correct letters (e.g. 'starze' for 'starve') despite good performance on spelling aloud (Goodman & Caramazza, 1986). This indicates that the grapheme level is functioning correctly, and well-formed letters shows that there is no motor pattern impairment. This points to difficulty in assigning the correct letter shape to the appropriate grapheme.

- *Motor pattern impairment.* In this disorder, patients have difficulty in retrieving graphic motor patterns to allow them to write. Patients can spell out loud and well as copy words but are not able to write spontaneously (e.g. Baxter & Warrington, 1986).

Summary

Studies of dysgraphic patients reveal that spelling and writing rely on multiple routes and that the functional architecture of spelling and writing is highly modular.

Evidence from surface dysgraphic and dyslexic patients suggests that there is more than one orthographic lexicon used for reading and writing, although this hypothesis awaits converging data from brain imaging studies.

Further reading Language disorders

Topic	Key reading
DRC model	Besner, D. & Roberts, M.A. (2003). Reading nonwords aloud: Results requiring change in the dual route cascaded model. *Psychonomic Bulletin & Review, 10*, 398–404. Available from: http://pbr.psychonomic-journals.org/content/10/2/398.full.pdf+html.
Dyslexia	Ramus, F., Rosen, S., Dakin, S.C. et al. (2003). Theories of developmental dyslexia: insights from a multiple case study of dyslexic adults. *Brain, 126*, 841–65. Available from: http://brain.oxfordjournals.org/content/126/4/841.long.
Dyslexia and dysgraphia	Rapcsak, S.Z., Beeson, P.M. & Henry, M.L. (2009). Phonological dyslexia and dysgraphia: Cognitive mechanisms and neural substrates. *Cortex, 45*, 575–91. Available from: http://www.ncbi.nlm.nih.gov/pmc/articles/PMC2689874/.
Disorders of reading and writing	Ellis, A.W. (1993). *Reading, writing and dyslexia.* 2nd ed. Hove: Psychology Press.

Test your knowledge

Language disorders

7.5 Describe auditory phonological agnosia.

7.6 What is the difference between Broca's aphasia and Wernicke's aphasia?

7.7 How do deep and surface dyslexia differ?

7.8 What is phonological dysgraphia?

Answers to these questions can be found on the companion website at:
www.pearsoned.co.uk/psychologyexpress

 Sample question   **Essay**

Discuss how studies of disorders have informed our knowledge of the processes involved in understanding and producing spoken words.

Neuropsychological aspects of memory

Brain damage has had a significant impact on our understanding of memory processes. In this section, we'll examine research on patients with amnesia.

Amnesias

Amnesia is a condition involving partial or total loss of memory, which may last a relatively short period of time or be permanent.

Causes of amnesia

Amnesia has several origins which can be divided into organic and psychogenic.

- *Organic causes* arise from injury to the brain through accidents or medical procedures, diseases (e.g. Alzheimer's), infections (e.g. viral encephalitis) or vitamin deficiency (e.g. Korsakoff's syndrome). The physiological basis of organic amnesia provides an insight into the location of memory processing through brain imaging.

- *Psychogenic causes* include psychological trauma, for example post-traumatic stress disorder (PTSD), dissociative amnesia where the traumatic events are forgotten, or dissociative fugue where stressful events lead to an inability to recall personal information, though this is usually limited to a few hours and the individual is always aware of the memory impairment.

The significant range of potential causes of amnesia, as well as issues like age of onset, makes interpreting the causes of the deficits seen in these patients difficult.

Types of amnesia

Memory is a complex process, and deficits can express themselves in many ways. One way of categorising memory deficits is by reference to whether the memory deficit is for information learned before or after the onset of amnesia.

- *Retrograde amnesia*: deficits recalling events occurring before the onset of amnesia. Note that this will not remove all memories prior to the onset of amnesia – a patient may retain clear memories of their childhood but have poorer memory for information learnt closer to when the amnesia occurred.

- *Anterograde amnesia*: deficits learning following the onset of the disorder. Patients will have good recall of events prior to the amnesia, but be unable to retain new information.

- *Post-traumatic amnesia*: refers to a range of cognitive impairments, including memory loss and confusion, following traumatic brain injury. Memory loss may be initially extensive (patients may be unable to remember their name) but will recover so that only the events that occurred just prior to the accident cannot be recalled.

- *Transient global amnesia (TGA)*: a temporary loss of all memory, especially the ability to form new memories, with milder loss of past memories, going back several hours. This form is rare and seen mostly in older people or those that have had electroconvulsive therapy. Unlike other types of amnesia, patients are usually aware of their memory loss.

The classic case of HM

One of the most well-known amnesic patients is HM, who underwent brain surgery to relieve the symptoms of severe epilepsy (Scoville & Milner, 1957). Although the surgery helped with his seizures, HM was left with profound episodic memory problems, including anterograde amnesia and some temporally graded retrograde amnesia (he was unable to recall any events from two years before his surgery but had better recall for events that took place prior to this). Despite these deficits, HM could learn new motor skills (e.g. mirror drawing), indicating his procedural memory was intact; he could also successfully perform tasks that relied only on short-term or working memory. Later research showed that HM could retain some information such as names of famous faces (Kensinger & Corkin, 2000) though these lacked detail and required cueing.

Findings from research on HM have been crucial to the development of cognitive neuropsychology, in particular the development of the modular understanding of memory function.

Amnesic syndrome

Most research on amnesia has focused on the amnesic syndrome. This is a permanent global disorder of memory following brain damage where patients are unable to learn new episodic information (i.e. anterograde amnesia). Patients have intact short-term and procedural memory as well as IQ, but may have some degree of retrograde amnesia. Patient HM (see the 'Key study') presented a classic case of amnesic syndrome. Patients with Korsakoff's disease are also usually considered to have amnesic syndrome. However, the widespread damage to cognitive regions of the brain in Korsakoff's may have an indirect impact on memory so it is difficult to make precise predictions about brain function, though Leng and Parkin (1988), found short-term memory deficits in Korsakoff's patients.

The amnesic syndrome

The amnesic syndrome is a broad category – compare this, for example, to the number of subtypes of dyslexia – and as such is of limited use in describing the specific problems faced by individual patients. Furthermore, it is unclear that the processes involved in anterograde and retrograde amnesia are functionally separate as patients rarely have one form of amnesia without at least elements of the other (Mayes & Downes, 1997).

One of the reasons that the amnesic syndrome is so broad is due to the difficulty in specifying the location of the damage in patients. The components associated with memory are numerous, often situated close together and, until recently, usually only accessible post-mortem. Although data from patients who have had brain injuries is useful, widespread damage makes it more difficult to determine which regions are associated with the impairment, which complicates life for the neuroscientist, though less so for the neuropsychologist. Advanced brain imaging techniques such as functional magnetic resonance imaging (fMRI) present an opportunity to move on from an overly broad term towards the specification of a range of amnesic syndromes.

Theories of amnesia

Research on amnesics has implications for the theories of general memory, for example anterograde amnesia cannot be accounted for by the multi-store model of long-term memory. Amnesics also show improvement with practice on puzzles such as the Towers of Hanoi, despite having no recollection of having practised the task. Such findings have led to the development of new theories of memory, using data from patients and non-brain-damaged individuals as well as an understanding of modularity. A central goal of theorists has been to explain why some information is lost and other information retained.

Episodic and semantic memory

Semantic memory is usually intact in amnesics – patients can usually converse without difficulty and perform well on IQ tests, but have pronounced deficits in episodic memory. However, making a comparison between the two is problematic, given that language and intellectual abilities are developed before the onset of amnesia, and semantic information is acquired afterwards. Nonetheless, research on patients with amnesia (e.g. Brandt, Gardiner, Vargha-Khadem, Baddeley & Mishkin, 2008) has shown that the processes underlying episodic and semantic memory do appear to be functionally, and probably anatomically, separate.

Explicit and implicit memory

Amnesics tend to show impairment on explicit tasks (e.g. recall, recognition), but will perform normally on implicit tests (e.g. priming). However, other studies have found both normal recognition memory in amnesics (Kopelman & Stanhope, 1998) and impaired priming (Schacter, Church & Bolton, 1995). These differences may be due to differences in the location of brain damage. Schacter et al. argue that the distinction between explicit and implicit is largely descriptive and does not explain why the memory impairments exist. Relational memory binding theory – where memory for items that are bound together such as letter and location is better than for separate items (see, e.g. Hannula, Tranel & Cohen, 2006) – gives a better account of the data. However, both this and implicit/explicit theory are problematic as neither considers the area and nature of the brain damage that has occurred.

Declarative and procedural knowledge

Some theorists have suggested that amnesia may be due to impairment of declarative (factual) knowledge while procedural (skill) knowledge remains intact (e.g. Cohen & Squire, 1980). Evidence to support this includes the acquisition of motor skills as quickly in amnesics as in healthy individuals, and improvement on tasks such as the Towers of Hanoi. The distinction between declarative and procedural knowledge hence appears useful for amnesia: nonetheless, tasks are rarely process-pure, so the appropriate focus is on the processes that underlie performance on various memory tasks.

Conclusions on neuropsychological findings on amnesia

One of the main difficulties with the study of amnesia has been the assumption that the deficits in memory would all stem from the same set of underlying causes. This is very different from other areas of cognition (see reading and attention, just within this chapter) where heterogeneity of impairments is the norm. As Ellis and Young (1988) point out, it would be very strange if long-term memory was the single exception to this rule, and it is likely that rather than a unitary form of amnesia, multiple syndromes exist.

Further reading Cognitive neuropsychology of memory

Topic	Key reading
Patient HM	Corkin, S. (2002). What's new with the amnesic patient H.M.? *Nature Reviews Neuroscience, 3,* 153–60.
Amnesia	Hannula, D.E., Tranel, D. & Cohen, N.J. (2006). The long and the short of it: Relational memory impairments in amnesia, even at short lags. *The Journal of Neuroscience, 26,* 8352–9. Available from: http://www.jneurosci.org/cgi/reprint/26/32/8352.
Retrograde amnesia	Levine, B., Black, S.E., Cabeza, R. et al. (1998). Episodic memory and the self in a case of isolated retrograde amnesia. *Brain, 121,* 1951–73. Available from: http://brain.oxfordjournals.org/content/121/10/1951.full.pdf.
Overview of cognitive neuropsychology of memory	Parkin, A.J. (1997). *Memory and amnesia: An introduction.* Oxford: Blackwell.
Case studies of patients with neuropsychological deficits	Sacks, O. (1985). *The man who mistook his wife for a hat.* London: Picador.

Test your knowledge

Neuropsychological aspects of memory

7.9 Explain the difference between organic and psychogenic amnesia.

7.10 What is transient global amnesia?

7.11 Define relational memory binding theory.

7.12 Describe the difference between the performance of amnesics on declarative and procedural tasks.

Answers to these questions can be found on the companion website at: **www.pearsoned.co.uk/psychologyexpress**

Chapter summary – pulling it all together

→ Can you tick all of the points from the revision checklist at the beginning of this chapter?

→ Attempt all of the Test yourself questions.

→ Attempt the essay questions within the chapter using the guidelines below.

→ Go to the companion website at www.pearsoned.co.uk/psychologyexpress to access more revision support online, including interactive quizzes, flash cards, You be the marker exercises as well as answer guidance for the Test yourself and Sample questions from this chapter.

Answer guidelines

 Sample question   *Essay*

Critically evaluate the usefulness of the amnesic syndrome to understanding amnesia.

Approaching the question

This question requires a description of amnesic syndrome, a recognition that as a term it is useful only in very general terms, and that further work is required to delineate this syndrome into more tightly defined disorders.

Important points to include

Start by defining amnesic syndrome, outlining its principal characteristics – permanent global disorder of memory following brain damage, anterograde amnesia, but intact short-term and procedural memory and IQ. Refer (briefly) to HM. The processes involved in anterograde and retrograde amnesia are unlikely to be functionally separate as patients rarely have one form of amnesia only. Also point out that some retrograde amnesia may exist. This last issue will lead you into a critique of the syndrome. The first thing to point out is the variability in symptoms observed in patients, even those having the same diagnosis (e.g. Korsakoff's). This indicates a lack of precision in the amnesic syndrome and a need for greater accuracy in describing patients' deficits. This requires a better taxonomy of amnesias, similar to that which exists for dyslexia. This is likely to only come about with converging data coming from cognitive neuropsychology and brain imaging data from cognitive neuroscience.

Make your answer stand out

One of the difficulties with the amnesic syndrome is that it does not include the full range of deficits that patients experience. Refer to research, such as Levine et al.'s (1998) paper referred to in the Further reading list above, which presents data on deficits outside the definition of the syndrome. In doing so you would point out the seemingly contradictory points that amnesic syndrome is too general to really be useful in specifying the deficits a specific patient will experience, but also that as a syndrome it ignores some important elements of memory dysfunction in some patients.

Explore the accompanying website at **www.pearsoned.co.uk/psychologyexpress**

→ Prepare more effectively for exams and assignments using the answer guidelines for questions from this chapter.
→ Test your knowledge using multiple choice questions and flashcards.
→ Improve your essay skills by exploring the You be the marker exercises.

Notes

Notes

Language 1: Language production and comprehension

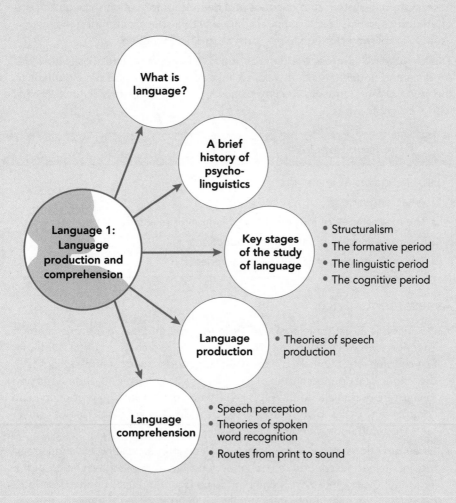

A printable version of this topic map is available from:
www.pearsoned.co.uk/psychologyexpress

Introduction

Language is central to life as a human being; in fact in many ways it is what separates us from the rest of the animal kingdom. It is how we communicate to others our intentions, instructions, desires, thoughts and dreams. It is fundamental to human civilisation, and is viewed as one of the key developments of human evolution.

Today the term language has many meanings, for example, spoken language, written language and other non-vocal forms of communication such as sign language. However, essential to all of these forms of language is the same basic system; a system that encodes and decodes information through the use of arbitrary symbols. Each symbol is paired with a specific intended meaning, usually established through some form of social convention.

This chapter will address the different forms of language, specifically how we produce and understand it. It will also look at the history and development of the study of language and the key stages in its formation as a distinct discipline within psychology.

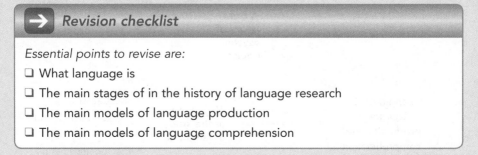

→ Revision checklist

Essential points to revise are:
- ❑ What language is
- ❑ The main stages of in the history of language research
- ❑ The main models of language production
- ❑ The main models of language comprehension

Assessment advice

- Language is a vast topic area, too large to cover in detail in a single chapter. Therefore, we've decided to split the topic into two chapters. This is the first chapter, which initially covers what language actually is and highlights definitions of language and the history of psycholinguistics. It then goes on to illustrate and evaluate the prominent theories of language production and comprehension. For all of these, we've provided key readings to give you a more in-depth understanding of the issues.

- **Essay questions:** most of the essays you'll encounter relating to language will require a clear description of each theory before a detailed evaluation of the individual theory. In essays a common issue is an emphasis on the description rather than the evaluation. Importantly, when appropriate the mechanisms behind the theories should also be highlighted. Within the evaluation process one should also always bear in mind if the model or theory is a plausible candidate for real life observations and the empirical data.

Sample question

Could you answer this question? Below is a typical essay question that could arise on this topic.

✱ *Sample question*	*Essay*

Critically contrast two models of speech production.

Guidelines on answering this question are included at the end of this chapter, whilst guidance on tackling other exam questions can be found on the companion website at: **www.pearsoned.co.uk/psychologyexpress**

What is language?

There are over 6,000 spoken languages in the world today, but the majority will share at least some properties. There have been many attempts to identify the properties that define a language. One of the most famous comes from Hockett (1960): he suggested that there were 13 linguistic universals – characteristics that were common to all human language:

1 *Arbitrariness.* There is no inherent connection between symbols and the objects they refer to.
2 *Broadcast transmission.* Messages are transmitted in all directions and can be received by any hearer.
3 *Cultural transmission.* Language is acquired through exposure to culture.
4 *Discreteness.* A distinct range of possible speech sounds exist in language.
5 *Displacement.* Messages are not tied to a particular time.
6 *Duality of structure.* A small set of phonemes can be combined and re-combined into an infinitely large set of meanings.
7 *Interchangeability.* Humans are both message perceivers and message producers.
8 *Productivity.* Novel messages can be produced according to the rules of the language.
9 *Semanticity.* Meaning is conveyed by the symbols of the language.
10 *Specialisation.* Sounds of a language are specialised to convey meaning (as compared with non-language sounds).
11 *Total feedback.* The speaker of a language has auditory feedback that occurs at the same time the listener receives the message.

12 *Transitoriness.* Linguistic messages fade rapidly.

13 *Vocal–auditory channel.* Means of transmission of the language is vocal–auditory.

There are a number of problems with this definition. One problem is that it applies only to verbal communication. Both British Sign Language (BSL) and American Sign Language (ASL) are recognised languages with their own vocabulary, grammar and phonology. Another problem that has been raised is related to the issue of 'total feedback,' audio feedback may not be available to all verbal language speakers. For example, an individual who is deaf may be able to produce verbal language without 'hearing' it in conventional terms (for a discussion of the linguistic universals of sign language see Fromkin, 1988).

Although there are many different definitions of what a language is, there are two fundamental aspects of language which the vast majority of psychologists do agree upon: language must involve the meaningful coding and production of a form of language output, and conversely, language must also entail active reception and comprehension through the decoding of the language output.

The study of the structure of language is also of great importance. There are a number of different components to what we would view as language (see Table 8.1).

Table 8.1 Components and definitions of language

Component	Definition
Phoneme	A phoneme is the smallest unit within a language system. These fundamental sound blocks are created by alternating the opening and closing of the vocal tract in set sequences. Different languages have different numbers of phonemes. The number of phonemes within the English language varies according to dialect, but most researchers would agree it is somewhere between 40 and 45.
Morpheme	The morpheme is the smallest unit within any language that can have meaning on its own. Morphemes are made up of combinations of phonemes. A morpheme is not always a word, as it can't always stand up on its own, for example, 'un', is not a word on its own, but it can change the meaning of a word from 'well' to 'unwell'. It is the smallest chunk of a language that can have semantic meaning.
The lexicon	Within any language the lexicon comprises the complete set of morphemes available within that language.
Syntax	Syntax is simply the rules for putting words together into a sentence.
Semantics	Semantics refer to the meaning of language.
Discourse	Any analysis of language beyond the level of the sentence is referred to as discourse.

Test your knowledge

What is language?

8.1 What are the main defining features of language?

8.2 What is a phoneme?

8.3 What is a morpheme?

8.4 What is the lexicon?

8.5 What is syntax?

8.6 What are semantics?

8.7 What is discourse?

Answers to these questions can be found on the companion website at:
www.pearsoned.co.uk/psychologyexpress

? *Sample question*   *Essay*

Critically evaluate Hockett's definition of language.

A brief history of psycholinguistics

Although psycholinguistics (the study of language) as we know it today is still a relatively young subdiscipline within the field of psychology, its beginnings date back to the end of the 19th century. Whilst many of the early Greek philosophers had a documented interest in language, many regard Wundt as the father of modern-day language research at the turn of the 20th century. The study of language has gone through a number of distinct stages or phases of development since then and has slowly evolved into what we would recognise as modern psycholinguistics today (see Figure 8.1).

Key stages of the study of language

- Structuralism
- Formative period
- Linguistic period
- Cognitive period
- Contemporary linguistics.

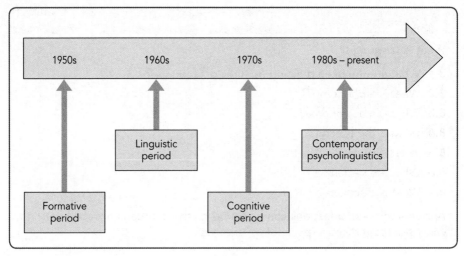

Figure 8.1 **The psycholinguistic timeline**

Structuralism

- Developed by Wilhelm Wundt (1832–1920)
- Emphasises the importance of the basic units of speech and language
- Production of speech involves progressing through a number of discrete stages or processes and language comprehension is simply the same process but in reverse
- Wundt suggested that the sentence was the most basic building block of language
- Hermann Paul (1886) disagreed with Wundt and claimed that the most basic building block was in fact the 'word'
- This shift to a focus on the word took the emphasis away from the language user and focused more on the formal representation of the language itself.

The formative period

- Began in the 1950s
- The term psycholinguistics is first used
- Language is seen as being distinct from other human behaviours
- Language is viewed as a form of information transference
- Emphasis is further removed from the producer and receiver of language
- Language is now viewed almost as an entity in its own right that can exist apart from a 'producer'.

The linguistic period

- Based mainly around the 1960s
- Noam Chomsky is the main architect of this period
- Chomsky believed there should be a focus on the 'grammar' of language
- Distinguished for the first time between 'deep structure' and the 'surface structure' of language
- Deep structure refers to the actual meaning that relates to the ideas and thoughts
- Surface structure refers simply to the final grammatical form
- Emphasised the syntactic, phonological and semantic components of grammar
- Introduced the idea of a phrase tree structure (see Figure 8.2).

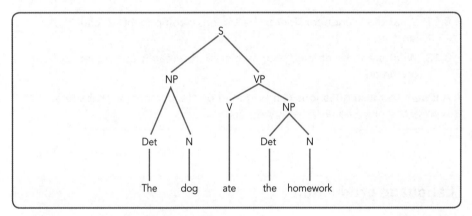

Figure 8.2 An example of a phase tree structure

The cognitive period

- Chomsky's work is still prevalent within this era
- Other influential thinkers of this time include Jerry Fodor and Dan Slobin
- Characterised by a search for generic cognitive foundations for linguistic structures
- Emphasis on the dependence of language on certain cognitive processes
- Importance of 'grammar' was reduced.

Contemporary psycholinguistics

- Psycholinguistics now has many branches within the discipline, including:
  - Language production
  - Language comprehension

- Language acquisition
- Biological aspects of language
- Language is viewed as just one form of information that we process
- Now psychology and linguistics are viewed as very separate and different disciplines

---

Test your knowledge

The history of psycholinguistic psychology

8.8 What are the five main stages of the development of psycholinguistics?

8.9 During which stage does grammar become important?

8.10 What are the two types of language structure suggested by Chomsky?

8.11 What did Wundt consider to be the basic component or 'chunk' of language?

8.12 What are the syntactic, phonological and semantic components of grammar?

Answers to these questions can be found on the companion website at: **www.pearsoned.co.uk/psychologyexpress**

Language production

Although language can be both written and spoken, for the vast majority speech is the primary way we communicate our ideas, beliefs, thoughts and intentions. Although there is no doubt that non-verbal communication (body language) plays a vital role in communication, it is spoken language and its production that we will be concentrating on within this section.

Theories and models of speech production

Spreading activation theory

The spreading activation theory of how we produce speech was put forward by Dell (1986) and Dell and O'Seaghdha (1991). It is based on connectionist principles, and considers speech as working on four levels (see Figure 8.3):

- Semantic level: the meaning of what is to be said
- Syntactic level: the grammatical structure of the words to be said
- Morphological level: the morphemes in the planned sentence
- Phonological level: the phonemes within the planned sentence.

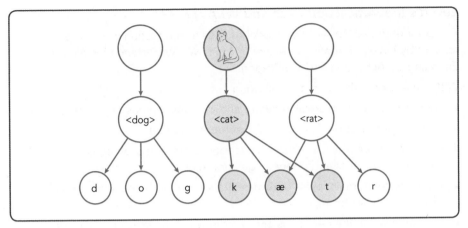

Figure 8.3 A spreading activation network (Dell, 1986)

Importantly, when planning what to say some form of representation is formed at each level simultaneously. This planning does not occur at separate times at the various different levels in the model but occurs at the same time at each level and operates in parallel.

- At each level there are a number of set defined 'categorical rules'
- The rules define categories that are appropriate at that level, for example whether a noun or verb is appropriate to use
- There is a 'lexicon' in the form of a network
- Within this network there are separate nodes for concepts, words, morphemes and phonemes
- When a node is activated it also spreads activation to other associated nodes connected to it
- Finally, using defined 'rules' the most appropriate node is selected
- The activation of the node returns to zero once it has been selected to avoid it being immediately selected again.

EVALUATION

+ It incorporates the mechanism of spreading of activation links which has parallels with other models of cognitive abilities

+ It is a testable model, for example, speech production errors can be predicted and tested empirically

− It has its focus mainly on the 'word' level and therefore has limitations when explaining the actual construction of the whole message and its links to the meaning of the communication

− It makes no predictions about the relative naming times for spoken words

Levelt's theoretical approach and WEAVER ++

The computational WEAVER++ model of speech production was first put forward by Levelt, Roelofs and Meyer in 1999. WEAVER stands for Word-form Encoding by Activation and Verification.

Within this model there are the following assumptions:

- Speech production is serial in nature and involves a series of processing stages
- Each stage has its own unique level of representation
- These representations are lexical concepts, lemmas, morphemes, phonological words and phonetic gestural scores
- There are three main levels of representation within the network: lexical, lemma and word forms
- Activation within the network is only 'feedforward', no activation goes backwards

Key terms

Lemma: the abstract form of a word containing information relating to the meaning of a word. A lemma contains no information relating to the sound of the word, and hence the word is not able to be pronounced in this form.

Figure 8.4 shows a more detailed account of the theory which involves six separate stages of processing:

1 Conceptual preparation: potential lexical concepts are activated on the basis of their meaning
2 Lexical selection is the retrieval of a 'lemma' from the mental lexicon
3 Morphological encoding involves the retrieval of the words' 'morphological shape'
4 Phonological encoding is the accessing of the syllables of the chosen word
5 Phonetics encoding: a word's 'gestural score' is computed
6 Articulation is when the planned gestural score is executed by the physical articulatory system.

Key terms

Gestural score: the physical plan of movement for the vocal tract.

EVALUATION

+ It can make predictions about the relative latency of word production
+ Much less reliant on data relating to errors in speech production
- Doesn't account for speech errors
- Focuses on 'words' and therefore there is a limited impact of context

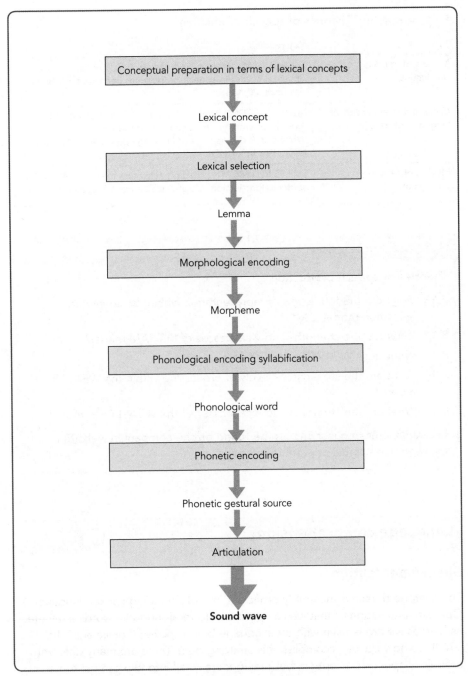

Figure 8.4 The components of the WEAVER++ model

Further reading Theories of speech production

Topic	Key reading
Models of speech production	Levelt, W.J.M., Roelofs, A. & Meyer, A.S. (1999). A theory of lexical access in speech production. *Behavioural & Brain Sciences, 22,* 1–38.
Computational models of language production	Roelofs, A. (2000). Weaver++ and other computational models of lemma retrieval and word form encoding. In L. Wheeldon (Ed.), *Aspects of language production* (71–114). Hove: Psychology Press.
Models of sentence production	Dell, G.S. (1986). A spreading-activation theory of retrieval in sentence production. *Cognitive Science, 93,* 283–321.

Test your knowledge

Theories of speech production

8.13 What are the four levels of representation within the spreading activation model (SAM)?

8.14 What are the strengths and weaknesses of the SAM model?

8.15 What does WEAVER++ stand for?

8.16 What are the six separate levels of processing within the WEAVER++ model?

8.17 What are the strengths and weaknesses of the WEAVER++ model?

Answers to these questions can be found on the companion website at: **www.pearson.co.uk/psychologyexpress**

Language comprehension

Speech perception

The average person is incredibly proficient in understanding spoken language. One estimate suggests that we can perceive up to around 250 words a minute, as long as we are familiar with the language being spoken (Foulke & Sticht, 1969). So how do we accomplish this amazing feat? There are many different models of speech perception, but they generally fall into two camps: those that view speech perception as being 'ordinary' and those that view speech perception as being 'special'.

The ordinary view of speech perception

- Speech perception is viewed as the same as the perception of any other non-speech sound.

- When we hear speech, we first split it down into its component parts (words), and then these sound components are compared with 'prototype' examples of the sounds of words. In this way we can assess which stored word each sound we hear is most similar to.

- This process is a bit like a computerised recycling system: first all of the rubbish has to be separated, to see what's actually there, it can then be compared with templates of what each type of rubbish is, e.g. an aluminium can, and then classified.

- Importantly, the theories within this school of thought also place much emphasis on the context of the sound, and suggest that what you perceive you hear can be very different from actual sounds that reach your eardrums! (See the Critical focus box on the McGurk effect.)

The special view of speech perception

- Speech is inherently perceived through specialised processes that are distinct from 'normal' auditory perceptual processes (e.g. Liberman, Cooper, Shankweiler & Studdert-Kennedy, 1967).

- Speech perception is special because it lies within the domain of language and is governed by principles that are different from general principles of perception. One example of this is the phenomenon of categorical perception – although the speech sounds we actually hear comprise a continuum of variation in sound waves, we perceive discontinuous categories of speech sounds. For instance, when a sound is slowly changed from one morpheme to another, we don't hear a slow change from one to another but a sudden switch. Although the speech sounds were physically equal in acoustic distance from one another, people only heard the 'sounds' that differed in phonetic label (Liberman, Harris, Hoffman & Griffith, 1957).

- Further evidence for language being a distinct specialised process comes from a study by McGurk and MacDonald (1976).

CRITICAL FOCUS

The McGurk effect

McGurk and MacDonald (1976) demonstrated that when visual and auditory perception are not synchronised, strange effects can occur. For example, if actors' lips pronounce the sound 'da' but the dubbed sound is 'ba' one may hear a compromise between the two, for example 'tha'. This sound was of course neither 'seen' nor 'heard' but appears to be some form of synthesis of the two types of perceptual inputs.

Theories of spoken word recognition

The cohort model of word recognition

Marslen-Wilson (1984, 1987), Marslen-Wilson and Tyler (1980) and Marslen-Wilson and Welsh (1978) proposed the cohort model of spoken word recognition (see Figure 8.5). Within this model, auditory lexical retrieval begins when the first phonemes are perceived, then the mental lexicon activates every possible word that begins with that phoneme. Each word is viewed as a potential candidate and this set of words is referred to as the 'cohort'. The number of candidates in the cohort is slowly whittled down as more phonological information is perceived, and also through the use of contextual information and information about the word itself, until only one candidate remains. This point is referred to as the 'recognition point'. Importantly, in later versions of this model (Marslen-Wilson, 1990; Marslen-Wilson & Warren, 1994) less emphasis was put on the importance of the initial part of the word. Also in the revised versions rather than there being a binary classification of words, being either in or out of the cohort, each word had an activation level, and hence only certain candidates with activations above a certain level were considered to be 'in the cohort'.

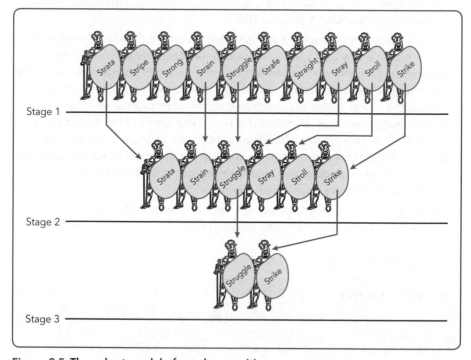

Figure 8.5 The cohort model of word recognition

EVALUATION

−/+ In the earlier version of the cohort model context effects occurred very early within the system, however in the later version this occurred much later in the process. This adaptation is much more in line with the data from word recognition experiments (e.g. Marslen-Wilson & Tyler, 1980).

−/+ The binary activation again seen in earlier versions, although similar to the firing or not-firing of neurons, was in contrast with the majority of other models of cognition; later versions removed this binary activation and brought the model in line with the majority of models that utilise 'activation' mechanisms.

− One problem with all versions of the cohort model is the reliance on the concept of the discrete 'word chunk', which necessitates a clear understanding of where a word begins and ends; however, the cohort model has no defined mechanism for accomplishing this process, and differentiating between word sounds.

The TRACE model

TRACE is a connectionist model of speech perception proposed by McClelland and Elman (1986) and McClelland (1991). As with the cohort model, it is based on the assumption that when the beginning of a word is heard, a set of words that share the same initial sound become activated. As more information is received by the system the potential candidates are slowly reduced until only a single candidate still stands. However, importantly, unlike the cohort model the TRACE model also makes some attempt at modelling the temporal dimensions of speech perception as well.

For example, a listener hears the beginning of *walk*, and the words walk, will, wash, went become active in memory. Then, as more of the word is perceived, only walk and wall remain in competition (wash and want have been eliminated because the third phoneme does not match). Soon after, 'walk' is recognised (see Figure 8.6). Importantly, the TRACE model is also able to represent a temporal element of speech comprehension, by allowing activation levels to vary over time, and also by including a competition feature between potential word candidates within the model. In this way how rapidly or easily a word can be recognised can be simulated.

TRACE also reliably simulates the effects of lexical context, in that it can decide between two ambiguous word endings according to the whether or not they create a 'real' word that is represented within the system. This is done by using a feedback method, where lexical units that are activated by a given word feedback to the phoneme level, and hence increase the activation of the phonemes that make up the word at the lexical level (see Figure 8.7).

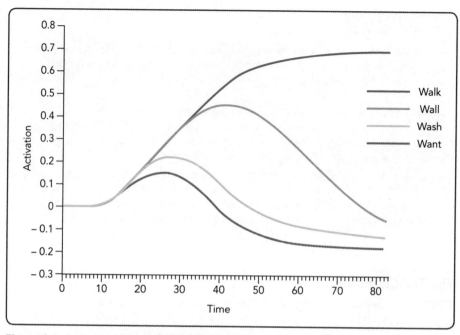

Figure 8.6 **Activation within the TRACE model**

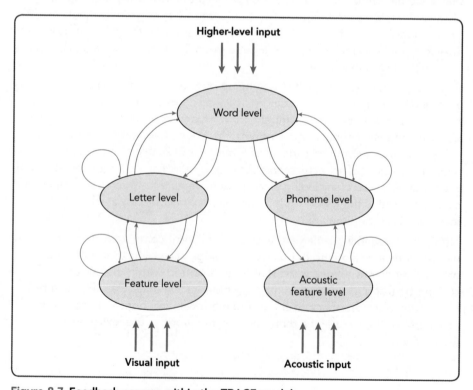

Figyre 8.7 **Feedback process within the TRACE model**

+ The TRACE model assumes that both top-down and bottom-up processes make a significant contribution to spoken word recognition, much as they do in actual human spoken word recognition.

+ Using activation thresholds, the model can reasonably successfully reproduce reaction times from a range of experimental data.

− The majority of tests of the TRACE model have relied upon a small number of single-syllable words, and it is not clear if the model's successes would continue with larger inputs.

− Importantly, the model cannot cope with any of the idiosyncrasies of speech production and relies upon distinct fixed time slots in which the input information is presented.

− Although based on connectionist principles, the TRACE model is not a learning network and does not employ any form of learning algorithm or mechanism, found in some other connectionist models (e.g. back-propagation). The consequence of this is that all the knowledge of spoken word perception is in essence programmed within the network and no further adaptation of learning can occur: hence the model struggles with the fuzziness of language perception.

Routes from print to sound

How many possible routes are available for reading a word aloud? A dual-route approach was initially proposed by Coltheart (1978). This model of reading proposed that there were two distinct processes for converting print to speech:

- a dictionary look-up process, also called the lexical semantic route, as it goes through the lexical and semantic systems, and
- a letter-to-sound conversion process, also called the sublexical route because it produces the sound of a word by mapping sublexical letter units (e.g. graphemes, syllables) onto sounds without consulting the dictionary (or lexicon) (see Figure 8.8).

In addition to the two routes described above, a third direct lexical route has also been proposed (e.g. Funnel, 1983; Coltheart & Funnel, 1987; Ellis & Young, 1988). It is suggested that this third route directly connects the visual word recognition to stored lexical phonology, bypassing the semantic system (see Figure 8.8).

As can be seen in Figure 8.8 there are a number of stages that are passed through in the naming of words.

- The grapheme analysis or visual analysis stage identifies groups of letters
- The visual word recognition stage recognises familiar written words
- Semantic representations contain word meanings
- Stored lexical phonology stores forms of spoken words
- Sublexical phonological recoding converts spelling into sounds
- Articulation

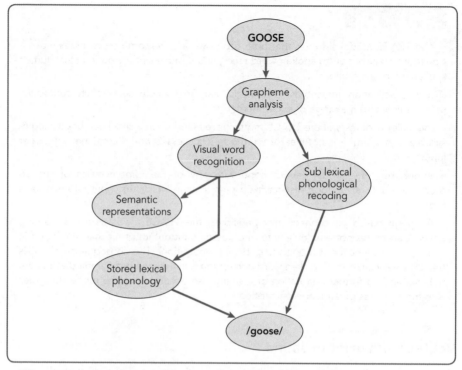

Figure 8.8 The dual route model of reading adapted from Ellis and Young's (1988) model for the recognition, comprehension and repetition of spoken words.

Adapted from Parkin, A. (1999). *Explorations in cognitive neuropsychology*. Hove: Psychology Press, page 155, Figure 8.1.

Figure 8.8 clearly shows that there are three possible routes that a word can take when being named.

1 Printed word to vocalisation (e.g. naming a pseudoword; a pronounceable non-word)

2 Through semantic representations (this is the most common route for reading words)

3 Bypassing semantic representations, these are usually rarely written words that are pronounced but are not understood, e.g. Quasar.

EVALUATION

One of the main pieces of empirical support for this model comes from the observed effect of priming in naming. There are many different ways to prime or facilitate naming. One of those is through phonemic priming, for example giving someone the first phoneme of the word to be named. If one is given the correct initial phoneme of a 'to-be named' word we are significantly faster at naming the word than when primed with an unrelated phoneme. Similarly, in general, if one is primed by the semantic category of the 'to-be-named' word (for example, being told 'It's a pet' priming the word 'cat') then this will facilitate the naming of the word, in contrast to if the word was to be primed by an unrelated semantic category. It appears that words (and pictures) can be primed at all of the levels of representation that they must pass through to be processed (see Figure 8.8) and this is a strong argument for the word having to actually pass through all of these distinct stages before being named.

Similarly, evidence for the three routes can also be supported through priming, as both nonsense words or a recognised but unknown word are found not to be primed by semantics, as the word doesn't necessitate access to the semantic representations in its journey through the model. There are also significant observed differences in the naming latencies of words being named through the three distinct routes outlined above.

Further reading Language comprehension

Topic	Key reading
Routes to reading and dyslexia	Wu, D.H., Martin, R.C. & Damian, M. (2002). A third route for reading? Implications from a case of phonological dyslexia. *Neurocase, 8*, 274–95.
Semantic processing	Shibahara, N., Zorzi, M., Hill, M.P., Wydell, T. & Butterworth, B. (2003). Semantic effects in word naming: Evidence from English and Japanese kanji. *The Quarterly Journal of Experimental Psychology, 56A (2)*, 263–86.
Dyslexia	Coltheart, M. (1980). Deep dyslexia: A right hemisphere hypothesis. In M. Coltheart, K.E. Patterson & J. Marshall (Eds), *Deep dyslexia* (pp. 326–80). London: Routledge & Kegan Paul.
Routes to language processing in reading	Coltheart, M. & Rastle, K (1994). Serial processing in reading aloud: Evidence for a dual route model of reading. *Journal of Experimental Psychology: Human Perception and Performance, 20*, 1197–211.

Test your knowledge

Language comprehension

8.18 What are the 'ordinary' and 'special' views of speech production?

8.19 Who created the cohort model?

8.20 Describe one strength and one weakness of the cohort model.

8.21 Briefly describe how candidate words were selected within the TRACE model.

8.22 Describe one strength and one weakness of the TRACE model.

8.23 What are the three routes to naming a word.

8.24 What is the main evidence for the necessity for three routes to naming?

Answers to these questions can be found on the companion website at: www.pearsoned.co.uk/psychologyexpress

? *Sample question* Essay

Critically evaluate two models of spoken word recognition.

Chapter summary – pulling it all together

→ Can you tick all of the points from the revision checklist at the beginning of this chapter?

→ Attempt all of the Test yourself questions.

→ Attempt the essay questions within the chapter using the guidelines below.

→ Go to the companion website at www.pearsoned.co.uk/psychologyexpress to access more revision support online, including interactive quizzes, flash cards, You be the marker exercises as well as answer guidance for the Test yourself and Sample questions from this chapter.

Answer guidelines

✱ *Sample question* Essay

Critically contrast two models of speech production.

Approaching the question

This question requires that you first think carefully about and then choose the two models that you wish to evaluate.

Important points to include

The models illustrated within this chapter are the spreading activation model and WEAVER++ models. Once two models have been identified, the key elements from each model should be highlighted. Then the strengths and weaknesses of each model should be discussed, remembering the practical plausibility of each model. If possible you can use a compare and contrast approach – pitting the two models against each other. Be careful to produce a conclusion where you sum up the findings of your evaluation.

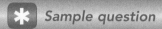 *Make your answer stand out*

Make sure that you read around the topic areas and get hold of some of the key papers. Make sure that you always back up your studies and evaluations

with appropriate studies/references to support your claims and statements. Specifically, when evaluating each model you need to explicitly focus on how testable each model is and also mention how good each model is at making predictions that can be extrapolated to real-life empirical observations.

Explore the accompanying website at **www.pearsoned.co.uk/psychologyexpress**

→ Prepare more effectively for exams and assignments using the answer guidelines for questions from this chapter.

→ Test your knowledge using multiple choice questions and flashcards.

→ Improve your essay skills by exploring the You be the marker exercises.

Notes

Notes

9

Language 2: Issues in language

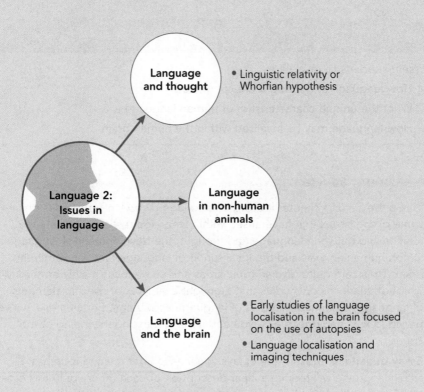

A printable version of this topic map is available from:
www.pearsoned.co.uk/psychologyexpress

Introduction

As well as our own specific experience of language, which will for most of us centre upon speech production and recognition, there are a number of other contemporary topic areas of interest within the sphere of language research.

For many years the issue of how language and thought are related has been debated at both the psychological and philosophical level. The issue of whether or not we are the only species that has a complex form of language is another question that has implications for how we view ourselves and other animals. And the possible location of language within the structure of the human brain can have huge implications and ramifications for the field of psychology and medicine. It is these contemporary issues that we will be discussing within this second chapter of language.

 Revision checklist

Essential points to revise are:

❑ How language and thought are connected
❑ What the unique characteristics of human language are
❑ How language may be localised within the human brain

Assessment advice

- This is the second chapter looking at language. This chapter focuses on some of the issues that have arisen within language research, namely the relationship between language and thought, the development of language in non-human animals and the localisation of language function within the brain. These are quite diverse topic areas and some focus mainly on theory, whilst others focus on studies that highlight examples of specific elements of language, e.g. animal studies of language acquisition. For all these, we've provided key readings to give you a more in-depth understanding of the issues.

- **Essay questions:** Most of the essays you'll encounter relating to issues within language will require a clear description of each theory or in this case of an important study, before giving a detailed evaluation of the theory or study. More often than not there is an over-reliance on description within student essays, and one must be careful to leave time and space for a critical review. This can of course include both the positive and negative, but again if possible must be supported by the literature, rather than all based on anecdotal evidence or personal opinion.

Sample question

Could you answer this question? Below is a typical essay question that could arise on this topic.

 Sample question *Essay*

Critically evaluate the statement 'Language is unique to humans'.

Guidelines on answering this question are included at the end of this chapter, whilst guidance on tackling other exam questions can be found on the companion website at: **www.pearsoned.co.uk/psychologyexpress**

Language and thought

One of the most hotly debated topics within the field of language is that of the relationship of language and thought. Which came first? And how are the two related?

Linguistic relativity or Whorfian hypothesis

Whorf (1956) claimed that language shapes the way people perceive and organise their world. Furthermore, his hypothesis states that language determines what thoughts we have about objects and events in our world. If we take the hypothesis to its extreme, it implies that if we do not have a word in our language to describe a perception or thought, we will have difficulty perceiving or thinking it. More recently this theory has been adapted and modified into two distinct strands; the strong and weak versions (Hunt & Agnoli, 1991).

The strong version suggests that language determines thinking

Early studies with Eskimos were often cited as evidence for this form of the hypothesis (Whorf, 1956). The studies stated that because Eskimos had many more words for different types of snow than the average non-Eskimo (e.g. snow on the ground, falling snow, etc.) they were also able to perceive and think about far more many types of snow as well. However, there have been a number of studies that have contradicted this evidence, suggesting that this is not in fact the case and that Eskimos have roughly as many words for snow as non-Eskimos (Pullum, 1991). Furthermore, today there is little support for this strong version of the Whorfian hypothesis.

149

The weak version suggests that language only influences thinking

One example comes from the Hanuxoo of the Philippine Islands who have 92 names for various kinds and states of rice. The Whorfian hypothesis suggests that the physical reality is translated, according to some internal representation of reality, into a perception that is consistent with long-standing cognitive structures. It is possible that these differences in language do influence thought; however, another, equally conceivable explanation for this observation could be simply that different environments affect the way that people think about and use language, and hence conversely it may be that even in this example thought has shaped language rather than vice versa.

Another study that demonstrates the influence of language of thinking comes from Hoffman, Lau and Johnson (1986). Bilingual English–Chinese speakers read descriptions of individuals, and were later asked to provide free interpretations of the individuals described. Hoffman et al. found that typically the descriptions conformed to either Chinese or English stereotypes of personality.

EVALUATION

Rosch (1973) suggests that our experience with colour and how we perceive it influences how we group certain colours into named categories, thus implying that our experience with the world shapes our linguistic categories. For example the Dani people have only two words for colours: 'mola' bright, warm and 'mili' dark, cool colours. However, they could more easily identify colours that were typical of colour categories that we have in English, i.e. a typical 'blue' was more easily distinguished as 'mili' than an off-blue. This should not happen if language strictly moulds thought as there would be no perception of 'our' different colours (Heider, 1972).

The cross-cultural research into colour perception and memory suggests that in spite of some cultures having many more available terms in their vocabulary to describe and name colours than others, the similarities between cultures are still far greater than their differences.

In conclusion, it may well be that the more significant an experience to us, the greater the number of ways it is expressed in our language rather than the other way around. The development of specific language systems, therefore, is dependent on cultural needs.

Further reading Language and thought

Topic	Key reading
Perception of colour	Davidoff, J., Davies, I. & Roberson, D. (1999). Colour categories in a stone-age tribe. *Nature*, 398 (6724), 203–4.
Perceptual categorisation	Davidoff, J. (2001). Language and perceptual categorisation. *Trends in Cognitive Science*, 5(9), 382–7.
Review of the Whorfian hypothesis	Hunt, E. & Agnoli, F. (1991). The Whorfian hypothesis: A cognitive psychology perspective. *Psychological Review*, 98, 377–89.

Test your knowledge

Language and thought

9.1 What are the differences between the strong and weak versions of the linguistic relativity hypothesis?

9.2 Describe one study that supports the weak version of the Whorfian hypothesis.

9.3 Describe one study that weakens the Whorfian hypothesis.

9.4 What are the weaknesses of the Whorfian hypothesis?

Answers to these questions can be found on the companion website at:
www.pearsoned.co.uk/psychologyexpress

 Sample question *Essay*

Critically evaluate the statement 'The development of language must precede the development of thinking in humans'.

Language in non-human animals

Apes have problems vocalising language in the same way that humans can, essentially because they do not have the physiological apparatus necessary to produce recognisable speech. However, although apes cannot speak vocally, a number of researchers have succeeded in teaching apes to communicate via sign language. For example, Allen and Beatrix Gardner (1969) managed to teach American Sign Language (ASL) to a chimpanzee named Washoe. After 4 years of training, Washoe knew over 100 signs to name objects and characteristics of objects.

There are many other cases of apes being taught to communicate: Table 9.1 gives some of the more famous examples.

The teaching of forms of language in other non-human animals other than apes has also had some success.

- **Dolphins** Hermann, Kuczaj and Holder (1993) examined the responses of a bottlenosed dolphin to sequences of gestures given within an artificial gestural language. The dolphin could discriminate between sequences that had meaning and those that had no meaning and respond appropriately.

- **Sea lions** Gisiner and Shusterman (1992) trained a sea lion to recognise a number of gestural signs. They then reported the sea lion's responses to

Table 9.1 Examples of animal communication

Francine Patterson	Koko the gorilla (born 1971) was said to be able to understand more than 300 ASL signs.
Ann and David Premack	Sarah the chimpanzee (born 1962) was able to communicate through sign language by using a series of coloured plastic chips to represent words.
Herbert Terrace	Nim Chimpsky the chimpanzee (born 1973) lived 24 hours a day with his human family from birth and was able to understand over 100 ASL signs.
Duane Rumbaugh	Lana the chimpanzee (born 1970) could use a computer-based sign board to create sentences.
Sue Savage-Rumbaugh	Kanzi the bonobo (born 1980) was able to learn to communicate through a sign board, but importantly learnt this skill by observing another ape being trained.

unfamiliar combinations of signs created by reordering, deleting or adding signs. The sea lion's responses to these unusual combinations demonstrated that she had learned a number of syntactic relations from the original training and only limited exposure to a limited set of standard examples.

- **Parrots** Irene Pepperberg trained an African Grey Parrot called Alex for 30 years (Pepperberg 2006). Alex could identify 50 different objects and number different quantities up to 6; he could distinguish seven colours and five shapes. Alex had a vocabulary of over 100 words and was able to combine words relating to objects he knew to create words for novel objects. He could also label items in terms of their shape and colour correctly.

EVALUATION

– Critics have suggested that in all of the above examples that the animals in question are simply being trained to respond to given cues to obtain rewards. For example Terrace (in the 1970s) suggested that the sentences that his chimpanzee 'Nim' was able to sign were simply his imitations of his trainers. Terrace claimed that Nim would rarely sign spontaneously or without prompting from trainers or the cue of potential food.

+ There are examples where animals have been observed to spontaneously create new words or new word sequences. One example of this comes from Koko, Patterson's Gorilla, who could create new sequences of words to describe objects e.g. calling a zebra a 'white tiger'.

+ Savage-Rumbaugh, Scanlon and Rumbaugh (1980) suggested that their apes could categorise and request objects from one another. Furthermore, they also propose that such abilities would seem to go beyond what one might expect purely on the basis of conditioning: instead, they suggest that these animals may have learned to use language as a tool.

+ Not only did Washoe learn to use sign language, but she also taught another chimpanzee Loulis to use approximately 50 signs. Importantly, Washoe's and Loulis' trainers did not sign in the presence of Loulis, so they knew that Washoe had taught him these signs.

▶

+ Premack and Premack (1983) claimed to find that language-trained chimpanzees appeared to have a variety of problem-solving abilities not possessed by chimps who were not language trained, suggesting that the acquisition of a form of language had a significant impact on other cognitive functions.

Further reading Language in non-human animals

Topic	Key reading
Sign language in a chimpanzee	Gardner, R.A. & Gardner, B.T. (1969), Teaching sign language to a chimpanzee, *Science*, 165, 664–72.
Sign language in chimpanzees	Gardner, R.A., Gardner, B.T. & Van Cantfort, T.E. (1989). *Teaching Sign Language to Chimpanzees*. Albany, NY: State University of New York Press.
Apes learning language	Savage-Rumbaugh, E.S., Rumbaugh, D.M. & McDonald, K. (1985). Language learning in two species of apes. *Neuroscience and Biobehavioral Reviews*, 9, 653–65.
Symbol and language acquisition in chimpanzees	Savage-Rumbaugh, E.S., McDonald, K., Sevcik, R.A., Hopkins, W.D. & Rupert, E. (1986). Spontaneous symbol acquisition and communicative use by pygmy chimpanzees *(Pan paniscus)*. *Journal of Experimental Psychology: General*, 115, 211–35.
Case study of chimpanzee learned sign language	Terrace, H.S. (1979). *Nim: A chimpanzee who learned sign language*. New York: Knopf.

Test your knowledge

Language in non-humans

9.5 Give three examples where apes have been taught to use sign language.

9.6 What are the major criticisms of studies where apes have learnt to use sign language?

9.7 What evidence is there to suggest that apes really can learn and use sign language?

9.8 Give details of three other types of non-human animal that have been taught to use language.

Answers to these questions can be found on the companion website at: www.pearsoned.co.uk/psychologyexpress

Language and the brain

Traditionally the left cerebral hemisphere is viewed as the part of the brain that controls the functions of language, which includes the production of both spoken and written language and comprehension of verbal information. This has been demonstrated through autopsy of patients who had functional language disorders, split brain studies and more recently brain scans.

Early studies of language localisation in the brain focused on the use of autopsies

The initial work centred on two physicians in the 19th century whose work suggested that there were two main areas in the left hemisphere associated with language: Broca's area and Wernicke's area (see Figure 9.1).

- Pierre Paul Broca (1824–1880) was a French surgeon who studied patients' behaviours and, when they died, performed autopsies. In the brains of most individuals with speech impairments, Broca found a lesion in the posterior section in the frontal lobe.

- The primary behaviours associated with Broca's patients were the ability to understand language along with an impaired ability to speak coherently.

- Carl Wernicke (1848–1904) was a German neurologist who examined and recorded patients' behaviour and discovered on autopsy that these patients had damage to the posterior section of the temporal lobe.

- Wernicke's patients were able to speak but could not understand language. Sometimes their choice of words to say was unusual and did not always make sense due to the patient not being able to fully understand their own speech.

There are of course limitations in the methodology of waiting for someone to die until investigating the potential locus of effect for language deficits, and more recently a number of experimental methods have been devised to assess

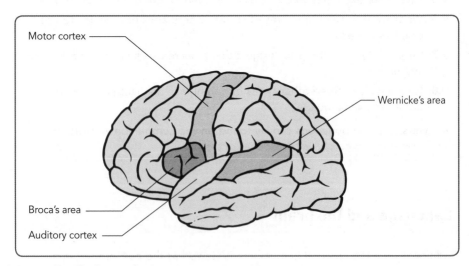

Figure 9.1 The human brain

localisation of function within the brain. One such method falls under the banner of 'split-brain' research; this is the sodium amytal (SA) or Wada test.

The Wada test

The Wada test or procedure, designed by Juhn Wada in 1949, involves the injection of barbiturate agents (typically sodium amytal) into either the left or right internal carotid arteries. This results in each hemisphere being temporarily anaesthetised, and permits functional assessment of the non-anaesthetised hemisphere.

Using the SA or Wada test cognitive functions can then be assessed. During the test, the patient is asked to recall well known series, e.g. letters of the alphabet. Wada (1949) found that in the majority of cases when SA is administered to the left hemisphere a patient is rendered completely mute for a minute or two and then speech gradually returns. In contrast, when the right hemisphere is anaesthetised speech remains unaffected.

Language localisation and imaging techniques

In recent years studies of language localisation in the brain have been enhanced through the use of new neuro-imaging techniques such as computed axial tomography (CAT), magnetic resonance imaging (MRI), positron emission tomography (PET) and functional magnetic resonance imaging (fMRI). These neuro-imaging technologies can at a very basic level be split into two categories, those that have a temporal element to them and those that do not.

1 CAT and MRI scans are in some ways like old fashioned X-rays, in that they both take a snapshot of your brain (of course in much better detail).

2 PET and fMRI scans can give some indication to the activity of the brain under certain conditions. The crude logic of these scans is that if a participant is engaged in a particular cognitive function and a certain part of their brain lights up (within the scan) then this part of the brain must be related to that particular function (see Figure 9.2).

Broca's brains

A fascinating example of the implementation of these new technologies comes from a study by Dronkers, Plaisant, Iba-Zizen and Cabanis in 2007. Within this study the preserved brains of two of Broca's original patients were reinspected using high-resolution MRI. The purpose of this study was to scan the brains in three dimensions and to identify the extent of the patient's brain lesions in more detail. The study also sought to locate the exact site of the lesion in the frontal lobe in relation to what is now called Broca's area.

▶

The MRI scans of the brains suggested that other areas besides Broca's may have had an impact on the patients' deficit in speech production. This is an important finding because it links in with a number of clinical studies that have demonstrated that although lesions to Broca's area alone can cause temporary speech disruption, they do not usually result in severe impediment to a patient's speech. Another significant finding was that the lesion was not in precisely the same region as what is now known as Broca's area. This study provides further evidence that language and cognition are far more complicated than once thought and involve various networks of brain regions.

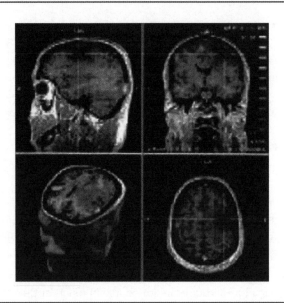

Figure 9.2 Examples of PET scans

EVALUATION

One of the often cited weaknesses and constraints of functional imaging techniques is that often the results of such scans are viewed far too simplistically. As mentioned above, the fact that a certain part of the brain is activated whilst performing a specific cognitive function does not necessarily imply that this area is the main locus for this function; it may be that the particular area acts as an intermediary area or as a link between other parts of the brain.

At a practical level knowing where a cognitive function occurs can be exceedingly helpful, but at a theoretical level it doesn't really tell us any more as to the nature, cause or development of that function.

Further reading Language and the brain

Key reading:

Binder, J.R., Swanson, S.J., Hammeke, T.A. et al. (1996). Determination of language dominance using functional MRI: A comparison with the Wada test. *Neurology, 46*, 978–84.

Binder, J.R., Frost, J.A.., Hammeke, T.A., Cox, R.W. et al. (1997). Human brain language areas identified by functional magnetic resonance imaging. *Journal of Neuroscience, 17*, 353–62.

Dronkers, N.F., Plaisant, O., Iba-Zizen, M.T. & Cabanis, E.A. (2007). Paul Broca's historic cases: High resolution MR imaging of the brains of Leborgne and Lelong. *Brain, 130*, 1432–41.

Wada, J. (1949). A new method of identifying the dominant hemisphere for language: Intracarotid sodium amytal injection in man. *Medical Biology, 14*, 221–2.

Wada, J. & Rasmussen, T. (1960). Intracortid injection of sodium amytal for the lateralisation of cerebral speech dominance. *Journal of Neurosurgery, 17*, 266–82.

 Sample question   *Essay*

Critically evaluate the evidence for the localisation of language function within the brain.

Chapter summary – pulling it all together

→ Can you tick all of the points from the revision checklist at the beginning of this chapter?

→ Attempt all of the Test yourself questions.

→ Attempt the two essay questions within the chapter using the guidelines below.

→ Go to the companion website at www.pearsoned.co.uk/psychologyexpress to access more revision support online, including interactive quizzes, flash cards, You be the marker exercises as well as answer guidance for the Test yourself and Sample questions from this chapter.

Answer guidelines

 Sample question   *Essay*

Critically evaluate the statement 'Language is unique to humans'.

Approaching the question

This question requires a description of language and then a critical review of whether or not it is limited to humans with reference to a range of other animals.

Important points to include

To answer this question one can draw information from more than one chapter within this book. To start with it would be helpful in defining what one actually means by language as this has a significant impact on whether or not it is an attribute unique to humans. Next, one should draw a selection of evidence from the various attempts to treat different animals to communicate with humans, both vocally and using sign language, and importantly critically evaluate these attempts, in relation to the established definition of language. Importantly, if possible you should aim for a final conclusion paragraph where you state whether or not your evidence supports the statement within the question.

| Make your answer stand out |

For the above question, make sure that you read around the topic and get hold of some of the key papers. Make sure that you always back up your studies and evaluations with appropriate studies/references to support your claims and statements, Specifically, make sure that you don't simply describe the accomplishments of researchers to teach apes sign language but evaluate the apes' abilities against a chosen set of criteria for language, e.g. Hockett. Critically evaluate each study including evidence of spontaneity, communication using sign language between apes and improvement of cognitive functions. Also don't forget to highlight any methodological flaws, e.g. sign language in apes possibly simply being a case of conditioning.

Explore the accompanying website at **www.pearsoned.co.uk/psychologyexpress**
→ Prepare more effectively for exams and assignments using the answer guidelines for questions from this chapter.
→ Test your knowledge using multiple choice questions and flashcards.
→ Improve your essay skills by exploring the You be the marker exercises.

Notes

Notes

Notes

10

Problem solving, thinking and reasoning

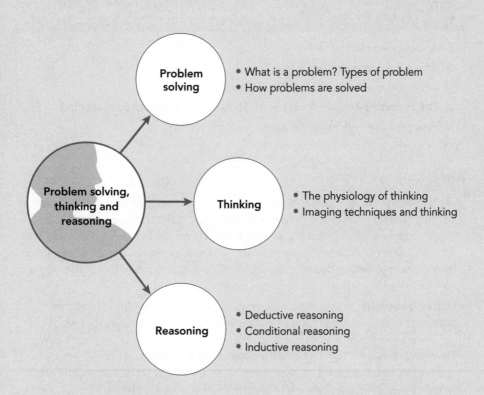

- **Problem solving**
  - What is a problem? Types of problem
  - How problems are solved

- **Problem solving, thinking and reasoning**

- **Thinking**
  - The physiology of thinking
  - Imaging techniques and thinking

- **Reasoning**
  - Deductive reasoning
  - Conditional reasoning
  - Inductive reasoning

A printable version of this topic map is available from:
www.pearsoned.co.uk/psychologyexpress

Introduction

Problem solving is a skill that we utilise in many different scenarios every day, whether it be juggling our schedule for the day or working through an essay plan. The majority of us go through these processes without contemplating the range of skills we are utilising in solving even the simplest of problems, and yet they are skills that for most we have developed over many years. Although many other species from the animal kingdom show behaviours that demonstrate problem solving it is only humans that have mastered the higher-level reasoning that is covered within this chapter. Specifically, this chapter will address how we define problems and how problems are solved along with the physiology of thinking. It will also look at different types of reasoning and judgement.

→ *Revision checklist*

Essential points to revise are
❑ How a problem can be defined
❑ What the main ways we problem solve are
❑ The strengths and weaknesses of deductive and inductive reasoning
❑ How problem solving is localised within the brain

Assessment advice

- This chapter focuses on problem solving, thinking and reasoning. The chapter is quite different from the majority of this book in that it focuses mainly on 'methods' of problem solving or reasoning. However, this does not mean that you shouldn't (as always) evaluate each of these methods. For all of the topic areas covered within this chapter we've provided key readings to give you a more in-depth understanding of the issues.

- **Essay questions:** most of the essays you'll encounter relating to problem solving or reasoning will require a clear description of the methods involved, and then a critique of each method. Weaker essays often simply give a very brief overview of a number of different methods. However, stronger essays give an in detail account of each method, including its various strengths and weaknesses, citing supporting literature/studies where possible. For essays relating to thinking and brain functioning, appropriate studies that highlight individuals' thinking deficits should be cited and of course sensitively critiqued.

Sample question

Could you answer this question? Below is a typical essay question that could arise on this topic.

Sample question **Essay**

Critically evaluate the statement 'the function of problem solving is localised within the human brain'.

Guidelines on answering this question are included at the end of this chapter, whilst guidance on tackling other exam questions can be found on the companion website at: **www.pearsoned.co.uk/psychologyexpress**

Problem solving

What is a problem? Types of problem

A problem occurs when there is something stopping you from getting from where you are at present to where you want to be – from your present state to your goal state – and you don't know how to get around this obstacle (Lovett, 2002). So in essence problems have three main components:

1 An initial start state – this is the state that we start at.

2 The goal state – this is the state that you wish to get to

3 The obstacles – are anything that lies between the initial start state and the goal state.

Problems can be very crudely split into two categories: those that are well defined and those that are not well defined. See box for some examples. Well-defined problems have completely specified initial conditions, goals and operators. Ill-defined problems have some aspects which are not completely specified and sometimes require insight to see the problem in a new way.

> #### Problem 1 – A well-defined problem
>
> A farmer is taking his produce to market. He has a fox, a hen and a bag of grain. Now, as I'm sure you all know, foxes like to eat hens. And hens (when they can avoid the foxes) love to snack on a bit of grain.
>
> As long as the farmer is watching over them, the fox and the hen will be as good as gold. But if he leaves them alone, then the hen will eat the grain or the fox will eat the hen.
>
> On the way to the market there is a river. When the farmer gets to the river, he sees that the ferry isn't there. The only way across is in a tiny rowing boat. But this boat is so small that he can only take one item at a time. He will have to make several trips. But wait! While he's in the boat with one item, how will he stop the two left on the bank from eating each other?
>
> How does the farmer get the fox, hen and grain across the river to market?

Problem 2

I want to move house into a nicer area than I live now but I can't afford the type of house that I really want. What shall I do?

How problems are solved

Before even attempting to solve a problem we need to create a representation of the problem: this is usually referred to as an 'internal representation'. This could be in the form of images, symbols or diagrams.

Once an internal representation has been created there are a number of strategies to actually solving the problem.

Problem solving using the problem-space analogy, means ends analysis and heuristics

Newell and Simon (1972) suggested that problems should be defined within something called 'problem space'. Within this problem space there is an 'initial state' and a 'goal state' and different paths that a would-be problem-solver can take. These different paths represent actions or technically 'operators' that one can take in an effort to get from the initial state to the goal state. This method of problem solving is called 'means ends analysis'. If we link this method with Problem 1 above this is how it might work (see Figure 10.1).

Means ends analysis is technically an algorithm for solving problems. The algorithm states:

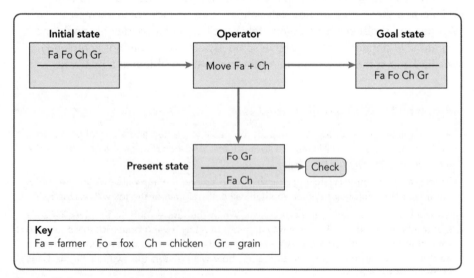

Figure 10.1 **Means ends analysis**

1 Make a move from the 'Present state' (which at the beginning will be the 'initial state').

2 Check, am I at the 'Goal state'? If so STOP – 'Mission accomplished'. Otherwise move to step 3.

3 Check if this move has brought you closer to the goal state – if Yes go to step 1, if No go to step 4.

4 Move back to previous state and then go to step 1.

Key terms

Algorithm: an algorithm is basically a method for solving a problem using a finite sequence of instructions.

In this way a problem space can be explored and hopefully the goal state will eventually be achieved. However, there are two main problems with the algorithm above – first, there is no mechanism for the algorithm to avoid getting into a loop where it either goes round in circles in the problem space, or simply goes backwards and forwards between states. Also if the problem space is large (e.g. chess) then just using an algorithm may take a very long time! A bigger problem is that the algorithm cannot move away from the goal state to achieve a solution. There are many problems where one has to move further away from the goal state before eventually achieving the goal. See Problem 3 for an example:

Problem 3 I live in Worcester but would like to travel to Barcelona

In reality the way I would tackle this problem would be to drive my car to Birmingham airport and take a plane directly to Barcelona. However, if we apply the means ends analysis strictly we run into trouble.

My initial state is 'In Worcester'. My first action is to get into my car and start to drive north on the M5. Step 2 checks if I'm at the goal state (No) so move on to step 3. Step 3 checks if I'm any closer to my Goal state (Barcelona). Well I am now 'technically' further away from Barcelona, so the answer to this check is No – so I turn the car around and head back to Worcester. If I abide strictly by this algorithm it looks like I'm driving to Barcelona!!

Using heuristics

As highlighted above there are a number of problems in only using algorithms to solve problems. One way around these problems is to use heuristics. A heuristic is a strategy for searching through the problem space in a meaningful way: it is sometimes likened to a 'rule of thumb', an obvious example comes from chess. In the opening move of chess (the first operation from the 'initial state') there are 20 possible moves that a player can make; however, an experienced chess player will discount all but perhaps six therefore dramatically reducing the search space. Another example is an anagram problem (see below).

Problem 4 Solve the anagram GTNEIAHC

If you use a simple algorithmic approach with this problem there are 40,320 permutations that can be developed and this could take some time. However, if we use heuristics this problem space can be significantly reduced – there are certain rules of thumb that we all know that we can utilise, e.g. there are certain non-valid letter pairings within the English language for the beginning and end of a word (e.g. GT, NH, HC, TN). Similarly, there are also some common letter pairings for the beginning of words (e.g. NE, TE, CH, HA).

Using these heuristics we can reduce the problem space and speed up the process of solving the problem. We use heuristics every day without even thinking about them, and almost never formally define them.

Using analogies to solve problems

When we are faced with a new problem and unsure how to proceed it may be helpful to draw upon experiences of previous problems that are similar to the present one. If one thinks back to how comparable problems were solved then these methods can be transferred to the present problem. In this way the problem can be said to be solved by analogy.

- Gick and Holyoak (1980) gave some participants the fortress problem (see Problem 5)
- Later in the study, they were given Duncker's radiation problem (see Problem 6)
- About 10 per cent of people solve the radiation problem spontaneously
- About 30 per cent of people solve it if they first read the story about the fortress
- Not much of a gain, but if given a hint to use the earlier stories, about 90 per cent of people solve the problem.

Problem 5 The fortress problem

A small country was ruled from a strong fortress by a dictator. The fortress was situated in the middle of the county, surrounded by farms and villages. Many roads led to the fortress through the countryside. A rebel general vowed to capture the fortress. The general knew that an attack by his entire army would capture the fortress. He gathered his army at the head of one of the roads, ready to launch a full-scale direct attack. However, the general then learned that the dictator had planted mines on each of the roads. The mines were set so that small bodies of men could pass over them safely, since the dictator needed to move his troops and workers to and from the fortress. However, any large force would detonate the mines. Not only would this blow up the road, but it would also destroy many neighbouring villages. It therefore seemed impossible to capture the fortress. However, the general devised a simple plan. He divided his army into small groups and dispatched each group to the head of a different road. Each group continued down its road to the fortress so that the entire army arrived together at the fortress at the same time. In this way, the general captured the fortress and overthrew the dictator (Gick & Holyoak, 1980, 1983).

Problem 6 The radiation problem

Suppose you are a doctor faced with a patient who has a malignant tumour in their stomach. It is impossible to operate on the patient, but unless the tumour is destroyed the patient will die. There is a special type of ray that can be used to destroy the tumour, as long as the rays reach it with sufficient intensity. However, at the necessary intensity, the healthy tissue that the rays pass through will also be destroyed and the patient will die. At lower intensities, the rays are harmless but they will not affect the tumour either. What procedure might the doctor employ to destroy the tumour with the rays, at the same time avoiding destroying any healthy tissue? (Duncker, 1945)

According to Gick and Holyoak, there are three steps to analogical problem solving.

1 *Noticing* – the participant needs to notice that there is an analogous relationship between the target problem and a previous problem.

2 *Mapping* – the participant needs to map corresponding elements from the previous problem to the target problem, by connecting elements from the two problems.

3 *Applying* – the participant needs to generate a parallel solution to the target problem by applying generalisations from the previous problem to the target problem.

Further reading Problem solving

Topic	Key reading
Solving problems by using analogies	Gick, M.L. & Holyoak, K.J. (1980). Analogical problem solving. *Cognitive Psychology, 12*, 306–55.
Problem solving	Lovett, M.C. (2002). Problem solving. In D.L. Medin (Ed.), *Steven's handbook of experimental psychology* (317–62). New York: Wiley.
Human problem solving	Newell, A. & Simon, H.A. (1972). *Human problem solving.* Englewood Cliffs, NJ: Prentice-Hall.

Test your knowledge

Problem solving

10.1 Define what is meant by means ends analysis.

10.2 What is an algorithm?

10.3 What is a heuristic?

10.4 How can one solve problems by analogy?

Answers to these questions can be found on the companion website at: www.pearsoned.co.uk/psychologyexpress

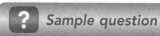

? *Sample question*   *Essay*

Compare and contrast two methods for solving problems.

Thinking

Thinking is a nebulous concept to try to pin down. One way of imagining it is that thinking is the process by which sense perceptions arise and are manipulated. Thinking enables us to be able to model our surrounding environment and to represent it according to our own plans and desires.

The physiology of thinking

We know that our problem solving is of course focused within our brains, but are there any specific parts of the brain that are crucial to these processes? Historically, the main focus has been on the role of the prefrontal cortex (PFC). As with much research into brain function, much of the work relies on observing the effects on cognitive processes of damage to specific parts of the brain.

Damage to the PFC has a significant impact on general planning ability (Owen, Downes, Sahakian, Polkey & Robbins, 1990), or in managing multiple task situations (e.g. Shallice & Burgess, 1991). It has also been found to impact on the completion of specific tasks, e.g., the Tower of Hanoi problem (Morris, Miotto, Feigenbaum, Bullock & Polkey, 1997) and the Luchins' water jug problem (Colvin, Dunbas & Grafman 2001; see Critical focus below). Goel, Grafman, Tajik & Danto (1997) demonstrated that damage to the PFC in patients had a detrimental impact on real-world planning tasks such as financial planning. They found that patient performance was reduced at a global level but not at the local level. Patients had difficulty in organising and structuring their problem space and they also had difficulty in allocating adequate resources to each problem-solving phase. Patients also had difficulty dealing with the fact that in real-life planning problems there are often no definitive right or wrong answers or necessarily conclusions to the problem.

Another real-world study by Goel and Grafman (2000) assessed the impact of PFC damage on an architectural task. They found that PFC damage caused problems in the transition from problem structuring to problem solving; as a result preliminary design did not start until two-thirds of the way into the session.

Imaging techniques and thinking

There have also been a number of studies that have used brain imaging techniques to assess the involvement of specific parts of the brain in problem solving. For example Newman, Carpenter, Varma & Just (2003) used fMRI to

Luchins' water jug problem

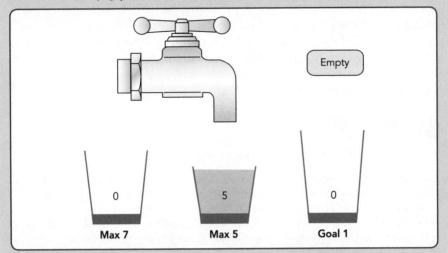

Figure 10.2 **Luchins' water jug problem**

The problem is to get exactly 1 litre of water from 7- and 5-litre jugs and another unknown volume jug.

Decision-making processes following damage to the prefrontal cortex

The aim of this study was to investigate the profile of cognitive deficits, with particular emphasis on decision-making processes, following damage to different sectors of the human **prefrontal cortex.**

Patients with discrete orbitofrontal (OBF) lesions, dorsolateral (DL) lesions, dorsomedial (DM) lesions and large frontal lesions (Large) were compared with matched controls on a number of different decision-making tasks: a gambling task and a battery of other tests including the assessment of recognition memory working memory, and planning ability was also administered.

Whilst combined frontal patients were impaired on several of the tasks, distinct profiles emerged for each patient group:

- DL patients showed greater impairment on working memory, planning and the gambling task.
- DM patients were impaired at the gambling task and also at planning.
- The Large group displayed diffuse impairment, but were the only group to exhibit risky decision making.

They concluded that ventral and dorsal aspects of prefrontal cortex must interact in the maintenance of rational and 'non-risky' decision making.

Manes, Sahakian, Clark, et al. (2002)

169

assess brain function when a participant was undertaking the 'Tower of London' task. There were a number of findings regarding the role of the PFC, including that while both the left and right prefrontal cortices were equally involved during the solution of moderate and difficult problems, the activation on the right was higher during the solution of the easy problems, also the activation observed in the right prefrontal cortex was highly correlated with individual differences in working memory. Crucially, these fMRI results suggested that the right prefrontal area may be more involved in the generation of a plan, whereas the left prefrontal area may be more involved in plan execution.

CRITICAL FOCUS

A functional MRI study of high-level cognition: The game of chess

Brain activity was compared (by using an fMRI technique) when a participant was playing the game of chess and when they were engaging with a spatial task with matched visual stimuli. Atherton and colleagues observed that there was bilateral activation in the superior frontal lobes, the parietal lobes and occipital lobes. Also some small areas of activation were observed unilaterally in the left hemisphere. Overall, they found that the left hemisphere showed more activation than the right.

Atherton, Zhuang, Bart, Hu & He (2003).

Further reading The physiology of thinking

Topic	Key reading
MRI	D'Esposito, M., Zarahn, E. & Aguirre, G.K. (1999). Event-related functional MRI: Implications for cognitive psychology. *Psychological Bulletin, 125*, 155–64.
MRI and planning	Fincham, J.M., Carter, C.S., van Veen, V., Strenger, V.A. & Anderson, J.R. (2002). Neural mechanisms of planning: A computational analysis using event-related fMRI. *Proceedings of the National Academy of Sciences of the United States of America, 99* (5), 3346–51.

Test your knowledge

The physiology of thinking

10.5 What is the PFC and where is it in the brain?

10.6 What is Luchins' water jug problem?

10.7 How can fMRI scans be used to assess localised thinking within the brain?

10.8 What are the limitations to brain imaging techniques in assessing problem solving?

Answers to these questions can be found on the companion website at: **www.pearsoned.co.uk/psychologyexpress**

Reasoning

At a very basic level reasoning can be split into two distinct categories: deductive and inductive reasoning.

Deductive reasoning

Deductive reasoning (see Figure 10.3) at its most basic level is simply reasoning from the general to the particular, for example, starting with a theory and looking for instances that confirm the deduction. One branch of deductive reasoning is that of syllogistic reasoning.

A syllogism or logical appeal is a kind of logical argument in which one proposition (the conclusion) is inferred from two others (the premises) of a certain form.

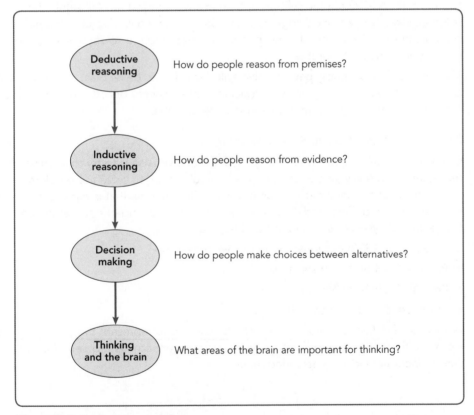

Figure 10.3 Deductive reasoning

> **Example 1**
>
> Premise 1:   All A are B
> Premise 2:   All B are C
> Conclusion: Therefore, all A are C
>
> *or*
>
> Premise 1:   All men are mortal.
> Premise 2:   Socrates is a man.
> Conclusion: Socrates is mortal.

There are a number of theories as to how people solve syllogisms. One of these is called the 'atmosphere bias' (e.g. Woodworth & Sells, 1935). There are two fundamental ideas to this theory; the first is that if there is at least one negative in the premises, then one will prefer a negative solution. Second, if there are two or more 'Alls' within the syllogism, then this will suggest an 'All' within the solution. Likewise, two 'Nos' suggest a 'No' solution and two 'Somes' a 'Some' solution. In this way a type of atmosphere is created and the solution is assumed to be congruous to the problem.

The second theory of how people solve syllogisms is the 'belief bias'. This simply states that if a syllogism agrees with a person's already held beliefs then it is more likely that the syllogism will be judged to be valid.

Mental models of deductive reasoning

One way of determining whether a syllogism is true or false is to try to imagine the situation. In this way one can utilise a 'mental model' to solve the problem. At a basic level a mental model is simply a specific situation that is represented in a person's mind. This model can then be utilised in helping one to determine the validity of syllogisms in deductive reasoning.

Johnson-Laird (1999) put forward the following example:

- Premise 1: all of the artists are beekeepers
- Premise 2: some beekeepers are chemists
- Question: are some artists chemists?

A number of different mental models can be created to represent this problem. However, there are many different ways of misrepresenting this problem that can lead to incorrect judgements being made:

> Incorrect mental model 1: A A A A
> B B B B
> C C

Incorrect mental model 2:	A A A A	
	B B B B B	
	C C C	
Correct mental model:	A A A A	
	B B B B B B	
	C C	

In the diagram above each letter represents an attribute – A represents artists, B, beekeepers and C, chemists. If they are in line vertically then they are classified as being a possible individual, for example on the first model, if you are a chemist then you must also be an artist and beekeeper. As can be seen in the diagram there are a number of ways that an incorrect mental model can be set up that will cause a wrong decision to be made about validity of the statement some of the chemists are artists.

Conditional reasoning

- The individual must attempt to draw a conclusion from an if–then proposition.
- A conditional syllogism is basically an if–then statement, e.g. If P then Q

if **antecedent – consequent**

There are a number of conclusions that can be made from an if–then statement, some valid and some invalid (see Figure 10.4).

If P then Q

First premise If P then Q		
VALID	**P implies Q**	**NOT Q implies NOT P**
NOT VALID	**NOT P implies NOT Q**	**Q implies P**

Figure 10.4 **Possible outcomes of a conditional syllogism**

173

This form of reasoning can be applied to a real-life problem. For example, Wason (1966) put forward a card selection task for which conditional reasoning can be used to solve (see Figure 10.5).

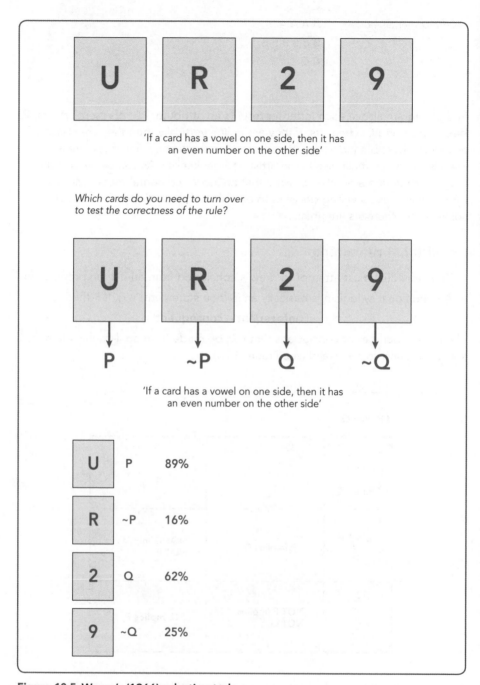

Figure 10.5 Wason's (1966) selection task

The answer to the Wason selection task is to choose U and 9, or the modus ponens and modus tollens.

Conclusions that can be taken from the Wason (1966) selection task are:

- People fail to reason appropriately within a deductive framework
- People tend to use an inductive method rather than a deductive method
- A probabilistic framework is implemented rather than a definitive binary true/false model
- This is unsurprising as it is much more akin to real-life situations that we might find ourselves in.

EVALUATION

− If either of the premises are false we cannot count on the conclusion being true, so we have to be sure of our facts

− It requires a complete and accurate set of data to work with

− Real life very seldom reflects the certainty associated with deductive reasoning

+ It works well within certain domains, e.g. mathematics, philosophy and computer science

+ It enables us to convert a disordered problem scenario into an ordered and uniform language which is transferable

Inductive reasoning

Inductive reasoning involves moving from specific facts to a conclusion. It involves going from a series of one-off observations of a specific event to a rule encompassing all such events (see Figure 10.6):

For example, if I find that multiplying 3 by 2 gives me an even number and 5 by 2, likewise 4 by 2, then I may put forward a hypothesis that says that if I have a number (n) and I multiply it by 2 the resulting number will always be an even one.

Or

Seawater is salty, in fact throughout my life every seawater sample I've experienced has been salty therefore, I can hypothesise that *all* seawater is salty.

In evaluating an inductive argument, we must decide how strong the argument is. A strong argument is defined as having an outcome that is likely to be true and a weak argument as having an outcome that is unlikely to be true. Inductive arguments deal with the probability of whether or not a statement is true rather than if a statement is actually definitely true.

There are a number of factors that can have in impact on the strength of an argument.

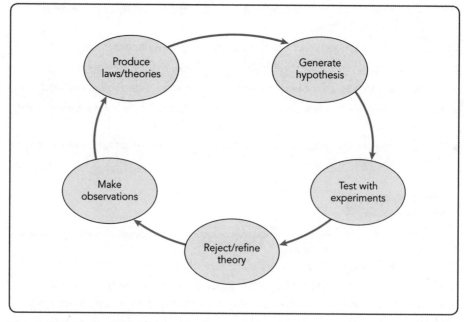

Figure 10.6 **The inductive process**

- How well does my observation fit all other observations, or is my observation a good example of category? E.g., if I see a person patting a lion in a zoo, I might induce that all lions are safe, but my observation was not a very good example of the group of 'lions'.

- How many observations have I made? If I've observed that every time I touch ice it is cold then this would start to create a strong argument for ice *always* being cold.

- Are my observations backed up any other scientific descriptions of the phenomenon or category that I'm observing? If I observe that every fish I have ever seen can survive underwater, and the biological evidence suggests that fish have gills that can absorb oxygen from water, then this may strengthen the argument for fish being able to breathe underwater.

EVALUATION

− Theories should be refutable and should aim to falsify rather than support theories.

− It is based on probability or likelihood, and therefore removes the certainty of situations.

+ It is much more similar to the problems we encounter in real life

+ It models the way that the majority of us attempt to make rational judgements about the world we live in.

Further reading **Reasoning**

Topic	Key reading
Deduction	Evans, J. St. B.T., Newstead, S.E. & Byrne, R.M.J. (1993). *Human reasoning: The psychology of deduction.* Hove: Lawrence Erlbaum Associates.
Reasoning	Johnson-Laird, P.N. (1999). Formal rules versus mental models in reasoning. In R Sternberg (Ed.), *The nature of cognition* (587–624). Cambridge, MA: MIT Press.
Structure of reasoning	Wason, P.C. & Johnson-Laird, P.N. (1972). *Psychology of reasoning: Structure and content.* Cambridge, MA: Harvard University Press.

Test your knowledge

Reasoning

10.9 What is deductive reasoning?

10.10 What are the strengths and weaknesses of deductive reasoning?

10.11 What is a syllogism?

10.12 What is inductive reasoning?

10.13 What are the strengths and weaknesses of inductive reasoning?

Answers to these questions can be found on the companion website at: **www.pearsoned.co.uk/psychologyexpress.**

 Sample question   *Essay*

Critically evaluate the use of two modes of reasoning in solving a real-life problem of your choice.

Chapter summary – pulling it all together

→ Can you tick all of the points from the revision checklist at the beginning of this chapter?

→ Attempt all of the Test yourself questions.

→ Attempt the essay questions within the chapter using the guidelines below.

→ Go to the companion website at www.pearsoned.co.uk/psychologyexpress to access more revision support online, including interactive quizzes, flash cards, You be the marker exercises as well as answer guidance for the Test yourself and Sample questions from this chapter.

Answer guidelines

 Sample question *Essay*

Critically evaluate the statement 'The function of problem solving is localised within the human brain'.

Approaching the question

This question requires a review of modularity of function within the brain focusing specifically on problem solving.

Important points to include

To answer this question you first need to describe the various parts of the brain that have been suggested as playing a role in problem solving, and then describe some of the evidence to support these claims. These will be based chiefly on imaging studies and assessment of brain-damaged patients. You must then attempt to evaluate this evidence in terms of strengths and weaknesses of the methodology employed and the extrapolations made from the findings. Be careful to produce a conclusion where you sum up the findings of your evaluation.

Make your answer stand out

For the above question, make sure that you read around the topic areas and get hold of some of the key papers. Make sure that you always back up your studies and evaluations with appropriate studies/references to support your claims and statements. Specifically, make sure that you don't simply describe the studies of imaging techniques and problem solving, but actually critically evaluate the different studies. This can be done in various ways, one of which could be by using a 'compare and contrast' approach where the different methodologies are assessed against each other. Furthermore, a good answer should also incorporate some of the contemporary research that looks at the modelling of brain functions relating to planning and problem solving.

Explore the accompanying website at **www.pearsoned.co.uk/psychologyexpress**

→ Prepare more effectively for exams and assignments using the answer guidelines for questions from this chapter.

→ Test your knowledge using multiple choice questions and flashcards.

→ Improve your essay skills by exploring the You be the marker exercises.

Notes

Notes

11

Learning

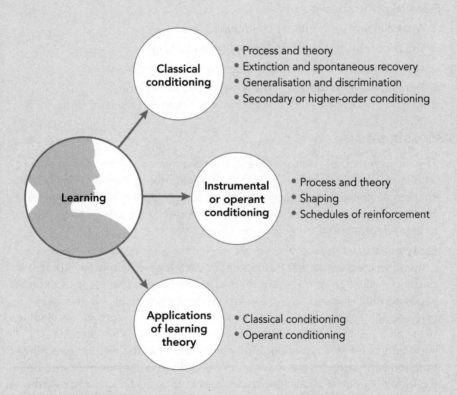

- Classical conditioning
  - Process and theory
  - Extinction and spontaneous recovery
  - Generalisation and discrimination
  - Secondary or higher-order conditioning

- Learning

- Instrumental or operant conditioning
  - Process and theory
  - Shaping
  - Schedules of reinforcement

- Applications of learning theory
  - Classical conditioning
  - Operant conditioning

A printable version of this topic map is available from:
www.pearsoned.co.uk/psychologyexpress

Introduction

The vast majority of our adult skills and knowledge can be attributed to the process of 'learning'. It is a process that is essential to our development and yet not one that we naturally spend much time contemplating. Although a cliché, it is true to say that we never stop learning: from the instant of birth until the moment of death we are constantly processing new information and therefore implicitly learning and developing as individuals. This chapter will address how different learning theories attempt to explain the process of learning and also how these theories can be applied within real-world settings.

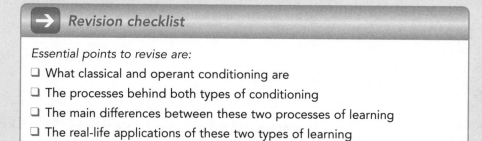

Revision checklist

Essential points to revise are:
- ❏ What classical and operant conditioning are
- ❏ The processes behind both types of conditioning
- ❏ The main differences between these two processes of learning
- ❏ The real-life applications of these two types of learning

Assessment advice

- This chapter focuses on learning and details a number of theories of how learning takes place. It then goes on to evaluate these theories. Finally the chapter illustrates some practical applications of learning within real-world settings. For all these topic areas, we've provided key readings to give you a more in-depth understanding of the issues.

- **Essay questions:** most of the essays you'll encounter relating to theories of learning will require a clear description of each theory or approach before a detailed evaluation of the strengths and weaknesses of the theory. Common issues are that students spend too long describing a theory which doesn't give enough space (or time, in an exam) to evaluate in depth, or get confused between the different mechanisms behind the theories. This raises an important point: it is not enough simply to 'describe' the experiments relating to theories of learning, the mechanism behind the processes must also be explained. Evidence should be drawn from both animal and human examples, and the problems relating to the extrapolation from animal to human behaviour should also always be borne in mind.

Sample question

Could you answer this question? Below is a typical essay question that could arise on this topic.

Guidelines on answering this question are included at the end of this chapter, whilst guidance on tackling other exam questions can be found on the companion website at: **www.pearsoned.co.uk/psychologyexpress**

 Sample question   *Essay*

Critically evaluate two psychological explanations of addiction.

Classical conditioning

Learning can be defined as a relatively permanent change in behaviour due to experience.

Associative learning is learning that occurs by making a connection or association between two events. There are two types of associative learning:

1 *Classical conditioning* – association between stimuli in the environment and involuntary reflexive behaviours such as salivation.

2 *Operant conditioning* – association between the consequences of our behaviours and our voluntary actions.

It is classical conditioning that we will focus on in the first section of this chapter.

Process and theory

● First studied by Pavlov (1849–1936).

● Presenting two stimuli close together allows a response to transfer from one to the other.

● Pavlov's explanation was that excitatory links formed between areas within the brain. Pavlov viewed this process as occurring automatically.

● He emphasised contiguity between the conditioned stimulus and unconditioned stimulus as the key requirement for conditioning to occur.

Key terms

Stimulus: an activating event in the environment.
Response: a reaction to the activating event.

Pavlov taught dogs to salivate in reaction to hearing a bell ring (see Figure 11.1). Eventually, after repeatedly pairing the bell with the food, the bell was able to act in the place of the food.

Bell [alone] = salivation

183

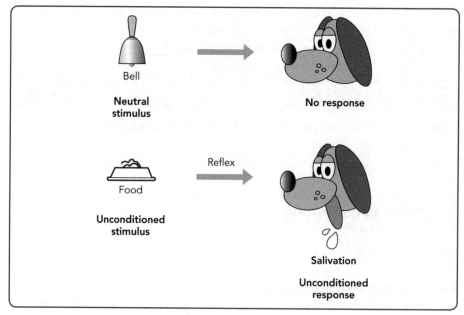

Figure 11.1 Classical conditioning

The dogs were able to salivate in response to just the bell ringing, without the food being present. This is known as *classical conditioning* (see Figure 11.2).

In classical conditioning, an involuntary or reflexive behaviour such as salivation is associated with another stimulus in the environment like a bell. An involuntary or reflexive behaviour is one that you do not have to learn how to do. It is instinctual or a passive response.

Examples of unconditioned responses include:

- Blinking – response to air puffs to the eye
- Shivering – response to cold
- Sweating – response to heat
- Emotional reactions such as fear
- Salivation – response to the sight or smell of food
- Nausea – response to certain smells or sights.

Can you think of any others?

CRITICAL FOCUS

The Little Albert experiment

John B. Watson and Rosalie Raynor (1920) chose Albert from a hospital for this study at the age of almost 9 months. Before the commencement of the experiment, Little Albert was given a battery of baseline emotional tests; the infant was exposed, briefly

▶

and for the first time, to a white rat, a rabbit, a dog, a monkey, masks with and without hair, cotton wool, burning newspapers, etc. During the baseline, Little Albert showed no fear toward any of these items. The next time Albert was exposed to the rat Watson made a loud noise by hitting a metal pipe with a hammer. Naturally, the child began to cry after hearing the loud noise. After repeatedly pairing the white rat with the loud noise, Albert began to cry simply after seeing the rat. After this conditioning session the instant the rat was shown, Little Albert began to cry.

- Introduction of a loud sound (unconditioned stimulus) resulted in fear (unconditioned response), a natural response.
- Introduction of a rat (neutral stimulus) paired with the loud sound (unconditioned stimulus) resulted in fear (unconditioned response).
- Successive introductions of a rat (conditioned stimulus) resulted in fear (conditioned response).

Furthermore, the experiment showed that Little Albert seemed to generalise his response to furry objects, so that when Watson sent a non-white rabbit into the room 17 days after the original experiment, Albert also became distressed. He showed similar reactions when presented with a furry dog, a sealskin coat, and even when Watson appeared in front of him wearing a Santa Claus mask with white cotton balls as his beard, although Albert did not fear everything with hair.

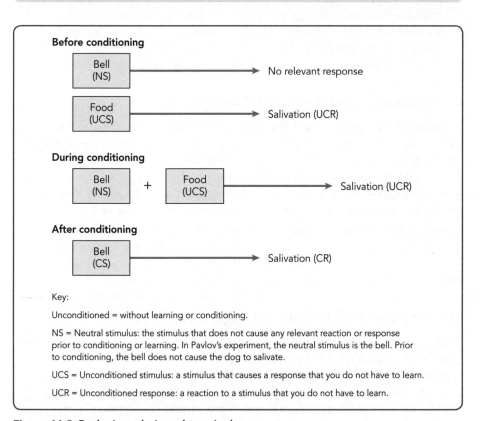

Before conditioning

Bell (NS) ⟶ No relevant response

Food (UCS) ⟶ Salivation (UCR)

During conditioning

Bell (NS) + Food (UCS) ⟶ Salivation (UCR)

After conditioning

Bell (CS) ⟶ Salivation (CR)

Key:

Unconditioned = without learning or conditioning.

NS = Neutral stimulus: the stimulus that does not cause any relevant reaction or response prior to conditioning or learning. In Pavlov's experiment, the neutral stimulus is the bell. Prior to conditioning, the bell does not cause the dog to salivate.

UCS = Unconditioned stimulus: a stimulus that causes a response that you do not have to learn.

UCR = Unconditioned response: a reaction to a stimulus that you do not have to learn.

Figure 11.2 Pavlov's analysis and terminology

> **Problem**
>
> *In the following example, see if you can work out what is the: NS, UCS, UCR, CS and CR.*
>
> You have a new job. The job is based in an office with large radiators, which are controlled centrally and for some inexplicable reason appear to be on all year round.
>
> Every day you go to work you notice that it is very hot, and even after several complaints nothing is done about it. You wear light clothing but still sweat profusely and leave your office feeling drained. After the first week of going to work, you eventually begin to sweat when you pull up outside your new office even before you go inside.

Extinction and spontaneous recovery

- Extinction is when a response that is no longer reinforced is weakened and less likely to occur again in the future, for example Pavlov's dogs would slowly 'unlearn' their response if no food was presented over a period of time.

- Spontaneous recovery is the sudden reappearance of a behaviour after extinction has taken place, for example when the initial salivating behaviour had become extinct through the removal of the food, once the food was returned the dog would very quickly return to a 'fully learned' state. Importantly, this process was much much quicker than the original learning curve, and hence was labelled 'spontaneous recovery'.

Generalisation and discrimination

Suppose a blue light was used as a CS in a conditioning experiment. If the light colour is changed slightly then it is likely that the desired response would still be observed, as the individual would have been able to generalise so that they responded not just to the original blue light, but to various shades of blue. Interestingly, different individuals have different cut-off points where they would no longer categorise the light as being blue and therefore respond to it.

In the same conditioning session if a green light is not reinforced, then the individual will learn to differentiate between the two different coloured lights and act accordingly. If the individual learns to respond to one colour and not the other then we can say that they can differentiate between them.

Secondary or higher-order conditioning

Once a conditioned stimulus (CS)–unconditioned stimulus (UCS) association has been learned, over time it is possible to form a secondary association with the conditioned stimulus and a second new stimulus even in the absence of the unconditioned stimulus. The first CS can act as a UCS for a new CS. Once an association has been established between the second CS and the CR, then it too can be used to condition a third CS, and this in theory can go on ad infinitum.

Secondary conditioning is basically learning through association in the absence of an unconditioned response, where a previously neutral stimuli may also acquire the ability to form further associations with other neutral stimuli.

A real-life example of this is 'money'. None of us actually wants money itself, we can't eat it or sleep under it, and yet we go to extraordinary lengths to gain it (e.g. working in an office for 40 hours a week). It is not the money we want, it's what we can buy with the money that is important, e.g. food and shelter. In this way we have been higher-order conditioned to respond to money, even though it does not elicit an automatic response itself.

Further reading Classical conditioning	
Topic	*Key reading*
Cognition and conditioning	Kirsch, I., Lynn, S.J., Vigorito, M. & Miller, R.R. (2004). The role of cognition in classical and operant conditioning. *Journal of Clinical Psychology*, 60, 369–92.
Reflexes	Pavlov, I.P. (1927/1960). *Conditioned reflexes*. New York: Dover. Available from: http://psychclassics.yorku.ca/Pavlov/).
Passive avoidance learning	Richard, S., Davies, D.C. & Faure, J.M. (2000). The role of fear in one-trial passive avoidance learning in Japanese quail chicks genetically selected for long or short duration of the tonic mobility reaction. *Behavioural Processes*, 48, 165–70.

Test your knowledge

Classical conditioning

11.1 What are some examples of other involuntary or reflexive unconditioned responses (UCRs)?

11.2 What are the necessary conditions for conditioning to occur?

11.3 What is the key association in Figure 11.1?

11.4 What was the UCS in Pavlov's study?

11.5 What was the UCR in Pavlov's study?

Answers to these questions can be found on the companion website at: **www.pearsoned.co.uk/psychologyexpress**

Instrumental or operant conditioning

Process and theory

- Focus is on voluntary behaviour.
- Behaviour that is learned only, *not* innate.

- Consequences shape voluntary behaviour.
- Operant conditioning: learning to perform a voluntary behaviour based upon the consequences.
- Behaviour is voluntary. You must think about doing it beforehand, it is not innate or passive.
- Example: raising your hand in class to answer a question. This is voluntary behaviour. It is not reflexive or involuntary. You are not born with this ability, you have to learn how (and why) to do this.
- Whether or not you will raise your hand again in the future has to do with the consequences of your actions.

Thorndike (1911) is really the grandfather of operant conditioning. He studied learning using puzzle boxes and observed a steady reduction in the time taken to escape, with no evidence of real insight. He put forward Thorndike's law of effect: that responses followed by positive outcomes have their links strengthened. Contemporary views of this form of learning have been shaped largely by the work of Skinner:

The main emphasis of Skinner's (1938) work was operant versus respondent behaviour.

- Free operants are emitted, rather than elicited by stimuli.
- Discriminative stimuli signal the operation of particular contingencies.
- Reward and punishment may be by delivery or omission of stimuli.
- Reward and punishment alter the likelihood that behaviour will be repeated.

According to Skinner there are two categories or types of consequences (see Figure 11.3):

1 Reinforcement
2 Punishment.

Reinforcement

- Reinforcement is any consequence that increases the probability of a response in the future.
- Reinforcement can be used to shape behaviours in both animals and people.

Reinforcement types

Reinforcement = any consequence that you like. Reinforcement is different for everyone; the trick to motivation is to try to work out what works for an individual – what are their likes and dislikes.

1 Positive reinforcement is when a consequence that you like is added, for example a treat – stickers, sweets, money, etc.
2 Negative reinforcement is when a consequence that you dislike is taken away, for example: if you manage to gain an average of an A grade in a particular

	Appetite	Aversive
Presented	*Positive reinforcement* Positive event follows response, e.g. reward	*Punishment* Discomfort follows response, e.g. smack
Removed	*Punishment* Positive state removed after response, e.g. making child go to room	*Negative reinforcement* Discomfort removed after response, e.g. escape or avoidance learning

Figure 11.3 **Processes of operant conditioning**

module then you will be exempt from the final exam and automatically get an A grade for the module. Other examples could be taking a painkiller for your headache or even using a snooze alarm.

Punishment

Punishment is any consequence that decreases the probability of a behaviour in the future. Something that you don't like is added, for example: getting smacked, etc.

Shaping

Shaping is a process first utilised by Skinner (1953). He rewarded a bird for turning slightly towards a spot in its cage. This increased the frequency of the behaviour. Rewards were then withheld until the behaviour was replicated. This process continued by reinforcing positions successively closer to the spot, and then only rewarding when the bird actually touched the spot.

In this way complicated behaviours can be created which would never appear in the natural behaviour of the animal otherwise. By reinforcing a series of successive approximations a very unlikely behaviour/event can become very likely in a relatively short time frame.

Researchers using Skinner's techniques have taught birds and animals to perform many behaviours that would appear to be unnatural to the species. Chickens have been taught to play toy pianos and dogs to climb ladders. These strange behaviours are taught through the process of shaping.

Schedules of reinforcement

- When teaching an individual a new skill, it is usually most effective to use continuous reinforcement. This means that the learner is rewarded every time they elicit the specific behaviour.
- Partial reinforcement is when the reinforcement is given but not every time the behaviour is elicited.
- Shaping is the reinforcement of successive approximations towards a targeted behaviour (see below).

Partial schedules of reinforcement

There are two main types of partial schedules:

- Ratio schedules, which depend upon the number of responses or behaviours that must occur between reinforcement.
- Interval schedules, which depend upon the amount of time that must elapse between reinforcement.

Both ratio and interval schedules can be either fixed or variable.

Ratio schedules

- **Fixed ratio**: the number of responses that must be made before reinforcement is given is fixed or constant, for example, every tenth time a pigeon pecks a bar they get a food pellet.
- **Variable ratio**: the number of responses that must be made before reinforcement is given is variable or changes, for example the first time the pigeon pecks a bar they get a food pellet. The next ten times, they receive nothing, the eleventh time they receive a food pellet. The next reward is given after 100 pecks.

Further reading Operant conditioning	
Topic	Key reading:
Trends in youth crime	Durant, J.E. (2000). Trends in youth crime and well-being since the abolition of corporal punishment in Sweden. *Youth and Society*, 31, 437–55.
Animal responses to food	Neuringer, A.J. (1969). Animals respond for food in the presence of free food. *Science*, 166, 399–401.
Animal intelligence and conditioning	Thorndike, E.L. (1901). Animal intelligence: An experimental study of the associative processes in animals. *Psychological Review Monograph Supplement*, 2, 1–109.

Test your knowledge

Operant conditioning

For each of the following examples, see if you can first work out if it is reinforcement or punishment. Is each example positive or negative?

11.6 Smacking a child for misbehaviour.

11.7 Taking an aspirin to make your headache go away.

11.8 Not having to do chores if you clean your room.

11.9 Getting shouted at by your lecturer for talking in classes.

11.10 Hitting the snooze button on your alarm clock in the morning.

11.11 Frequent flier miles.

11.12 Being given £10 for every A grade at university.

11.13 Being assigned an extra test because the class was behaving badly.

11.14 Detention for misbehaviour in school.

11.15 A speeding ticket.

Answers to these questions can be found on the companion website at:
www.pearsoned.co.uk/psychologyexpress

 Sample question *Essay*

What are the strengths and weaknesses of classical and operant conditioning in explaining complex human behaviour?

Applications of learning theory

Classical conditioning

Advertising

Through imagery and/or music, smells, sounds, advertisers attempt to manipulate the emotions of consumers. The goal is to make the consumer associate a specific emotion with their product, for example using humour or attractive individuals within an advertisement in order to sell a specific product.

Over time the neutral stimulus (e.g. a car) can elicit a conditioned response that was at first associated with the unconditioned response (e.g. a party or adventure).

Reducing prejudice

Studies such as that by Olson and Fasio (2006; see Critical focus box) illustrate how prejudice can be classically conditioned through repeated pairings of characteristics or traits with one group of people.

CRITICAL FOCUS

Reduction of automatically activated racial prejudice

In a series of experiments Olson and Fasio (2006) used a conditioning procedure to reduce automatically activated racial prejudice in White participants.

Stimuli consisted of 16 photos (8 Black and 8 White) of clearly Black and White individuals in different occupational roles. The Black photos were shown with positive words and the White with neutral words. The procedure was found to be effective in reducing prejudice. Furthermore, this reduction in prejudice was found to persist throughout a two-day separation between the conditioning procedure and the attitudinal evaluation procedure.

Participants in the experimental condition showed less negative, automatically activated racial attitudes than control participants.

Behavioural therapy

Wolpe (1958) originally coined the term 'systematic desensitisation'. Systematic desensitisation can be used to associate a feared object with something positive and/or liked. For example, Jones (1924) used this method to eliminate fear of rabbits in a young boy. A rabbit was gradually introduced to the boy over a period of a few days, and each time that the rabbit appeared it was accompanied by a positive activity (e.g. eating something nice). Over time it was demonstrated that the boy's fear of rabbits was significantly reduced.

Aversion therapy is aimed at weakening or reducing unwanted behaviours such as addictions or unwanted habits. The technique of counter-conditioning is used to associate the negative behaviours with a really negative consequence or an 'extremely aversive' consequence. A good example comes from Raymond in 1964, who used aversion therapy to assist a 14-year-old boy to quit smoking. The boy was given injections of apomorphine (a substance that induces nausea), while he was smoking. Subsequently, the boy felt sick the next few times he smoked, and over time the habit was significantly reduced.

Medical matters

● *Allergic reactions.* Dekker and Groen (1956) demonstrated that allergic reactions could occur from a secondary stimulus that the patient was not actually allergic to. For example they found that a patient who developed asthma when near goldfish, also developed an asthma attack when in the presence of a plastic goldfish. The patient had created a stimulus generalisation from a genuine stimulus to one that would not normally have caused an allergic reaction.

- *The immune system.* Ader (2001) demonstrated that if a sweet liquid was given to a rat at the same time as it was injected with a drug that suppresses an immune system, over time the sweet liquid itself would start to depress the rat's immune system. This finding is particularly pertinent as there are many environmental situations which can also suppress human immune systems and some of these will have been conditioned.

Operant conditioning

Prejudice

Prejudice and discrimination can be learned through positive reinforcement (e.g. positive attention or acceptance by others).

Biofeedback

A bodily function (such as blood pressure or heart rate) is recorded and the information is fed back to an organism to increase voluntary control over the bodily function.

- Positive reinforcement: feedback is added as a way to increase the likelihood that the behaviour will be repeated.
- Secondary reinforcement: the value we place on health.
- Shaping: the information gained through data helps the organism approximate the desired outcome.

Superstition

- Behaviours get accidentally reinforced such that the organism associates the reinforcement with the behaviour.
- Can also become conditioned through partial schedules of reinforcement.

CRITICAL FOCUS

The long-term effects of a token economy on safety performance in open-pit mining

A token economy that used trading stamps as tokens was instituted at two open-pit mines (Fox, Hopkins and Anger, 1987). Employees earned stamps for a number of safety positive behaviours, including: working without injuries, being in work groups in which all other workers had no injuries, and for not being involved in equipment-damaging accidents. They lost stamps if they or other workers in their group were injured, caused equipment damage, or failed to report accidents or injuries. The stamps could be exchanged for a selection of items at redemption stores. They found that implementation of the token economy was followed by large reductions in the number of days lost from work because of injuries the number of lost-time injuries and the costs of accidents and injuries. The reductions in costs far exceeded the costs of operating the token economy. Furthermore, the improvements were maintained over several years.

Education

Through the use of token economies, student behaviour and performance have been shown to improve. These tokens can be points, gold stars, stamps, etc., but importantly can be stored up to obtain something desirable. This has also been shown to be effective in workplaces; one study showed that a token economy among miners reduced accidents (Fox et al., 1987; see the Critical focus box).

Further reading Applications of learning theory

Topic	Key reading
Psychoneuroimmunology	Ader, R. (2001). Psychoneuroimmunology. *Current Directions in Psychological Science*, 10, 94–8.
Improving classroom control	Hall, R.V., Panyan, M., Rabon, D. & Broden, M. (1968). Instructing beginning teachers in reinforcement procedures which improve classroom control. *Journal of Applied Behavior Analysis*, 1, 315–22.
Conditioning and treating cancer	Stockhorst, U., Spennes-Saleh, S., Körholz, D., et al. (2000). Anticipatory symptoms and anticipatory immune responses in pediatric cancer patients receiving chemotherapy: Features of a classically conditioned response? *Brain, Behavior, and Immunity*, 14, 198–218.
Conditioning and drug addiction	Kreek, M.J., Nielsen, D.A., Butelman, E.R. & LaForge, K.S. (2005). Genetic influences on impulsivity, risk taking, stress responsivity and vulnerability to drug abuse and addiction. *Nature Neuroscience*, 8, 1450–7.

Test your knowledge

Applications of learning theory

11.16 What is aversion therapy?

11.17 What is biofeedback?

11.18 What is systematic desensitisation?

11.19 How can conditioning make allergies worse?

11.20 What is a token economy?

Answers to these questions can be found on the companion website at: **www.pearsoned.co.uk/psychologyexpress**

? Sample question   Essay

Critically evaluate the contribution of classical and operant conditioning to human health (both physical and psychological).

Chapter summary – pulling it all together

→ Can you tick all of the points from the revision checklist at the beginning of this chapter?

→ Attempt all of the Test yourself questions.

→ Attempt the essay questions within the chapter using the guidelines below.

→ Go to the companion website at **www.pearsoned.co.uk/psychologyexpress** to access more revision support online, including interactive quizzes, flash cards, You be the marker exercises as well as answer guidance for the Test yourself and Sample questions from this chapter.

Answer guidelines

 Sample question   *Essay*

Critically evaluate two psychological explanations of addiction.

Approaching the question

This question requires the application and evaluation of psychological theories of learning to the specific behaviour of addiction.

Important points to include

To answer this question the obvious approach is to use both classical and operant conditioning to explain addiction. Focus on two or three examples of addiction, e.g. smoking, gambling, and then explain how both theories can explain this addiction. Importantly, embed your example into the processes and terminology of classical and operant conditioning described in this chapter. Evaluation can be completed through comparing and contrasting the two theories; make sure you refer to both the biological and psychological processes involved. Be careful to produce a conclusion where you sum up the findings of your evaluation.

Make your answer stand out

For the above question, make sure that you read around the topic areas and get hold of some of the key papers. Make sure that you always back up your studies and evaluations with appropriate studies/references to support your claims and statements. Specifically, make sure that you don't simply describe the process of conditioning and all of the terminology and stimuli and responses, but that you actually critically assess the strengths and weaknesses of each approach. As mentioned this can be completed using a 'compare

195

and contrast' approach where the different theories are assessed against each other, but also use previous research to assess the effectiveness of each approach. Furthermore, a good answer could also incorporate some of the contemporary research that examines the impact of genetics on conditioning and addiction (see the Further reading list on applications of learning theory on p. 194).

Explore the accompanying website at **www.pearsoned.co.uk/psychologyexpress**

→ Prepare more effectively for exams and assignments using the answer guidelines for questions from this chapter.

→ Test your knowledge using multiple choice questions and flashcards.

→ Improve your essay skills by exploring the You be the marker exercises.

Notes

12

Human and computer intelligence

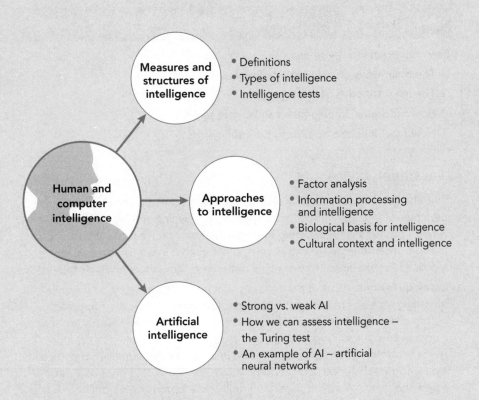

- **Measures and structures of intelligence**
  - Definitions
  - Types of intelligence
  - Intelligence tests

- **Human and computer intelligence**

- **Approaches to intelligence**
  - Factor analysis
  - Information processing and intelligence
  - Biological basis for intelligence
  - Cultural context and intelligence

- **Artificial intelligence**
  - Strong vs. weak AI
  - How we can assess intelligence – the Turing test
  - An example of AI – artificial neural networks

A printable version of this topic map is available from:
www.pearsoned.co.uk/psychologyexpress

Introduction

Intelligence is one of the most difficult attributes to define. Although we all have a good idea of what we mean by intelligence and can quite easily categorise those that we would deem to exhibit intelligence, this can vary from person to person and hence it has historically been difficult to take a firm grasp of this most nebulous of concepts. One of the major issues within this field is the vast number of spheres of experience where intelligence may manifest itself. We describe great musicians as musical geniuses and chefs as culinary geniuses. This chapter will attempt to address this issue and specifically look at the differences between general and specific intelligences and multiple intelligences. We will also consider if we are alone in displaying intelligence, specifically asking the question will computers ever display intelligent behaviour?

> **→** *Revision checklist*
>
> *Essential points to revise are:*
> ❑ The main ways of defining intelligence
> ❑ The main theories of intelligence
> ❑ How machines' intelligence can be measured
> ❑ How machines can appear to be intelligent

Assessment advice

- This chapter focuses primarily on intelligence in humans. The majority of the content highlights theories or approaches towards intelligence and also ways of measuring or assessing intelligence. Later on we highlight attempts to reproduce intelligence within computers. For all these topic areas, we've provided key readings to give you a more in-depth understanding of the issues.

- **Essay questions**: most of the essays you'll encounter relating to theories of intelligence will require a clear description of each theory or approach before a detailed evaluation of the shortcomings. Common issues are that students spend too long describing a theory which doesn't give enough space (or time, in an exam) to evaluate in depth or get confused between measuring intelligence and theories of intelligence. Remember one must follow the other. We can't measure intelligence before we've defined it. It is always appropriate to point out the weaknesses in intelligence measurement, particularly those relating to cultural or societal bias.

Sample question

Could you answer this question? Below is a typical essay question that could arise on this topic.

Sample question   *Essay*

Critically evaluate two psychological theories of intelligence.

Guidelines on answering this question are included at the end of this chapter, whilst guidance on tackling other exam questions can be found on the companion website at: **www.pearson.co.uk/psychologyexpress**

Measures and structures of intelligence

Definitions

There are two big questions when it comes to defining intelligence: what is intelligence and is there one intelligence or multiple intelligences? This section attempts to illustrate the main attempts that researchers have made to answer these questions. To start, below is one of the more famous definitions of intelligence made by Sternberg:

> Mental activity directed towards purposive adaptation to, and selection and shaping of, real-world environments relevant to one's life. (Sternberg, 1984)

One of the first actual tests of intelligence was designed by Binet (1916) and subsequently developed by Binet and Simon (1916). It measured memory, comprehension, mathematical ability and visual ability. Specifically, Stern (1912) suggested that intelligence could be measured by using an intelligence quotient (IQ) where

$$IQ = MA/CA \times 100$$

where MA is the mental age as measured by an IQ test and CA referred to actual chronological age.

Types of intelligence

One of the most influential individuals in defining intelligence is Spearman. In 1923 using a form of factor analysis he claimed that all of the individual facets of what we would view as intelligence could indeed be brought down to just one general factor of intelligence, which he denoted as *g*. However, not everyone agreed with this single factor perspective.

Sternberg (1983) claimed that there were three types of intelligence in his 'triarchic theory:'

1 Analytic
2 Creative
3 Practical.

Analytical intelligence

- Analytic intelligence corresponds roughly to IQ
- Analytic tends to correlate moderately with creative, but poorly with practical.

Creative intelligence

- Focuses on discovering, exploring, creating and imagining.

Practical intelligence

- Solving problems that may be encountered in any given task, for example, changing a tyre.
- Sternberg (1993) finds relatively low correlations with IQ scores.

Going even further, Thurstone (1938) suggested seven factors:

1 Numerical ability
2 Inductive reasoning
3 Verbal fluency
4 Verbal meaning
5 Perceptual speed
6 Memory
7 Spatial ability.

Gardner's (1999) theory also suggests that there are multiple intelligences:

- Spatial, musical, linguistic, logical–mathematical, interpersonal, intrapersonal, bodily–kinaesthetic
- Naturalist was a recent proposed addition to the list by Gardner
- Spiritual and existential were also later additions to Gardner's original list.

Spatial intelligence

This area deals with spatial judgement. Individuals that have high spatial intelligence would suit careers such as designers and architects.

Linguistic intelligence

This area is to do with spoken or written words. People with high verbal–linguistic intelligence are typically good at reading, writing, telling stories and memorising words.

They also have high verbal memory and recall, and an ability to understand and manipulate syntax and structure.

Hierarchical model

Carroll (1993) suggested that intelligence wasn't a single entity but could be defined within a hierarchy of intelligence (see Figure 12.1).

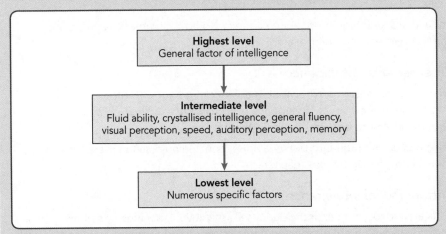

Figure 12.1 Carroll's (1993) hierarchical model of intelligence

Individuals with high linguistic intelligence would suit careers such as teachers, journalists and lawyers.

Logical–mathematical intelligence

This area is connected to the use of logic, abstractions, reasoning and numbers. It places emphasis on reasoning capabilities, abstract patterns of recognition, scientific thinking and investigation and the ability to perform complex calculations.

Individuals with high logical–mathematical intelligence would suit careers such as physicists, mathematicians, doctors and economists.

Kinaesthetic intelligence

This area has is linked to an individual's ability to control one's bodily motion and capacity to handle objects skilfully.

Individuals who have high kinaesthetic intelligence tend to be good at physical activities such as sports or dance. Those with strong bodily–kinaesthetic intelligence seem to be able to have a high level of 'muscle memory' which is essential in many sports, for example, playing golf.

Individuals with high kinaesthetic intelligence would suit careers such as sportsmen/women, dancers, musicians and surgeons.

Musical intelligence

This area has to do with sensitivity to sounds, rhythms, tones and music. People with a high musical intelligence normally have a high sensitivity to pitch.

High musical intelligence is usually linked with highly developed language skills

Individuals with high musical intelligence would suit careers as musicians, singers, writers and composers.

Interpersonal intelligence

This area focuses on an individual's ability to interact with others. Individuals who have high interpersonal intelligence tend to have excellent communication skills and the ability to empathise with others.

Individuals with high interpersonal intelligence would suit careers such as politicians, managers and teachers.

Intrapersonal intelligence

This area focuses on an individual's self-reflective capacities or self-awareness. Individuals with high intrapersonal intelligence tend to be intuitive and typically are skilful at deciphering their own feelings and motivations. Individuals having high intrapersonal intelligence would suit careers such as psychologists, lawyers and possibly writers.

EVALUATION

+ It encompasses far more aspects of human personality and individual differences then previous definitions of intelligence
+ It approaches intelligence in a far more holistic manner
− It's not clear what the relative importance of all the types is
− All of the multiple intelligences tend to correlate − g?
− The theory is descriptive rather than explanatory
− Lack of any empirical evidence

Intelligence tests

Wechsler intelligence tests

Wechsler first developed his intelligence test in 1939. He originally created these tests to find out more about his patients at the Bellevue clinic in response to the then current Binet IQ test which did not meet his needs.

The Wechsler scales assigned a value of 100 to the mean intelligence and added or subtracted another 15 points for each standard deviation an individual was above or below the mean. Rejecting the concept of global intelligence, he divided the concept of intelligence into two main areas: verbal and performance. Each area was then further subdivided and consequently could be tested with a different subtest.

The WAIS-III, a revision of the Wechsler Adult Intelligence Scale (WAIS-III) was released in 1997 (see Figure 12.2). It provided scores for verbal IQ and performance IQ along with four secondary indices (verbal comprehension, working memory, perceptual organisation and processing speed).

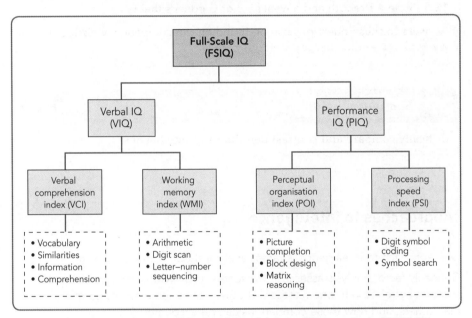

Figure 12.2 A representation of the Wechsler Adult Intelligence Scale (WAIS-III)

Further reading Measures and structures of intelligence

Topic	Key reading
Human cognitive abilities	Carroll, J.B. (1993). *Human cognitive abilities: A survey of factor analytic studies.* New York: Cambridge University Press.
Multiple intelligences in a school setting	Gardner, H. & Hatch, T. (1989). Multiple intelligences go to school: Educational implications of the theory of multiple intelligences. *Educational Researcher, 18,* 4–10.
Sternberg's triarchic theory of intelligence	Sternberg, R.J. (1985). *Beyond IQ: A triarchic theory of human intelligence.* New York: Cambridge University Press.

Test your knowledge

Measures and structures of intelligence

12.1 According to Stern how would you calculate IQ?

12.2 What are the three types of intelligence within Sternberg's 'triarchic theory'?

12.3 What are Thurstone's seven factors of intelligence?

12.4 Which intelligence factors are associated with the different levels in Carroll's Hierarchy of intelligence?

12.5 State a strength and a weakness of Gardner's theory.

Answers to these questions can be found on the companion website at: **www.pearsoned.co.uk/psychologyexpress**

 Sample question Essay

Critically compare and contrast definitions of intelligence.

Approaches to intelligence

One approach to intelligence is factor analysis theories of intelligence.

Generally factor analysis assesses how scores on individual test items or on subtests correlate with one another, whether or not some scores correlate more than others, and how these correlations can be accounted for.

Factor analysis

An example of factor analysis theory comes from Spearman, who proposed a two-factor theory of intelligence, where:

1 Every activity involves a general factor + a specific factor (g + s)

2 g = general intelligence and is innate

3 s = the specific factors and need not be innate

Spearman had noted that results of different 'intelligence' tests almost always correlated positively. His principal components version of factor analysis found a factor (g) that accounts for these correlations.

Thurstone put forward the idea of primary mental abilities. He thought g was not a realistic concept that could be applied to real-life settings, and that abilities should be identified positively.

He started with 56 different tests and identified 7 primary mental abilities, which he originally wanted to claim were independent.

Thurstone (1924) argued that g has no real significance, but merely reflects correlations between test results (which may change if different tests are used).

Guilford's (1967) structure of intelligence attempted a different way of accounting for intelligence. He classified tests according to:

- content (4 types), e.g. verbal meanings and visual figures
- operations (5 types), e.g. memory
- products (6 types), e.g. implications

and so, identified $4 \times 5 \times 6 = 120$ distinct mental abilities. Guilford tried to develop tests for each, but importantly he found that the scores on his tests were often strongly correlated!

Cattell

Cattell (1963) suggested that we should view intelligence as two separate elements:

1 Crystallised intelligence which represents cumulative learning experience or wisdom/expertise and increases with age, and

2 Fluid intelligence which deals with abstract relations and represents the ability to deal with new problems. This intelligence is mainly not taught, is culture free, and generally declines with age.

Information processing and intelligence

These approaches are originally based on ideas from developmental psychology, e.g. Piaget (1896–1980) and Vygotsky (1896–1934). Importantly, unlike psychometric approaches, information-processing approaches focus on the mental processes underlying intelligent behaviour, not on individual differences per se.

Choice reaction times

Jensen (1979) proposed that intelligence can be understood in terms of speed of neuronal conduction. What this means in practice is that intelligent people have neural circuits that conduct information more rapidly. Jensen (1982) found that reaction times in response to a light activation were correlated with higher IQ. However, more recent studies have shown that when the task becomes more difficult than a single stimulus–response the correlation figures are reduced (e.g. Bors, MacLeod & Forrin, 1993).

Lexical access speed and intelligence

Hunt (1980) suggested that speed of retrieval from memory can be used as an index of intelligence. He used the Posner and Mitchell physical match (AA) and name match (Aa) task for letters. However, it may be that participants could also be using higher-level intelligent processes to decide the best strategy for the task.

CRITICAL FOCUS

Attention

Posner and Mitchell (1967) showed participants a series of paired letters to which participants must respond 'same' or 'different' as quickly as possible. Levels of instruction are physical identity (e.g. AA), name identity (e.g. Aa), and rule identity (e.g. both vowels). The variable of interest is the difference between their naming speeds for the first and second examples. The theory states that the first task involves only structural information, whereas the second example involves some access to lexical information, hence Posner and Mitchell suggest that this difference is a measure of an individual's speed of lexical access.

Biological basis for intelligence

Vernon, Wickett, Bazana and Stelmack (2000) suggest that there is a significant statistical relationship between brain size and intelligence. However, it's not clear whether big brains cause intelligence or intelligence causes big brains. This relationship does not work across species, where it appears that it is the ratio of brain size to body size that is the most important factor (e.g. Jerison, 2000), otherwise sperm whales (which have the largest brain) might be super-intelligent and be silently making their plans against us!

Duncan, Emslie and Williams (1996) argued that g is largely a reflection of certain activity levels within frontal lobes. They found that patients with damage to their frontal patients do not have normal intelligence (particularly not normal g). Furthermore, Duncan et al. (2000) compared three 'high g' and 'low g' tasks in a PET study. 'High g' tasks were found to be associated with selective recruitment of lateral frontal cortex in one or both hemispheres.

Imaging studies of intelligence and brain structure

Magnetic resonance imaging (MRI) studies show a significant correlation between general intelligence abilities (g) and total brain volume. Furthermore, MRI-based studies have estimated a moderate correlation between brain size and intelligence of 0.40 to 0.51. Gray and Thompson (2004) found that g was significantly linked to differences in the volume of frontal grey matter, which were mainly determined by genetic factors. They also found a correlation between the volume of each brain region and g, independent of other brain regions. In essence this means that the volume of frontal grey matter had additional predictive validity for g even when the predictive effect of total brain volume was factored out. Hence, the volume of frontal grey matter appears to be one of the better structural indicators of general intelligence abilities (Gray & Thompson, 2004).

Another MRI study found strong evidence that hemispheric size asymmetry was correlated with verbal IQ. In men, a relatively larger left hemisphere predicted better verbal than non-verbal ability, whereas in women a larger left hemisphere predicted relatively better non-verbal than verbal ability (Willerman, Schultz, Rutledge & Bigler 1992).

Cultural context and intelligence

According to 'contextualism', intelligence must be understood in its real-world context. Contextualism views intelligence as being inextricably linked to culture. People in different cultures may have quite different ideas of what it means to be intelligent. For example one of the more interesting cross-cultural studies of intelligence was by Cole, Gay, Glick and Sharp (1971).

CRITICAL FOCUS

Culture and intelligence

Cole et al. (1971) asked adult members of the Kpelle tribe in Africa to undertake a task in which they had to categorise concepts. For example, they may sort names of different kinds of birds together. Then they place the word 'bird' over that. They place the name 'animal' over 'bird' and over 'insects' and so on. Individuals with lower IQ tend to sort functionally. They may sort 'fish' with 'eat', etc. The Kpelle sorted functionally, even after the investigators attempted to train them to sort hierarchically. However, this is not the end of the story. Finally, they asked the Kpelle to sort the concepts as a foolish person would do. In response the Kpelle quickly and easily sorted hierarchically. They had just not done it because they viewed the questions as being stupid.

The Cole study demonstrates why it is so difficult to assess intelligence in a 'culturally neutral' manner. There are generally two main ways that the issue of cultural context within intelligence testing can be approached. First, a test can be created that is adapted to measure the kinds of skills and knowledge base that are prized within any particular culture. The second option is to try to create a test that is not tied to any particular cultural knowledge base, but that reflect a general 'non-cultural-specific' ability to process and evaluate stimulus patterns in a universal way.

One such attempt at creating a cultural neutral assessment of intelligence comes from Raven (1982), who developed an intelligence test that assessed an individual's ability to detect relationships between patterns of drawings and then to attempt to create rules that linked to different patterns in order to pick the missing pattern form a choice of potential patterns. This test has been used in many cultures and measures a general mental capacity that is also measured by traditional intelligence tests in our culture (Jensen, 1998).

Further reading Approaches to intelligence

Key reading

Cole, M., Gay, J., Glick, J. & Sharp, D.W. (1971). *The cultural context of learning and thinking*. New York: Basic Books.

Posner, M.J. & Mitchell, R.F. (1967). Chronometric analysis of classification. *Psychological Review, 74*, 392–409.

Vernon, P.E. (1979). *Intelligence: Heredity and environment*. San Francisco, CA: W.H. Freeman & Company.

Test your knowledge

Approaches to intelligence

12.6 What are the strengths and weaknesses of factor analysis approaches to intelligence?

12.7 What evidence is there for physiological indicators of intelligence?

12.8 What links have MRI studies made between *g* and brain structure?

12.9 What are the cultural problems associated with intelligence testing?

12.10 What are two possible ways of tackling the problems of cultural bias within tests of intelligence?

Answers to these questions can be found on the companion website at:
www.pearsoned.co.uk/psychologyexpress

 Sample question   *Essay*

Critically evaluate two approaches to intelligence testing.

Artificial intelligence

Artificial intelligence (AI) has been defined as the study of how to do things which at the moment people do better (Rich & Knight, 1991), and also as the science of making machines do things that would require intelligence if done by men (Minsky, 1961). AI can relate to attempting to automate common-sense activities that everyone can do.

Strong vs. weak AI

This important distinction is due to the philosopher John Searle.

Weak AI is like cognitive science (i.e. about people): it uses the machine representations and hypotheses to mimic human mental function on a computer, but never ascribes those mental properties to the machine.

Strong AI is the claim that machines programmed with the appropriate behaviour are having the same mental states as people would who had the same behaviour – i.e. that machines can have mental states.

How we can assess intelligence – the Turing test

1 In 1950 Turing published a paper designed to end once and for all the debate concerning whether or not machines could think.

2 Turing proposed a test, which is what is now called the 'Turing test'.

Turing's proposed test was a variation on a common game called the imitation game (see Figure 12.3):

1 An interrogator in a room asks questions of an individual (in a second room) by computer to guess their gender. Importantly the interrogator cannot see or hear the other individual.

2 The individual is sometimes a man and sometimes a woman.

3 Turing suggested a computer could replace the individual and then one could ask whether the interrogator would notice.

4 If, after some agreed time, the interrogator cannot distinguish when a machine has been substituted for the man/woman, then we would be able to say that the machine can truly be said to be intelligent.

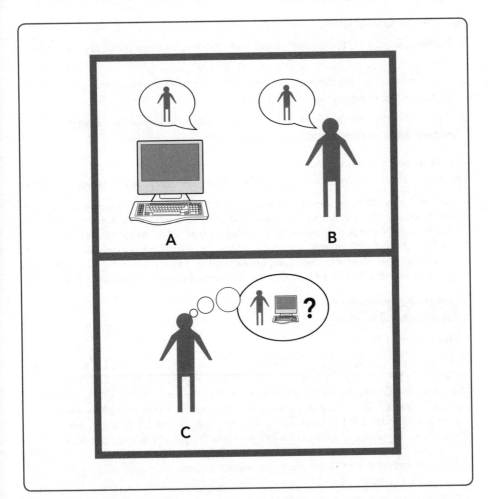

Figure 12.3 **The Turing test**

Turing's own objections to his test

Turing considered, and dismissed, some possible objections to the idea that computers can think. Some of these objections might still be raised today; some objections are easier to refute than others.

Objections considered by Turing

1 The theological objection
2 The 'heads in the sand' objection
3 The argument from consciousness

The theological objection

One objection that Turing considered was that thinking is a function of man's immortal soul, that God has given an immortal soul to every man and woman, and not to any other animal or to machines. Hence no animal or machine can think.

Heads in the sand objection

1 Thinking would be too dreadful. Let us hope and believe that they cannot do so.

2 This is related to the theological argument; the idea that humans are superior to the rest of creation, and must stay so.

3 Those who believe in this and the previous objection would probably not be interested in any criteria for deciding if machines could think.

The argument from consciousness

This argument is very well expressed in Professor Jefferson's Lister Oration for 1949.

> Not until a machine can write a sonnet or compose a concerto because of thoughts and emotions felt, and not by the chance fall of symbols, could we agree that machine equals brain – that is not only write it but know that it had written it. No mechanism could feel (and not merely artificially signal, an easy contrivance) pleasure at its successes, grief when its valves fuse, be warmed by flattery, be made miserable by its mistakes, be charmed by sex, be angry or depressed when it cannot get what it wants.

CRITICAL FOCUS

The Loebner Prize

The Loebner Prize for artificial intelligence is the first formal instantiation of a Turing test. In 1990 Hugh Loebner agreed with The Cambridge Center for Behavioral Studies to underwrite a contest designed to implement the Turing Test. Dr Loebner pledged a grand prize of $100,000 and a gold medal for the first computer whose responses were indistinguishable from a human's. Such a computer can be said 'to think'. Each year an annual prize of $2,000 and a bronze medal is awarded to the most human-like computer. The winner of the annual contest is the best entry relative to other entries that year, irrespective of how good it is in an absolute sense.

Cited from the Home Page of The Loebner Prize in Artificial Intelligence. See http://www.loebner.net/ Prizef/loebner-prize.html for more details of the Loebner Prize.

An example of AI – artificial neural networks

Artificial neural networks (see Figure 12.4) are based upon our own neural networks – namely the human brain. Features of the brain:

- 10 billion neurons
- Averaging several thousand connections each
- Hundreds of operations per second
- Low reliability
- Neurons die frequently and are never replaced
- Problems are compensated for by massive parallelism.

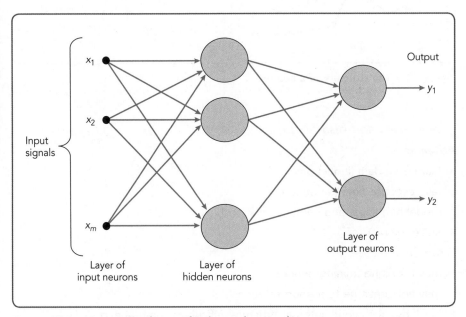

Figure 12.4 An example of an artificial neural network

The brain is made of neurons (see Figure 12.5 for their structure). A neuron only 'fires' if its input signal exceeds a threshold level within a short time period. Synapses can vary in strength; good connections allow a large signal and slight connections only allow a weak signal. Importantly, synapses can be either exhibitory or inhibitory

What do neural networks do?

- They are good at pattern recognition
- Any kind of pattern
- And good at generalising …
- Therefore any information that can be represented as a pattern can be learned!?

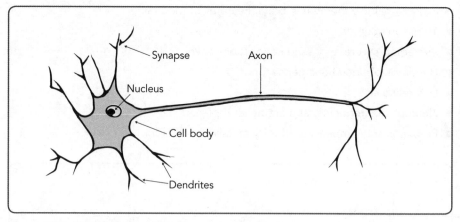

Figure 12.5 **The structure of a neuron**

Advantages and disadvantages

Advantages:

- learn from data (induction)
- fast response time (operation)
- model non-linear and complex relationships
- noise tolerant.

Disadvantages:

- may take long training periods
- may not converge to a good solution
- black box technique, internal structure difficult to comprehend.

Key concepts

- *Learn from experience*: through examples, analogy or discovery.
- *To adapt*: changes in response to interaction.
- *Generalisation*: to use experience to form a response to novel situations.

Summary

- Neural networks involve parallel processing
- They are good at pattern matching
- They are reasonably resistant to damage and error
- In some ways they can be said to 'learn'.

Further reading **Artificial intelligence**

Topic	Key reading
Philosophy of artificial intelligence	Boden, M. (1977). *Artificial intelligence and natural man*. Cambridge, MA: MIT Press.
Good introduction to artificial intelligence	Rich, F. & Knight, K. (1991). *Artificial intelligence*. New York: McGraw-Hill Inc.
Testing artificial intelligence	Turing, A.M. (1950) Computing machinery and intelligence. *Mind, 49*, 433–60.

Test your knowledge

Artificial intelligence

12.11 What is the difference between 'weak' and 'strong' AI?

12.12 What is the Turing test?

12.13 Name three objections to the Turing test.

12.14 What is a neural network?

12.15 Name one strength and one weakness of a neural network.

Answers to these questions can be found on the companion website at:
www.pearsoned.co.uk/psychologyexpress

 Sample question   *Essay*

Critically evaluate the Turing test.

Chapter summary – pulling it all together

→ Can you tick all of the points from the revision checklist at the beginning of this chapter?

→ Attempt all of the Test yourself questions.

→ Attempt the essay questions within the chapter using the guidelines below.

→ Go to the companion website at www.pearsoned.co.uk/psychologyexpress to access more revision support online, including interactive quizzes, flash cards, You be the marker exercises as well as answer guidance for the Test yourself and Sample questions from this chapter.

Answer guidelines

 Sample question   *Essay*

Critically evaluate two psychological theories of intelligence.

Approaching the question

This question requires a description of two psychological theories of intelligence and then a critical evaluation of how well these theories can explain intelligence.

Important points to include

To answer this question the first step is to choose wisely your two theories of intelligence. One good place to start might be to compare and contrast a theory that suggests a general concept of intelligence against one that puts forward multiple theories of intelligence, for example, Spearman vs. Gardner. Be careful not to spend all of your time describing the two approaches (although a brief description is essential), but utilise evidence for and against each one, e.g. the results of factor analysis of intelligence tests. Be careful to produce a conclusion where you sum up the findings of your evaluation. You don't have to come out for one approach but finish by giving a brief summary of what you have written about and the strengths of the arguments on both sides.

Make your answer stand out

For the above question, make sure that you read around the topic areas and get hold of some of the key papers. Make sure that you always back up your studies and evaluations with appropriate studies/references to support your claims and statements. Specifically, make sure that you don't simply describe the theories but that you actually critically assess the strengths and weaknesses of each approach. As mentioned this can be completed using a 'compare and contrast' approach where the different theories are assessed against each other, but also use previous research to assess the effectiveness of each approach. Furthermore, a good answer could also incorporate some of the contemporary research that looks at the impact of imaging studies and the biological basis for intelligence.

Explore the accompanying website at **www.pearsoned.co.uk/psychologyexpress**
→ Prepare more effectively for exams and assignments using the answer guidelines for questions from this chapter.
→ Test your knowledge using multiple choice questions and flashcards.
→ Improve your essay skills by exploring the You be the marker exercises.

Notes

Notes

And finally, before the exam ...

How to approach revision from here

You should be now at a reasonable stage in your revision process – you should have developed your skills and knowledge base over your course and used this text judiciously over that period. Now, however, you have used the book to reflect, remind and reinforce the material you have researched over the year/ seminar. You will, of course, need to do additional reading and research to that included here (and appropriate directions are provided) but you will be well on your way with the material presented in this book.

It is important that in answering any question in psychology you take a research- and evidence-based approach to your response. For example, do not make generalised or sweeping statements that cannot be substantiated or supported by evidence from the literature. Remember as well that the evidence should not be anecdotal – it is of no use citing your mum, dad, best friend or the latest news from a celebrity website. After all, you are not writing an opinion piece – you are crafting an argument that is based on current scientific knowledge and understanding. You need to be careful about the evidence you present: do review the material and from where it was sourced.

Furthermore, whatever type of assessment you have to undertake, it is important to take an evaluative approach to the evidence. Whether you are writing an essay, sitting an exam or designing a webpage, the key advice is to avoid simply presenting a descriptive answer. Rather, it is necessary to think about the strength of the evidence in each area. One of the key skills for psychology students is critical thinking and for this reason the tasks featured in this series focus upon developing this way of thinking. Thus you are not expected to simply learn a set of facts and figures, but to think about the implications of what we know and how this might be applied in everyday life. The best assessment answers are the ones that take this critical approach.

It is also important to note that psychology is a theoretical subject: when answering any question about psychology, not only refer to the prevailing theories of the field, but outline the development of them as well. It is also important to evaluate these theories and models either through comparison with other models and theories or through the use of studies that have assessed them and highlighted their strengths and weaknesses. It is essential to read widely – within each section of this book there are directions to interesting and pertinent papers relating to the specific topic area. Find these papers, read these papers and make notes from these papers. But don't stop there. Let them lead you to other sources that may be important to the field. One thing that an examiner hates to see is the same old sources being cited all of the time: be innovative and, as well as reading the seminal works, find the more obscure and interesting sources as well – just make sure they're relevant to your answer!

How not to revise

- **Don't avoid revision.** This is the best tip ever. There is something on the TV, the pub is having a two-for-one offer, the fridge needs cleaning, your budgie looks lonely ... You have all of these activities to do and they need doing now! Really ...? Do some revision!
- **Don't spend too long at each revision session.** Working all day and night is not the answer to revision. You do need to take breaks, so schedule your revision so you are not working from dawn until dusk. A break gives time for the information you have been revising to consolidate.
- **Don't worry.** Worrying will cause you to lose sleep, lose concentration and lose revision time by leaving it late and then later. When the exam comes, you will have no revision completed and will be tired and confused.
- **Don't cram.** This is the worst revision technique in the universe! You will not remember the majority of the information that you try to stuff into your skull, so why bother?
- **Don't read over old notes with no plan.** Your brain will take nothing in. If you wrote your lecture notes in September and the exam is in May is there any point in trying to decipher your scrawly handwriting now?
- **Don't write model answers and learn by rote.** When it comes to the exam you will simply regurgitate the model answer irrespective of the question – not a brilliant way to impress the examiner!

Tips for exam success

What you should do when it comes to revision

Exams are one form of assessment that students often worry about the most. The key to exam success, as with many other types of assessment, lies in good preparation and self-organisation. One of the most important things is knowing what to expect – this does not necessarily mean knowing what the questions will be on the exam paper, but rather what the structure of the paper is, how many questions you are expected to answer, how long the exam will last and so on.

To pass an exam you need a good grasp of the course material and, obvious as it may seem, to turn up for the exam itself. It is important to remember that you aren't expected to know or remember everything in the course, but you should be able to show your understanding of what you have studied. Remember as well that examiners are interested in what you know, not what you don't know. They try to write exam questions that give you a good chance of passing – not ones to catch you out or trick you in any way. You may want to consider some of these top exam tips.

- Start your revision in plenty of time.
- Make a revision timetable and stick to it.
- Practise jotting down answers and making essay plans.
- Practise writing against the clock using past exam papers.
- Check that you have really answered the question and have not strayed off the point.
- Review a recent past paper and check the marking structure.
- Carefully select the topics you are going to revise.
- Use your lecture/study notes and refine them further, if possible, into lists or diagrams and transfer them on to index cards/Post-it notes. Mind maps are a good way of making links between topics and ideas.
- Practise your handwriting – make sure it's neat and legible.

One to two days before the exam

- Recheck times, dates and venue.
- Actively review your notes and key facts.
- Exercise, eat sensibly and get a few good nights' sleep.

On the day

- Get a good night's sleep.
- Have a good meal, two to three hours before the start time.
- Arrive in good time.
- Spend a few minutes calming and focusing.

In the exam room

- Keep calm.
- Take a few minutes to read each question carefully. Don't jump to conclusions – think calmly about what each question means and the area it is focused on.
- Start with the question you feel most confident about. This helps your morale.
- By the same token, don't expend all your efforts on that one question – if you are expected to answer three questions then don't just answer two.
- Keep to time and spread your effort evenly on all opportunities to score marks.
- Once you have chosen a question, jot down any salient facts or key points. Then take five minutes to plan your answer – a spider diagram or a few notes

may be enough to focus your ideas. Try to think in terms of 'why and how' not just 'facts'.

- You might find it useful to create a visual plan or map before writing your answer to help you remember to cover everything you need to address.
- Keep reminding yourself of the question and try not to wander off the point.
- Remember that quality of argument is more important than quantity of facts.
- Take 30–60-second breaks whenever you find your focus slipping (typically every 20 minutes).
- Make sure you reference properly – according to your university requirements.
- Watch your spelling and grammar – you could lose marks if you make too many errors.

→ *Final revision checklist*

❏ Have you revised the topics highlighted in the revision checklists?
❏ Have you attended revision classes and taken note of and/or followed up on your lecturers' advice about the exams or assessment process at your university?
❏ Can you answer the questions posed in this text satisfactorily? Don't forget to check sample answers on the website too.
❏ Have you read the additional material to make your answer stand out?
❏ Remember to criticise appropriately – based on evidence.

Test your knowledge by using the material presented in this text or on the website: **www.pearsoned.co.uk/psychologyexpress**

Glossary

affordance The potential uses of an object.

agrammatism A type of aphasia associated with an inability to speak grammatically.

AI or artificial intelligence The attempt to get computers to do things that humans can do.

algorithm A method for solving a problem using a finite sequence of instructions.

amnesia Memory loss caused by brain damage.

amnesic syndrome A condition characterised by significant impairment to long-term memory.

anomia Difficulty with object naming, but not comprehension.

anterograde amnesia A reduced ability to retain information presented after the onset of amnesia.

aphasia Impairment of language ability due to brain damage.

artificial neural networks Computer models networks of artificial neurons or nodes that can be used for pattern recognition or problem solving.

autobiographical memory Part of episodic memory consisting of recollections of personal experiences.

automatic processes Processing of information without conscious awareness, and without interfering with other conscious activity.

aversion therapy A type of behavioural therapy based on the principles of learning (conditioning) undertaken to eliminate the presence of some maladaptive behaviour. This is done by pairing the maladaptive behaviour with a stimulus that is unpleasant. The pleasant behaviour then becomes less pleasant and decreases over time until it is completely gone.

Broca's area Named after Paul Broca, who delineated this area of the brain. It is located in the frontal lobe of the brain and acts as one of the speech centres.

blindsight The ability of patients with no conscious perception of stimuli to be able to discriminate between them.

bottom-up processing Processing influenced by environmental information.

bump effect The disproportionably higher likelihood that individuals will recall memories from between the ages of 10 and 30 in individuals aged over 35.

CAT scan Computerised axial tomography (also known as a CT scan), which utilises a process of using computers to make a three-dimensional image from a two-dimensional picture (X-ray). During the process a series of X-ray photographs are taken from different angles and then combined by computer into a composite three-dimensional representation.

central executive A component of working memory involved in the coordination of the slave systems as well as for reasoning and language coordination. It directs attentional resources to the other subsystems of working memory, as well as being responsible for higher-level thought processes involved in reasoning and language comprehension.

classical conditioning Conditioning based on associating a new neutral stimulus with an established 'involuntary' or 'reflexive' response.

cognitive interview An interview procedure for eliciting information.

cognitive neuropsychology A branch of cognitive psychology which uses data from individuals with impairments to learn more about cognitive processes.

cognitive science The interdisciplinary scientific study of how information concerning human cognitive abilities such as language, reasoning and perception is represented and manipulated within the human brain or computer. It consists of multiple research disciplines, including artificial intelligence, psycholinquistics, psychology, philosophy, education, neuroscience and anthropology.

computational theory of vision A theory of how information might be extracted from images.

conditioned response In classical conditioning, the conditioned response is the

Glossary

learned response (reflexive behaviour) to a conditioned stimulus. This response is almost identical to the unconditioned stimulus except that now the reflexive behaviour occurs in response to a conditioned stimulus as opposed to an unconditioned stimulus.

conditioned stimulus In classical conditioning, a formerly neutral stimulus that, after association with an unconditioned stimulus, comes to produce a conditioned response.

constructivist theory Proposes that the perceiver has an internal constructive (problem-solving) process to transform an incoming stimulus into a percept.

contextualism Is the view that human attributes (such as intelligence) are inextricably linked to culture, and hence can only be truly understood within its real-world context.

declarative knowledge Factual information, divided into semantic and episodic memory.

deductive reasoning Reasoning from the general to the particular, for example, starting with a theory and looking for instances that confirm the deduction.

deep dyslexia A condition involving impaired naming of unfamiliar words as well as semantic errors (e.g. reading 'sapling' as 'tree')

dichotic listening Different messages are played to each ear; allows investigation of selective attention.

direct perception The use of environmental cues to generate a percept through bottom-up processing only.

discourse Any analysis of language beyond the level of the sentence is referred to as discourse.

divided attention Where two tasks are performed simultaneously.

double dissociation Where two related mental processes are shown to operate independently of each other.

DRM effect The high-confidence but false recall of prototypes, such as recalling 'sleep' from a list of words highly associated with sleep but not containing that word.

dysgraphia An impairment in spelling or writing.

dysphasia Impaired ability to communicate.

dyslexia A condition where reading is impaired (see *deep dyslexia* and *surface dyslexia*).

echoic memory Memory for auditory stimuli, typically very brief.

ecological validity The degree to which the methods used or behaviours observed in research relate to those in the real world.

encoding The process of receiving or registering stimuli through one or more of the senses and modifying that information.

encoding specificity principle Contextual information affects memory. The principle states that memory is improved when information available at encoding is also available at retrieval.

environmental or context reinstatement Recreating the state at encoding as a means of improving recall.

episodic buffer A slave system in working memory controlled by the central executive which acts as an interface between the other slave systems and LTM, and is used as a modelling space to assist learning.

episodic memory The storage and retrieval of specific events.

explicit memory Conscious recall of information; explicit or declarative memory is further divided into episodic and semantic components.

extinction When a response that is no longer reinforced is weakened and less likely to occur again in the future, for example Pavlov's dogs would slowly 'unlearn' their response if no food was presented over a period of time.

field perspective Where an autobiographical memory is seen from the viewpoint of the individual whose memory it is.

flashbulb memories Vivid snapshots of the circumstances in which we heard consequential or traumatic information.

fMRI (functional magnetic imaging) A special type of MRI that specifically measures blood flow in the brain, hence it can measure brain activity as well as brain structures

forgetting The loss of information already stored in long-term memory.

fovea (or macula) A small depression in the retina densely packed with photoreceptors.

generalisation A process within operant and classical conditioning, where a conditioned response starts occurring in response to the presentation of other, similar stimuli, not just the conditioned stimulus. For example, a dog is trained to sit when the note middle C is played, but may also respond to notes very close to this as well, e.g. C sharp.

Gestalt approach A theory emphasising active cognition.

Gestalt principles of organisation A series of factors believed to aid the perception of forms and promote their grouping.

gestural score The physical plan of movement for the vocal tract.

heuristics A potential strategy or 'rule of thumb' for searching through a problem space in a meaningful way.

iconic memory Memory for visual stimuli, occurring in the form of mental pictures.

implicit memory Automatic or unconscious memory in which previous knowledge aids task performance without conscious awareness.

inductive reasoning This involves moving from specific facts to a conclusion. It involves going from a series of one-off observations of a specific event to a rule encompassing all such events.

infantile or childhood amnesia The inaccessibility of memories for events occurring in infancy and early childhood.

IQ or intelligence quotient A measure of intelligence derived from a standardised intelligence test – where the mean is 100. In children the child's IQ can be derived by the quotient of 'mental age' and 'chronological age' – again the mean is 100.

isomorphism The assumption that the organisation of the mind resembles that of the brain.

Korsakoff's syndrome Impaired long-term memory usually caused by heavy alcohol consumption.

lateral geniculate nucleus (LGN) Part of the brain where the retinal axons terminate, and where cortical axons originate.

lemma A lemma is the abstract form of a word containing information relating to the meaning of a word.

levels-of-processing (LOP) framework Proposes that memory is a continuum along which depth of encoding varies.

lexicon Within any language the lexicon comprises the complete set of morphemes available within that language.

linguistic relativity hypothesis The hypothesis that language shapes the way people perceive and organise their world.

long-term memory A system of storage and retrieval of information over an extended period of time.

macrosmatic A highly developed sense of smell.

microsmatic A poor sense of smell.

misinformation (or false memory effect) Recall of an event is influenced by information received after the event.

modularity The idea that the cognitive system consists of largely independent, functionally specific processors.

mood A transient emotional state, such as joy.

morpheme The morpheme is the smallest unit within any language that can have meaning on its own. Morphemes are made up of combinations of phonemes.

multi-store model A theory proposing memory consists of interlinked components, the sensory register, short-term and long-term memory.

negative reinforcement When a consequence of a behaviour that you dislike is taken away, for example: if you manage to gain an average of an A grade in a particular module then you will be exempt from the final exam and automatically get an A grade for the module.

neurophysiology The study of the responses of the nervous system to external stimulation.

neutral stimulus In classical conditioning this is a stimulus which initially produces no specific response. However, when used together with an unconditioned stimulus, the neutral stimulus becomes a conditioned stimulus.

observer perspective Where an autobiographical memory is pictured from another person's viewpoint.

operant conditioning Conditioning of a new neutral stimulus with a 'voluntary' or 'active' response.

optic chiasm The part of the visual system where the optic nerves partially split.

Glossary

optic flow pattern Changing elements of the visual field.

organic amnesia Memory loss resulting from physical trauma to the brain.

percept The perceived form of an external stimulus.

PET (positron emission tomography) An imaging technique that produces a three-dimensional image or picture of functional processes in the body. To conduct the scan, a short-lived radioactive tracer isotope is injected into the patient. This radioactivity is then picked up by the scanner to create the image.

PFC (prefrontal cortex) The anterior part of the frontal lobes of the brain lying in front of the motor and pre-motor areas. It has been implicated in the planning of complex cognitive behaviours.

phoneme A phoneme is the smallest unit within a language system. These fundamental sound blocks are created by alternating the opening and closing of the vocal tract in set sequences.

phonological (or articulatory) loop Stores a limited number of speech sounds for a short period of time. It consists of two components, the passive phonological store and an articulatory or subvocal control process supporting mental rehearsal.

Pollyanna principle The tendency to forget less pleasant events

positive reinforcement When a consequence that you like is associated with a behaviour, for example a treat – stickers, sweets, money, etc.

post-traumatic amnesia Transient global amnesia.

Prägnanz The fundamental principle of perceptual segregation proposed by gestalt psychologists which states that the simplest and most stable shape will be perceived.

primacy effect Earlier-presented items are remembered better.

procedural knowledge Memory for 'procedures' or for basic associations between stimuli and responses, such as how to ride a bike.

props Physical cues which mimic some aspect of a situation. May be specific to a particular environment, such as a model of a particular scene of crime, or be more general, such as anatomically correct dolls.

prospective memory (PM) The process of remembering to do things at some future point in time.

psychogenic amnesia Amnesia due to psychological trauma, rather than brain injury.

psychological refractory period (PRP) The delay in the response to the second of two closely spaced stimuli when two tasks overlap temporally.

recency effect Most recently presented items tend to be remembered well.

reinforcement Any consequence that increases the probability of a response in the future.

reinstatement In context or environmental reinstatement, witnesses are returned to the location where they originally experienced a particular event. This reinstatement may occur physically or mentally.

response A reaction to an activating event.

retina An outgrowth of the brain consisting of a thin and complex network of photoreceptor cells.

retrieval Recall of stored information in response to some cue.

retrograde amnesia Inability to retrieve or recall information before the traumatic event.

retrospective memory Memory for information encountered in the past, subdivided into episodic, semantic and procedural.

SAS (supervisory attentional system) A limited capacity system used for a variety of purposes, including planning or decision making; similar in function to the central executive of working memory.

schemas (or schemata) Mental models or representations used to assimilate, organise and simplify knowledge. They develop through experience and are unique to each individual.

scripts Contain generic information about frequently occurring events.

selective attention Focusing on one source of information, while ignoring others.

semantic memory Knowledge that does not have contextual elements like time or place; can be viewed as general knowledge, e.g. capital cities.

semantics Relates to meaning.

sensory register The part of the memory system which is the initial store for perceived stimuli.

short-term store/memory The part of the memory system where information is stored for brief periods; information can be retained for longer through rehearsal.

simultanagnosia A neurological disorder characterised by the inability of an individual to perceive more than one object at a time.

spontaneous recovery The sudden reappearance of a behaviour after extinction has taken place, for example when the initial salivating behaviour had become extinct through the removal of the food, once the food was returned the dog would very quickly return to a 'fully learned' state.

stimulus An activating event in the environment.

storage Creation of a permanent record of encoded information.

strong AI The claim that machines programmed with the appropriate behaviour, are having the same mental states as people would who had the same behaviour, i.e. that machines can have mental states.

subtractivity The idea that brain damage removes modules, or connections between them, but cannot add new modules or connections.

superior colliculus Part of the visual system responsible for reflexive orienting towards novel information, usually movement.

surface dyslexia A condition where regular words (e.g. stem) can be read but there are problems with irregular words (e.g. cough).

syllogism A kind of logical argument in which one proposition (the conclusion) is inferred from two others (the premises) of a certain form.

syntax The rules for constructing meaningful sentences in language.

texture gradient A monocular depth cue in which there is a gradual change in appearance of objects from coarse to fine, with nearer objects coarser than more distant ones.

top-down processing Processing influenced by stored knowledge.

transduction The conversion of energy (light, sound, etc.) into electrical signals.

transfer-appropriate processing (TAP) People are more efficient performing a task when there has been previous experience in performing the same task, regardless of whether the task was explicit or implicit.

transient global amnesia Temporary but almost complete disruption of short-term memory, as well as difficulties accessing older memories.

transparency The view in cognitive neuropsychology that deficits and normal function should indicate which module is damaged.

two-process (or dual-process) model In memory and problem solving, the two processes consist of an implicit (automatic), unconscious process and an explicit (controlled), conscious process.

two-process theory States that recall consists of two stages, the first is search and retrieval, the second, recognition.

unconditioned response In classical conditioning, there are stimuli that can produce responses by themselves and without any prior learning. These types of stimuli are called unconditioned stimuli and they evoke unconditioned responses, or responses that are completely natural and occur without an organism going through any prior learning.

unconditioned stimulus In classical conditioning, an unconditioned stimulus is any stimulus that can evoke a response without the organism going through any previous learning; the response to the unconditioned stimulus (the unconditioned response) occurs naturally.

universality assumption The assumption that there is no difference in cognitive processing or related processes between individuals prior to brain damage.

visual cliff A test given to infants to see if depth perception has developed.

visual cortex The part of the brain responsible for processing visual information.

visuospatial sketchpad (or visuospatial working memory) Temporarily holds and manipulates visual and spatial information, similar to the phonological loop speech.

weak AI Uses the machine representations and hypotheses to mimic human mental function on a computer, but never ascribes those mental properties to the machine.

Glossary

weapon focus The tendency for witnesses to violent crime to focus their attention on the weapon used at the expense of other information.

Wernicke's area Named after Carl Wernicke. It is located on the left temporal lobe, is one of the language centres of the brain, and is specifically important to the development of language.

working memory A memory system that provides temporary storage and allows manipulation of the information necessary for complex cognitive tasks such as reasoning.

References

Ader, R. (2001). Psychoneuroimmunology. *Current Directions in Psychological Science, 10,* 94–98.

Anderson, J. R. (1996). ACT: A simple theory of complex cognition. *American Psychologist, 51,* 355–365.

Andrade, J. (2001). An introduction to working memory. In J. Andrade (Ed.), *Working memory in perspective* (pp. 3–30). Hove and New York: Psychology Press.

Atherton, M., Zhuang, J., Bart, W. M., Hu, X., & He, S. (2003). A functional MRI study of high-level cognition. I. The game of chess. *Cognitive Brain Research, 16*(1), 26–31.

Atkinson, J., & Braddick, O. (1981). Acuity, contrast, sensitivity, and accommodation in infancy. In R. Aslin, J. Alberts, & M. Petersen (Eds.), *Development of perception: Psychological perspectives: Vol. 2. The visual system* (pp. 243–278). New York: Academic Press.

Atkinson, R. C., & Shiffrin, R. M. (1968). Human memory: A proposed system and its control processes. In K. W. Spence and J. T. Spence, *The psychology of learning and motivation: Vol. 2* (pp. 89–195). New York: Academic Press.

Bäckman, L., Nilsson, L., & Chalom, D. (1986). New evidence on the nature of encoding action events. *Memory & Cognition, 14,* 339–346.

Baddeley, A. D. (1990). *Human memory: Theory and practice.* London: Lawrence Erlbaum.

Baddeley, A. D. (1997). *Human memory: Theory and practice.* (2nd ed.). Hove: Psychology Press.

Baddeley, A. D. (2000). The episodic buffer: A new component of working memory? *Trends in Cognitive Science, 4,* 417–423.

Baddeley, A., D., & Hitch, G. J. (1974). Working memory. In G. H Bower (Ed.), *The psychology of learning and motivation, 8* (pp. 67–89). London: Academic Press.

Baddeley, A. D., Thomson, N., & Buchanan, M. (1975). Word length and the structure of short-term memory. *Journal of Verbal Learning and Verbal Behavior, 14,* 575–589.

Baker-Ward, L., Hess, T. M., & Flannagan, D. A. (1990). The effects of involvement on children's memory for events. *Cognitive Development, 5,* 55–69.

Banaji, M. R., & Crowder, R. G. (1989). The bankruptcy of everyday memory research. *American Psychologist, 44,* 1185–1193.

Barbur, J. L., Ruddock, K. H., & Waterfield, V. A. (1980). Human visual responses in the absence of the geniculo-calcarine projection. *Brain, 103,* 905–928.

Bartlett, F. C. (1932). *Remembering: A study in experimental and social psychology.* Cambridge, UK: Cambridge University Press.

Battermanfaunce, J. M., & Goodman, G. S. (1993). Effects of context on the accuracy and suggestibility of child witnesses. In G. S. Goodman & B. L. Bottoms (Eds.), *Child victims, child witnesses* (pp. 301–330). New York: Guilford Press.

Baxter, D. M., & Warrington, E. K. (1986). Ideational agraphia: A single case study. *Journal of Neurology, Neurosurgery, & Psychiatry, 49,* 369–374.

Beauvois, M.-F. & Dérousené, J. (1979). Phonological alexia: Three dissociations. *Journal of Neurology, Neurosurgery and Psychiatry, 42,* 1115–1124.

Bekerian, D. A., & Dennett, J. L. (1993). The cognitive interview: Reviving the issues. *Applied Cognitive Psychology, 7,* 275–298.

Bicego, M., Brelstaff, G., Brodo, L., Grosso, E., Lagorio, A., & Tistarelli, M. (2008). Distinctiveness of faces: A computational approach. *ACM Transactions on Applied Perception, 5,* 1–18.

Binet, A. (1916). New methods for the diagnosis of the intellectual level of subnormals. In E. S. Kite (Trans.), *The development of intelligence in children.* Vineland, NJ: Publications of the Training School at Vineland. (Originally published 1905 in *L'Année Psychologique, 12,* 191–244.)

Binet, A., & Simon, T. (1916). *The development of intelligence in children.* Baltimore: Williams & Wilkins. (Reprinted 1973, New York: Arno Press; 1983, Salem, NH: Ayer Company).

Blumer, D., Zorick, F., Heilbronn, M., & Roth, T. (1982). Biological markers for depression in chronic pain. *Journal of Nervous and Mental Disease, 170,* 425–438.

Bohannon, J. N. (1988). Flashbulb memories for the space shuttle disaster: a tale of two stories. *Cognition, 29,* 179–196.

Bors, D. A., MacLeod, C. M., & Forrin, B. (1993). Eliminating the IQ-RT correlation by eliminating an experimental confound. *Intelligence, 17,* 475–500.

Bower, G. H. (1981). Mood and memory. *American Psychologist, 36,* 129–148.

Bower, G. H., Black, J. B., & Turner, J. T. (1979). Scripts in text comprehension and memory. *Cognitive Psychology, 11,* 177–220.

Bower, T. G. R. (1965). Stimulus variables determining space perception in infants. *Science, 149,* 88–89.

Brand, G., & Millot, J.-L. (2001). Sex differences in human olfaction: Between evidence and enigma. *Quarterly Journal of Experimental Psychology B, 54B,* 259–270.

Brandt, K. R., Gardiner, J. M., Vargha-Khadem, F., Baddeley, A. D., & Mishkin, M. (2008). Impairment of recollection but not familiarity in a case of developmental amnesia. *Neurocase, 15,* 60–65.

Braun, M. (1996). Impediment of basilar membrane motion reduces overload protection but not

References

threshold sensitivity: vidence from clinical and experimental hydrops. *Hearing Research, 97,* 1–10.

Bregman, A. S. (1990). *Auditory scene analysis.* Cambridge, MA: MIT Press.

Brewer, W. F., & Treyens, J. C. (1981). Role of schemata in memory for places. *Cognitive Psychology, 13,* 207–230.

Broadbent, D. E. (1958). *Perception and communication.* London: Pergamon Press.

Broadbent, D. E. (1971). *Decision and stress.* London: Academic Press.

Brooks, L. R. (1967). The suppression of visualization by reading. *Quarterly Journal of Experimental Psychology, 19,* 289–299.

Brown, R., & Kulik, J. (1977). Flashbulb memories. *Cognition, 5,* 73–99.

Bruce, V., Georgeson, M. A., & Green, P. R. (2003). *Visual perception: Physiology, psychology and ecology.* (4th ed.). New York: Psychology Press.

Bub, D., & Kertesz, A. (1982). Evidence for lexicographic processing in a patient with preserved written over oral single word naming. *Brain, 105,* 697–717.

Cain, W. S. (1982). Odor identification by males and females: Predictions vs performance. *Chemical Senses, 7,* 129–142.

Calabria, M., Cotelli, M., Adenzato, M., Zanetti, O., & Miniussi, C. (2009). Empathy and emotion recognition in semantic dementia: A case report. *Brain and Cognition, 70,* 247–252.

Caramazza, A. (1986). On drawing inferences about the structure of normal cognitive systems from the analysis of patterns of impaired performance: The case for single-patient studies. *Brain & Cognition, 5,* 41–66.

Carroll, D. (1994). *Psychology of language.* Pacific Grove, CA: Brooks/Cole.

Carroll, J. B. (1993). *Human cognitive abilities.* Cambridge, UK: Cambridge University Press.

Cattell, R. B. (1963). Theory of fluid and crystallized intelligence: A critical experiment. *Journal of Educational Psychology, 54,* 1–22.

Ceci, S. J., Toglia, M. P., & Ross, D. F. (Eds.). (1987). *Children's eyewitness memory.* New York: Springer-Verlag.

Cherry, E. C. (1953). Some experiments on the recognition of speech with one and two ears. *Journal of the Acoustic Society of America, 25,* 975–979.

Chomsky, N. (1956). Three models for the description of language. *IRE Transactions on Information Theory, 2,* 113–124.

Christianson, S. A., & Hübinette, B. (1993). Hands up! A study of witnesses' emotional reactions and memories associated with bank robberies. *Applied Cognitive Psychology, 7,* 365–379.

Chun, M. M., & Wolfe, J. M. (2000). Visual attention. In E. B. Goldstein (Ed.) *Blackwell handbook of perception* (pp. 272–310). Oxford: Blackwell.

Cohen, C. E. (1981). Goals and schemata in person perception: Making sense from the stream of behavior. In N. Cantor & J. F. Kihlstrom (Eds.), *Personality, cognition, and social interaction* (pp. 45–68). Hillsdale, NJ: Lawrence Erlbaum.

Cohen, N. J., & Squire, L. R. (1980). Preserved learning and retention of pattern-analysing skill in amnesia using perceptual learning. *Cortex, 17,* 273–278.

Cole, C. B., & Loftus, E. F. (1987). The memory of children. In S. J. Ceci, M. P. Toglia, & D. F. Ross (Eds.), *Children's eyewitness memory* (pp. 178–208). New York: Springer-Verlag.

Cole, M., Gay, J., Glick, J., & Sharp, D. W. (1971). *The cultural context of learning and thinking.* New York: Basic Books.

Coltheart, M. (1978). Lexical access in simple reading tasks. In G. Underwood (Ed.), *Strategies of information processing* (pp. 151–216). London: Academic Press.

Coltheart, M. (2006). Acquired dyslexias and the computational modelling of reading. *Cognitive Neuropsychology, 23,* 96–109.

Coltheart, M., & Funnel, E. (1987). Reading and writing: One lexicon or two? In D. A. Allport, D. G. MacKay, W. Prinz, & E. Scheerer (Eds.), *Language perception and production: Shared mechanisms in listening, reading and writing* (pp. 313–39). London: Academic Press.

Coltheart, M., Rastle, K., Perry, C., Langdon, R., & Ziegler, J. (2001). The DRC model: A model of visual word recognition and reading aloud. *Psychological Review, 108,* 204–258.

Colvin, M. K., Dunbar, K., & Grafman, J. (2001). The effects of frontal lobe lesions on goal achievement in the water jug task. *Journal of Cognitive Neuroscience, 13*(8), 1129–1147.

Conrad, R., & Hull, A. J. (1964). Information, acoustic confusion and memory span. *British Journal of Psychology, 55,* 429–432.

Conway, M. A. (1996). Autobiographical memories and autobiographical knowledge. In D. C. Rubin. (Ed.), *Remembering our past: Studies in autobiographical memory* (pp. 67–93). Cambridge, UK: Cambridge University Press.

Conway, M. A., & Pleydell-Pearce, C. W. (2000). The construction of autobiographical memories in the self-memory system. *Psychological Review, 107,* 261–288.

Conway, R. A., Cowan, N., & Bunting, M. F. (2001). The cocktail party phenomenon revisited: The importance of working memory capacity. *Psychonomic Bulletin & Review, 8,* 331–335.

Cornell, E. H., & Hay, D. H. (1984). Children's acquisition of a route via different media. *Environment & Behavior, 16,* 627–641.

Corteen, R. S., & Wood, B. (1972). Autonomous responses to shock associated word in an unattended channel. *Journal of Experimental Psychology, 94,* 308–313.

Cowan, N. (2001). The magical number 4 in short-term memory: A reconsideration of mental storage capacity. *Behavioral and Brain Sciences, 24,* 87–185.

Cowan, N. (2005). *Working memory capacity.* New York: Psychology Press.

Cowey, A., & Stoerig, P. (2001). Detection and discrimination of chromatic information in monkeys with unilateral striate cortical ablation. *European Journal of Neuroscience, 14,* 1320–1330.

Craik, F. I. M., & Lockhart, R. S. (1972). Levels of

processing: A framework for memory research. *Journal of Verbal Learning and Verbal Behavior*, *11*, 671–684.

Craik, F. I. M., & Tulving, E. (1975). Depth of processing and the retention of words in episodic memory. *Journal of Experimental Psychology: General*, *104*, 268–294.

Crowder, R. G. (1996). The trouble with prospective memory: A provocation. In M. Brandimonte, G. O. Einstein, & M. A. McDaniel (Eds.), *Prospective memory: Theory and applications* (pp. 143–147). Hillsdale, NJ: Erlbaum.

D'Argembeau, A., Comblain, C., & van der Linden, M. (2002). Phenomenal characteristics of autobiographical memories for positive, negative, and neutral events. *Applied Cognitive Psychology*, *17*, 281–94.

Davidson, P. S. R., & Gilsky, E. L. (2002). Is flashbulb memory a special instance of source memory? Evidence from older adults. *Memory*, *10*, 99–100.

Davidson, R. J. (2003). Seven sins in the study of emotion: Correctives from affective neuroscience. *Brain and Cognition*, *52*, 129–132.

Day, R. H. (1972). Visual spatial illusions: A general explanation. *Science*, 175, 1335–1340.

Deco, G., & Rolls, E. T. (2007). Decision-making mechanisms in the brain. *American Institute of Physics Conference Proceedings*, *887*, 21–28.

Deese, J. (1959). On the prediction of occurrence of particular verbal instructions in immediate recall. *Journal of Experimental Psychology*, *58*, 17–22.

Deffenbacher, K. A. (1983). The influence of arousal on reliability of testimony. In S. M. A. Lloyd-Bostock & B. R. Clifford (Eds.), *Evaluating witness evidence* (pp. 235–254). Chichester: Wiley.

Deffenbacher, K. A. (1994). Effects of arousal on everyday memory. *Human Performances*, *7*, 141–161.

Dekker, E., & Groen, J. (1956). Reproducible psychogenic attacks of asthma. *Journal of Psychomatic Research*, *1*, 58–67.

Dell, G. S. (1986). A spreading-activation theory of retrieval in sentence production. *Psychological Review*, 93, 283–321.

Dell, G. S., & O'Seaghdha, P. G. (1991). Mediating lexical priming in language production: Comments on Levelt et al. (1991). *Psychological Review*, 98 (4), 604–614.

Della Sala, S., & Logie, R. H. (1993). When working memory does not work: The role of working memory in neuropsychology. In F. Boller & H. Spinnler (Eds.), *Handbook of neuropsychology*, 8 (pp. 1–63). Amsterdam: Elsevier.

Dent, H., & Flin, R. (Eds.). (1992). *Children as witnesses*. Chichester: Wiley.

Deutsch, J. A., & Deutsch, D. (1963). Attention, some theoretical considerations. *Psychological Review*, *70*, 80–90.

Dronkers, N. F., Plaisant, O., Iba-Zizen, M. T., & Cabanis, E. A. (2007). Paul Broca's historic cases: High resolution MR imaging of the brains of Leborgne and Lelong. Brain, 130, 1432–1441.

Duncan, J., & Humphrey, G. W. (1992). Visual search and visual similarity. *Psychological Review*, *96*, 433–458.

Duncan, J., Emslie, H., & Williams, P. (1996).

Intelligence and the frontal lobe: The organization of goal-directed behavior. *Cognitive Psychology*, *30*, 257–303.

Duncan, J., Seitz, R., Kolodny, J., Bor, D., Herzog, H., Ahmed, A., Newell, F., & Emslie, H. (2000). A neural basis for general intelligence. *Science*, *289*(5478), 457–460.

Duncker, K. (1945). On problem solving. *Psychological Monographs*, *58*(5, Whole no. 270).

Eastwood, J. D., Smilek, D., & Merikle, P. M. (2001). Differential attentional guidance by unattended faces expressing positive and negative emotion. *Perception and Psychophysics*, *63*, 1004–1013.

Einstein, G. O., & McDaniel, M. A. (1996). Retrieval processes in prospective memory: Theoretical approaches and some new empirical findings. In M. Brandimonte, G. O. Einstein, & M. A. McDaniel (Eds.), *Prospective memory: Theory and applications* (pp. 115–141). Mahwah, NJ: Lawrence Erlbaum.

Einstein, G. O., Holland, L. J., McDaniel, M. A., & Guynn, M. J. (1992). Age-related deficits in prospective memory: The influence of task complexity. *Psychology and Aging*, *7*, 471–478.

Ellis, A. W., & Young, A. W. (1988). *Human cognitive neuropsychology*. Hove: Psychology Press.

Ellis, A. W., Miller, D., & Sin, G. (1983). Wernicke's aphasia and normal language processing: A study in cognitive neuropsychology. *Cognition*, *15*, 111–144.

Ellis, J. (1996). Prospective memory or the realization of delayed intentions: A conceptual framework for research. In M. Brandimonte, G. O. Einstein, & M. A. McDaniel (Eds.), *Prospective memory: Theory and applications* (pp. 1–22). Mahwah, NJ: Lawrence Erlbaum.

Engle, R. W. (2001). What is working memory capacity? In H. L. Roediger, J. S. Nairne, I. Neath, & A. M. Suprenant (Eds.), *The nature of remembering: Essays in honor of Robert G. Crowder* (pp. 297–314). Washington, DC: American Psychological Association.

Ericsson, K. A., & Kintsch, W. (1995). Long-term working memory. *Psychological Review*, *102*, 211–245.

Eriksen, C. W., & St. James, J. D. (1986). Visual attention within and around the field of focal attention: A zoom lens model. *Perception and Psychophysics*, *40*, 225–240.

Evans, J., Heron, J., Lewis, G., Araya, R., & Wolke, D. (2005). Negative self-schemas and the onset of depression in women: Longitudinal study. *British Journal of Psychiatry*, *186*, 302–307.

Eysenck, M. W. (1997). *Anxiety and cognition: A unified theory*. Hove: Psychology Press.

Eysenck, M. W., & Eysenck, M. C. (1980). Effects of processing depth, distinctiveness, and word frequency on retention. *British Journal of Psychology*, *71*, 263–274.

Eysenck, M. W., & Keane, M. T. (1995). *Cognitive psychology*. Hove: Lawrence Earlbaum.

Fantz, R. L. (1961). The origin of form perception. *Scientific American*, *204*, 66–72.

Farrin, L., Hull, L., Unwin, C., Wykes, T., & David, A. (2003). Effects of depressed mood on objective and subjective measures of attention. *Journal of*

Neuropsychiatry & Clinical Neurosciences, 15, 98–104.

Fisher, R. P., & Geiselman, R. E. (1992). *Memory-enhancing techniques for investigative interviewing: The cognitive interview.* Springfield, IL: Thomas.

Fodor, J. A. (1983). *Modularity of mind.* Cambridge, MA: MIT Press.

Fodor, J. A., & Pylyshyn, Z. W. (1981). How direct is visual perception? Some reflections on Gibson's 'ecological approach'. *Cognition, 9,* 139–196.

Foulke, E. A., & Sticht, T. G. (1969). A review of research on the intelligibility and comprehension of accelerated speech. *Psychological Bulletin, 72*(1), 50–62.

Fox, D. K., Hopkins, B. L., & Anger, W. K. (1987). The long-term effects of a token economy on safety performance in open-pit mining. *Journal of Applied Behavior Analysis, 20,* 215–224.

Fromkin, V. A. (1988). Sign language: Evidence for language universals and the linguistic capacity of the human brain. *Sign Language Studies, 59,* 115–127.

Funnel, E. (1983). Phonological processing in reading: New evidence from acquired dyslexia. *British Journal of Psychology, 74*(2), 159–180.

Gallo, D. A. (2010). False memories and fantastic beliefs: 15 years of the DRM illusion. *Memory & Cognition, 38,* 833–848.

Galton, F. (1879). Psychometric experiments. *Brain: A Journal of Neurology, 2,* 149–162.

Gardiner, J. M. (1988). Functional aspects of recollective experience. *Memory & Cognition, 16,* 309–313.

Gardner, H. (1999). *Intelligence reframed: Multiple intelligences for the 21st century.* New York: Basic Books.

Gardner, R. A., & Gardner, B. T. (1969). Teaching sign language to a chimpanzee. *Science, 165,* 664–672.

Gasper, K. (2003). When necessity is the mother of invention: Mood and problem solving. *Journal of Experimental Social Psychology, 39,* 248–262.

Gazzaley, A., & D'Esposito, M. (2007). Unifying prefrontal cortex function: Executive control, neural networks and top-down modulation. In B. L. Miller & J. L. Cummings (Eds.), *The human frontal lobes* (pp. 187–206). New York: Guilford Press.

Gibson, E. J., & Walk, R. D. (1960). The 'visual cliff'. *Scientific American, 202,* 67–71.

Gibson, J. J. (1979). *The ecological approach to visual perception.* Boston, MA: Houghton Mifflin.

Gick, M. L., & Holyoak, K. J. (1980). Analogical problem solving. *Cognitive Psychology, 12*(3), 306–355

Gick, M. L., & Holyoak, K. J. (1983). Scheme induction and analogical transfer. *Cognitive Psychology, 15*(1), 1–38.

Gisiner, R. and Schusterman, R. J. (1992b). Combinatorial relationships learned by a language trained sea lion. In J. A. Thomas, R. A. Kastelein, & Y. A. Supin (Eds.), *Marine Mammal Sensory Systems,* New York: Plenum Press.

Gisiner, R., & Schusterman, R. J. (1992a). Sequence, syntax and semantics: Responses of a language trained sea lion (*Zalophus californianus*) to novel sign combinations. *Journal of Comparative Psychology, 106,* 78–91

Glanzer, M., & Cunitz, A. R. (1966) Two storage mechanisms in free recall. *Journal of Verbal Learning and Verbal Behaviour, 5,* 351–60.

Glushko, R. J. (1979). The organisation and activation of orthographic knowledge in reading aloud. *Journal of Experimental Psychology: Human Perception & Performance, 5,* 674–691.

Godden, D. R., & Baddeley, A. D. (1975). Context-dependent memory in two natural environments: On land and underwater. *British Journal of Psychology, 66,* 325–331.

Goel, V., & Grafman, J. (2000). Role of the right prefrontal cortex in ill-structured planning. *Cognitive Neuropsychology, 17*(5), 415–436.

Goel, V., Grafman, J., Tajik, J., & Danto, D. (1997). A study of the performance of patients with frontal lobe lesions in a financial planning task. *Brain, 120*(10), 1805–1822.

Goodglass, H., & Kaplan, E. (1972). *The assessment of aphasia and related disorders.* Philadelphia, PA: Lea and Febiger.

Goodman, G. S., Rudy, L., Bottoms, B. L., & Aman, C. (1990). Children's concerns and memory: Issues of ecological validity in the study of children's eyewitness testimony. In R. Fivush & J. A. Hudson (Eds.), *Knowing and remembering in young children* (pp. 249–284). Cambridge, UK: Cambridge University Press.

Goodman, R. A., & Caramazza, A. (1986). Aspects of the spelling process: Evidence from a case of acquired dysgraphia. *Language and Cognitive Processes, 1,* 263–296.

Gray, J. A., & Wedderburn, A. A. (1960). Grouping strategies with simultaneous stimuli. *Quarterly Journal of Experimental Psychology, 12,* 180–184.

Gray, J. R., & Thompson, P. M. (2004). Neurobiology of intelligence: Science and Ethics. *Neuroscience, 5,* 471–842.

Gregory, R. L. (1997). *Eye and brain: The psychology of seeing.* Oxford: Oxford University Press.

Guilford, J. P. (1967). *The nature of human intelligence.* New York: McGraw-Hill.

Guynn, M. J., McDaniel, M. A., & Einstein, G. O. (2001). Remembering to perform actions: A different type of memory? In H. D. Zimmer, R. L. Cohen, M. J. Guynn, et al. (Eds.), *Memory for action: A distinct form of episodic memory?* (pp. 25–48). New York: Oxford University Press.

Hannula, D. E., Tranel, D., & Cohen, N. J. (2006). The long and the short of it: Relational memory impairments in amnesia, even at short lags. *Journal of Neuroscience, 26,* 8352–8359.

Harley, T. A. (1995). *The psychology of language: From data to theory.* Hove: Psychology Press.

Harris, J. E. (1980). Memory aids people use: Two interview studies. *Memory & Cognition, 8,* 31–38.

Harris, J. E. (1983). Remembering to do things: A forgotten topic. In J. E. Harris & P. E. Morris (Eds.), *Everyday memory, actions, and absentmindedness* (pp. 71–92). New York: Academic Press.

Hartlage, S., Alloy, L. B., Vazquez, C., & Dykman,

B. (1993). Automatic and effortful processing in depression. *Psychological Bulletin, 113*, 247–278.

Hasher, L., & Zacks, R. T. (1979). Automatic and effortful processes in memory. *Journal of Experimental Psychology: General, 108*, 356–388.

Heffernan, T. M., Moss, M., & Ling, J. (2002). Subjective ratings of prospective memory deficits in chronic heavy alcohol users. *Alcohol and Alcoholism, 37*, 269–271.

Heider, E. A. (1972) Probabilities, sampling and ethnographic method: The case of Dani colour names. *Man, 7*, 448–466.

Henry, J. D. et al. (2004). A meta-analysis review of prospective memory in aging. *Psychology and Aging, 19*, 27–39.

Herman, L. M., Kuczaj, S., II, & Holder, M. D. (1993). Responses to anomalous gestural sequences by a language-trained dolphin: Evidence for processing of semantic relations and syntactic information. *Journal of Experimental Psychology: General, 122*, 184–194.

Hillis, A. E., & Caramazza, A. (1991). Category-specific naming and comprehension impairment: A double dissociation. *Brain, 114*, 2081–2094.

Hillis, A. E., Newhart, M., Heidler, J., Parker, P. B., Herskovits, E. H., & Degaonkar, M. (2005). Anatomy of spatial attention: Insights from perfusion imaging and hemispatial neglect in acute stroke. *Journal of Neuroscience, 25*, 3161–3167.

Hitch, G. J., Halliday, M. S., Schaafstal, A., & Schraagen, J. M. (1988). Visual working memory in young children. *Memory and Cognition, 16*, 120–132.

Hockett, C. F. (1960). The origins of speech. *Scientific America, 203*, 321–332.

Hoffman, T. W., Lau, I., & Johnson, D. R. (1986). The linguistic relativity of person cognition. *Journal of Personality and Social Psychology, 51*, 1097–1105.

Holst, V. F., & Pezdek, K. (1992). Scripts for typical crimes and their effects on memory for eyewitness testimony. *Applied Cognitive Psychology, 6*, 573–587.

Hubel, D. H., & Wiesel, T. N. (1962). Receptive fields, binocular interaction and functional architecture in the cat's visual cortex. *Journal of Physiology, 160*, 106–154.

Hubel, D. H., & Wiesel, T. N. (1977). Functional architecture of macaque monkey visual cortex. *Proceedings of the Royal Society of London, Series B, 198*, 1–59.

Hunt, E. (1980). Intelligence as an information-processing concept. *British Journal of Psychology, 71*(4), 449–474.

Hunt, E., & Agnoli, F. (1991). The Whorfian hypothesis: A cognitive psychology perspective. *Psychological Review, 98*, 377–389.

Hyde, T. S., & Jenkins, J. J. (1969). Recall for words as a function of semantic, graphic, and syntactic orienting tasks. *Journal of Verbal Learning and Verbal Behavior, 12*, 471–480.

Hyman, I. E., & Loftus, E. F. (2002). False childhood memories and eyewitness memory errors. In M. L. Eisen, J. A. Quas, & G. S. Goodman (Eds.), *Memory and suggestibility in the forensic interview* (pp. 63–84). Mahwah, NJ: Lawrence Erlbaum.

Iakovides, S. A., Iliadou, V. T. H., Bizeli, V. T. H., Kaprinis, S. G., Fountoulakis, K. N., & Kaprinis, G. S. (2004). Psychophysiology and psychoacoustics of music: Perception of complex sound in normal subjects and psychiatric patients. *Annals of General Hospital Psychiatry, 3*, 6.

Isen, A. M., Daubman, K. A., & Nowicki, G. P. (1987). Positive affect facilitates creative problem solving. *Journal of Personality & Social Psychology, 52*, 1122–1131.

James, W. (1890). *The principles of psychology.* New York: Holt.

Jefferson, G. (1949). The mind of mechanical man: Lister oration for 1949. *British Medical Journal, 1*, 1105–21.

Jenkins, J., & Dallenbach, K. (1924). Obliviscence during sleep and waking. *American Journal of Psychology, 35*, 605–612.

Jensen, A. R. (1979). *G*: Outmoded theory or unconquered frontier? *Creative Science and Technology, 2*, 16–27.

Jensen, A. R. (1982). The chronometry of intelligence. In R. J. Sternberg (Ed.), *Advances in the psychology of human intelligence Vol. 1* (pp. 255–310). Hillsdale, NJ: Erlbaum.

Jensen, A. R. (1998). *The g factor.* Westport, CT: Praeger/Greenwood.

Jerison, H. J. (2000). Evolution of intelligence. In Sternberg, R. (Ed.) *Handbook of human intelligence* (2nd ed.) (pp. 216–244). Cambridge, UK: Cambridge University Press.

Johnston, W. A., & Heinz, S. P. (1978). Flexibility and capacity demands of attention. *Journal of Experimental Psychology: General, 107*, 420–435.

Jones, D. M., & Macken, W. J. (1993). Irrelevant tones produce an irrelevant speech effect: Implications for coding in phonological memory. *Journal of Experimental Psychology: Learning, Memory and Cognition, 19*, 369–381.

Jones, D. M., Beaman, C. P., & Macken, W. J. (1996). The object-oriented episodic record model. In S. Gathercole (Ed.), *Models of short-term memory.* London: Lawrence Erlbaum.

Jones, G. V. (1982). Tests of the dual-mechanism theory of recall. *Acta Psychologica, 50*, 61–72.

Jones, M. C. (1924). A laboratory study of fear: The case of Peter. *Pedagogical Seminary, 31*, 308–315.

Julesz, B. (1975). Experiments in the visual perception of texture. *Scientific American, 212*, 38–48.

Kahneman, D. (1973). *Attention and effort.* Englewood Cliffs, NJ: Prentice Hall.

Kazui, H., Matsuda, A., Hirono, N., et al. (2005). Everyday memory impairment of patients with mild cognitive impairment. *Dementia and Geriatric Cognitive Disorders, 19*, 331– 337.

Kendzierski, D., & Costello, M. C. (2004). Healthy eating self-schema and nutrition behavior. *Journal of Applied Social Psychology, 34*, 2437–2451.

Kenealy, P. M. (1997). Mood-state-dependent

retrieval: The effects of induced mood on memory reconsidered. *Quarterly Journal of Experimental Psychology, 50A,* 290–317.

Kensinger, E. A., Corkin S. 2000. Retrograde memory in amnesia: A 'famous faces' study with the amnesic patient H. M. *Society for Neuroscience Abstracts, 26,* 463.

Keppel, G., & Underwood, B. J. (1962). Proactive inhibition in short-term retention of single items. *Journal of Verbal Learning & Verbal Behavior, 1,* 153–161.

Khalfa, S., Bruneau, N., Roge, B., Georgieff, N., Veuillet, E., et al. (2004). Increased perception of loudness in autism. *Hearing Research, 198,* 87–92.

Kliegel, M. I., McDaniel, M. A., & Einstein, G. O. (Eds.) (2008). *Prospective memory: Cognitive, neuroscience, developmental, and applied perspectives.* New York: Taylor & Francis.

Knowles, W. B. (1963). Operator loading tasks. *Human Factors, 5,* 151–161.

Knowlton, B. J., & Squire, L. R. (1995). Remembering and knowing: Two different expressions of declarative memory. *Journal of Experimental Psychology: Learning, Memory, & Cognition, 21,* 699–710.

Kopelman, M. D., & Stanhope, N. (1998). Recall and recognition memory in patients with focal frontal, temporal lobe and diencephalic lesions. *Neuropsychologia, 36,* 785–95.

Kripke, S. (1980). *Naming and necessity.* Cambridge, MA Harvard University Press.

Kvavilashvili, L. (1987). Remembering intention as a distinct form of memory. *British Journal of Psychology, 78,* 507–518.

Kvavilashvili, L., & Ellis, J. (2004). Ecological validity and the real-life/laboratory controversy in memory research: A critical and historical review. *History & Philosophy of Psychology, 6,* 59–80.

LaBerge, D., & Buchsbaum, J. L. (1990). Positron emission tomography measurements of pulvinar activity during an attention task. *Journal of Neuroscience, 10,* 613–619.

Lang, P. J., Öhman, A., & Vaitl, D. (1988). *The international affective picture system.* Gainesville, FL: The Center for Research in Psychophysiology, University of Florida.

Lavie, N., Hirst, A., de Fockert, J., & Viding, E. (2004). Load theory of selective attention. *Journal of Experimental Psychology: General, 133,* 339–354.

Lazarus, R. S. (1982). Thoughts on the relations between emotion and cognition. *American Psychologist, 37,* 1019–1024.

LeDoux J. E. (1987). Emotion. In F. Plum (Ed.) *Handbook of physiology. 1: The nervous system: Vol. V. Higher functions of the brain* (pp. 419–460). Bethesda, MD: American Physiological Society.

LeDoux, J. E. (1996). *The emotional brain: The mysterious underpinnings of emotional life.* New York: Simon & Schuster.

Leibowitz, H., & Gwozdecki, J. (1967). The magnitude of the Poggendorff illusion as a function of age. *Child Development, 38,* 573–580.

Leichtman, M. D., & Ceci, S. J. (1995). The effects of stereotypes and suggestions on preschoolers' reports. *Developmental Psychology, 31*(4), 568–578.

Lemogne, C., Piolino, P., Friszer, S., Claret, A., Girault, N., Jouvent, R., et al. (2006). Episodic autobiographical memory in depression: Specificity, autonoetic consciousness, and self-perspective. *Consciousness and Cognition, 15,* 258–268.

Leng, N. R. C., & Parkin, A. J. (1988). Amnesic patients can benefit from instructions to use imagery: Evidence against the cognitive mediation hypothesis. *Cortex, 24,* 33–39.

Levelt, W. J. M., Roelofs, A., & Meyer, A. S. (1999). A theory of lexical access in speech production. *Behavioral and Brain Sciences, 22*(1), 1–75.

Leventhal, A. G., & Hirsch, H. V. B. (1977). Effects of early experience upon orientation sensitivity and binocularity of neurons in visual cortex of cats. *Proceedings of the National Academy of Science, 74,* 1272–1276.

Levine, B., Black, S. E., Cabeza, R., et al. (1998). Episodic memory and the self in a case of isolated retrograde amnesia. *Brain, 121,* 1951–1973.

Lewis, T. L., & Maurer, D. (2005). Multiple sensitive periods in human visual development: Evidence from visually deprived children. *Developmental Psychobiology, 46,* 163–183.

Liberman, A. M., Cooper, F. S., Shankweiler, D. P., & Studdert-Kennedy, M. (1967). Perception of the speech code. *Psychological Review, 74*(6), 431–461

Liberman, A. M., Harris, K. S., Hoffman, H. S., & Griffith, B. C. (1957). The discrimination of speech sounds within and across phoneme boundaries. *Journal of Experimental Psychology, 53,* 358–368.

Lindsay, D. S., Hagen, L., Read, J. D., Wade, K. A., & Garry, M. (2004). True photographs and false memories. *Psychological Science, 15,* 149–154.

Ling, J., Campbell, C., Heffernan, T. M., & Greenough, C. G. (2007). Short-term prospective memory deficits in patients with chronic back pain. *Psychosomatic Medicine, 69,* 144–148.

Linton, M. (1986). Ways of searching and the contents of memory. In D. C. Rubin (Ed.) *Autobiographical memory* (pp. 50–70). Cambridge, UK: Cambridge University Press.

Lockhart, R. S., & Craik, F. I. M. (1990). Levels of processing: A retrospective commentary on a framework for memory research. *Canadian Journal of Psychology, 44,* 87–112.

Loftus, E. F. (2003). Our changeable memories: Legal and practical implications. *Nature Reviews: Neuroscience, 4,* 231–234.

Loftus, E. F., & Palmer, J. C. (1974). Reconstruction of automobile destruction: An example of the interaction between language and memory. *Journal of Verbal Learning and Verbal Behavior 13,* 585–589.

Logie, R. H. (1991). Visuo-spatial short term memory: Visual working memory or visual buffer. In C. Cornoldi & M. McDaniel (Eds.), *Imagery and cognition* (pp. 77–102). New York: Springer-Verlag.

Logie, R. H. (1995). *Visuo-spatial working memory*. Hove: Lawrence Erlbaum.

Logie, R. H., & Duff, S. C. (1996). Processing and storage in working memory: Multiple components? Poster presented at the annual meeting of the Psychonomic Society, Chicago IL.

Lovett, M. C. (2002). Problem solving. In D. L. Medin (Ed.), *Steven's handbook of experimental psychology*. New York: Wiley.

Lovett, M. C. (2005). A strategy-based interpretation of Stroop. *Cognitive Science, 29*, 493–524.

Maass, A., & Kohnken, G. (1989). Eyewitness identification: Simulating the weapon effect. *Law and Human Behavior, 13*, 397–408.

MacLeod, C., Mathews, A., & Tata, P. (1986). Attentional bias in emotional disorders. *Journal of Abnormal Psychology, 95*, 15–20.

MacLeod, M. D. (2002). Retrieval-induced forgetting in eyewitness memory: Forgetting as a consequence of remembering. *Applied Cognitive Psychology, 16*, 135–149.

MacLeod, P. D. (1978). Does probe RT measure central processing demand? *Quarterly Journal of Experimental Psychology, 30*, 83–89.

MacLin, O. H., MacLin, M. K., & Malpass, R. S. (2001). Race, arousal, attention, exposure and delay: An examination of factors mediating face recognition. *Psychology, Public Policy and Law, 7*, 134–152.

Manes, F., Sahakian, B., Clark, L., Rogers, R., Antoun, N., Aitken, M., & Robbins, T. (2002). Decision-making processes following damage to the prefrontal cortex. *Brain, 125*(3), 624–639.

Marin, B. V. O., Holmes, D. L., Guth, M., & Kovac, P. (1979). The potential of children as eyewitnesses. A comparison of children and adults on eyewitness tasks. *Law and Human Behaviour, 3*, 295–306.

Marr, D. (1982). *Vision: A computational investigation into the human representation and processing of visual information*. San Francisco, CA: W. H. Freeman.

Marr, D., & Hildreth, E. (1980). Theory of edge detection. *Proceedings of the Royal Society of London, B207*, 187–217.

Marr, D., & Nishihara, K. (1978). Representation and recognition of the spatial organisation of three-dimensional shapes. *Philosophical Transactions of the Royal Society, Series B, 200*, 269–294.

Marsh, R. L., & Hicks, J. L. (1998). Event-based prospective memory and executive control of working memory. *Journal of Experimental Psychology: Learning, Memory, and Cognition, 24*, 336–349.

Marsh, R. L., Hicks, J. L., Cook, G. I., Hansen, J. S., & Pallos, A. L. (2003). Interference to ongoing activities covaries with the characteristics of an event-based intention. *Journal of Experimental Psychology: Learning, Memory & Cognition, 29*, 861–870.

Marshall, J. C., & Halligan, P. W. (1988). Blindsight and insight in visuo-spatial neglect. *Nature, 336*, 766–767.

Marshall, J. C., & Halligan, P. W. (1988). Independent properties of normal hemispheric specialization predict some characteristics of visuospatial neglect. *Cortex, 30*, 509–517

Marshall, J. C., & Newcombe, F. (1973). Patterns of paralexia: A psycholinguistic approach, *Journal of Psycholinguistic Research, 2*, 175–199.

Marslen-Wilson, W. D. (1984). Spoken word recognition: A tutorial review. In H. Bouma & D. G. Bouwhis (Eds.), *Control and Performance X: Control of Language Processes* (pp. 125–150). Hove: Lawrence Erlbaum Associates Ltd.

Marslen-Wilson, W. D. (1987). Functional parallelism in spoken word recognition. *Cognition, 25*(1), 71–102.

Marslen-Wilson, W. D. (1990). Activation, competition, and frequency in lexical access. In G. M. T. Altmann (Ed.), *Cognitive models of speech production* (pp. 148–172), Cambridge, MA: MIT Press.

Marslen-Wilson, W. D., & Tyler, L. K. (1980). The temporal structure of spoken language understanding. *Cognition, 8*(1), 1–71.

Marslen-Wilson, W. D., & Warren, P. (1994). Levels of perceptual representation and process in lexical access: Words, phonemes, and features. *Psychological Review, 101*, 653–675.

Marslen-Wilson, W. D., & Welsh, A. (1978). Processing interactions and lexical access during word recognition in continuous speech. *Cognitive Psychology, 10*(1), 29–63.

Martin, C. L., & Halverson, C. F. (1983). The effects of sex-typing schemas on young children's memory. *Child Development, 54*, 563–574.

Mayes, A. R., & Downes, J. J. (1997). What do theories of the functional deficit(s) underlying amnesia have to explain? *Memory, 5*, 3–36.

McClelland, J. L. (1991). Stochastic interactive processes and the effect of context on perception. *Cognitive Psychology, 23*(1), 1–44.

McClelland, J. L., & Elman, J. L. (1986). The TRACE model of speech perception. *Cognitive Psychology, 18*(1), 1–87.

McClelland, J. L., & Rumelhart, D. E. (1985). Distributed memory and the representation of general and specific information. *Journal of Experimental Psychology: General, 114*, 159–197.

McFarland, C., & Buehler, R. (1998). The impact of negative affect on autobiographical memory: The role of self-focused attention to moods. *Journal of Personality and Social Psychology, 75*, 1424–1440.

McGurk, H., & MacDonald, J. (1976). Hearing lips and seeing voices. *Nature, 264*, 746–748.

Meacham, J. A., & Leiman, B. (1982). Remembering to perform future actions. In U. Neisser (Ed.), *Memory observed: Remembering in natural contexts* (pp. 327–336). San Francisco, CA: W. H. Freeman.

Mehler, J., & Dupoux, E. 1994. *What infants know: The new cognitive science of early development*. Cambridge, MA: Blackwell.

Memon, A., & Vartoukian, R. (1996). The effects of repeated questioning on young children's eyewitness memory. *British Journal of Psychology, 87*, 403–415.

Memon, A., Cronin, O., Eaves, R., & Bull, R. (1993). The cognitive interview and child witnesses. In G. M. Stephenson & N. K. Clark (Eds.), *Children,*

References

evidence and procedure. *Issues in criminological and legal psychology, no. 20* (pp. 3–9). Leicester: British Psychological Society.

Mercado E. (2008). Neural and cognitive plasticity: from maps to minds. *Psychological Bulletin, 134,* 109–137.

Miceli, G., & Capasso R. (2006). Spelling and dysgraphia. *Cognitive Neuropsychology, 23,* 110–134.

Miller, G. A. (1956). The magical number seven, plus or minus two: Some limits on our capacity for processing information. *Psychological Review, 63,* 343–355.

Minsky, M. (1961). Steps towards artificial intelligence. *Proceedings of the IRE, 49,* 8–30.

Mitchell, D. G. V., Richell, R. A., Leonard, A., & Blair, R. J. R. (2006). Emotion at the expense of cognition: Psychopathic individuals outperform controls on an operant response task. *Journal of Abnormal Psychology, 115,* 559–566.

Mitchell, K. J., Livosky, M., & Mather, M. (19998). The weapon focus effect revisited: The role of novelty. *Legal and Criminological Psychology, 3,* 287–303.

Möller, R. (2000). Perception through anticipation: A behaviour-based approach to visual perception. In A. Riegler, M. Peschl, & A. von Stein (Eds.), *Understanding representation in the cognitive sciences* (pp. 169–176). New York: Kluwer Academic.

Moors, A., & De Houwer, J. (2006). Problems with dividing the realm of cognitive processes. *Psychological Inquiry, 17,* 199–204.

Moray, N. (1959). Attention in dichotic listening: Affective cues and the influence of instructions. *Quarterly Journal of Experimental Psychology, 11,* 56–60.

Moray, N. (1967). Where is capacity limited? A survey and a model. *Acta Psychologia, 27,* 84–92.

Morgan, C. A., Hazlett, G., Doran, A. et al. (2004). Accuracy of eyewitness memory for persons encountered during exposure to highly intense stress. *International Journal of Law and Psychiatry, 27,* 265–279

Morris, C. D., Bransford, J. D., & Franks, J. J. (1977). Levels of processing versus transfer-appropriate processing. *Journal of Verbal Learning and Verbal Behavior, 16,* 519–533.

Morris, R. G., Miotto, E. C., Feigenbaum, J. D., Bullock, P., & Polkey, C. E. (1997). Planning ability after frontal and temporal lobe lesions in humans: The effects of selection equivocation and working memory load. *Cognitive Neuropsychology, 14,* 1007–1027.

Moston, S. (1992). Social support and children's eyewitness testimony. In H. Dent & R. Flin (Eds.), *Children as witnesses* (pp. 33–46). Chichester: Wiley.

Murphy, S. T., & Zajonc, R. B. (1993). Affect, cognition, and awareness: Affective priming with suboptimal and optimal stimulus. *Journal of Personality and Social Psychology, 64,* 723–739.

Naismith, S. L., Hickie, I. B., Ward, P. B., Scott, E., & Little, C. (2006). Impaired implicit sequence learning in depression: A probe for frontostriatal dysfunction? *Psychological Medicine, 36,* 313–323.

Neisser, U. (1967) *Cognitive psychology.* New York: Appleton-Century-Crofts.

Neisser, U. (1986). Nested structure in autobiographical memory. In D. C. Rubin (Ed.) *Autobiographical memory* (pp. 71–81). Cambridge, UK: Cambridge University Press.

Neisser, U., & Becklen, R. (1975). Selective looking: Attending to visually specified events. *Cognitive Psychology, 7,* 480–494.

Nelson, T. O. (1977). Repetition and depth of processing. *Journal of Verbal Learning and Verbal Behavior, 16,* 151–171.

Neuman, O. (1984). Automatic processing: A review of recent findings and a plea for an old theory. In W. Printz and A. Sanders (Eds.), *Cognition and motor process* (pp. 225–293). Berlin: Springer.

Newcombe, N., Drummey, A. B., Fox, N. A., Lie, E., & Ottinger-Alberts, W. (2000). Remembering early childhood: How much, how, and why (or why not). *Current Directions in Psychological Science, 9,* 55–58.

Newell, A., & Simon, H. A. (1958). Simulation of cognitive processes: A report on the summer research training institute. *Items, 12,* 37–40.

Newell, A., & Simon, H. A. (1972). *Human problem solving.* Englewood Cliffs, NJ: Prentice Hall.

Newman, S. D., Carpenter, P. A., Varma, S., & Just, M. A. (2003). Frontal and parietal participation in problem solving in the Tower of London: fMRI and computational modelling of planning and high-level perception. *Neuropsychologia, 41,* 1668–1982.

Norman, D. A., & Bobrow, D. G. (1975). On data-limited and resource-limited processes. *Cognitive Psychology, 7,* 44–64.

Norman, J. (2002). Two visual systems and two theories of perception: An attempt to reconcile the constructivist and ecological approaches. *Behavioral and Brain Sciences 25,* 73–144.

Norman, S., Tröster, A. I., Fields, J. A., & Brooks, R. (2002). Effects of depression and parkinson's disease on cognitive functioning. *Journal of Neuropsychiatry and Clinical Neurosciences, 14,* 31–36.

Norman, W., & Shallice, T. (1986). Attention to action. In R. J. Davidson, G. E. Schwartz, & D. Shapiro (Eds.), *Consciousness and self regulation: Advances in research and theory, 4* (pp. 1–18). New York: Plenum Press.

Öhman, A., & Mineka, S. (2001). Fears, phobias, and preparedness: Toward an evolved module of fear and fear learning. *Psychological Review, 108,* 483–522.

Olson, M. A., & Fazio, R. H. (2006). Reducing automatically-activated racial prejudice through implicit evaluative conditioning. *Personality and Social Psychology Bulletin, 32,* 421–433.

Owen, A. M., Downes, J. J., Sahakian, B. J., Polkey, C. E., & Robbins, T. W. (1990). Planning and spatial working memory following frontal lobe lesions in man. *Neuropsychologia, 28,* 1021–1034.

Park, J., Newman, L. I., & Polk, T. A. (2009). Face processing: The interplay of nature and nurture. *Neuroscientist, 15,* 445–449.

Parkin, A. (1999). *Explorations in cognitive neuropsychology.* Hove, UK: Psychology Press.

Parkinson, B., & Manstead, A. S. R. (1992). Appraisal as a cause of emotion. In M. S. Clark (Ed.), *Review of personality and social psychology Vol. 13.* New York: Sage.

Pashler, H. (1990). Do response modality effects support multiprocessor models of divided attention? *Journal of Experimental Psychology: Human Perception and Performance, 16,* 826–842.

Patel, H., Blades, M., & Andrade, J. (2002). Children's incidental recall of the colours of objects and clothing. *Cognitive Development, 16,* 965–985.

Patterson, K. E. (1986). Lexical but non-semantic spelling? *Cognitive neuropsychology, 3,* 341–367.

Pepperberg, I. M. (2006a). Ordinality and inferential abilities of a grey parrot (*Psittacus erithacus*). *Journal of Comparative Psychology, 120,* 205–216.

Pepperberg, I. M. (2006b). Grey parrot (*Psittacus erithacus*) numerical abilities: Addition and further experiments on a zero-like concept. *Journal of Comparative Psychology, 120,* 1–11.

Perry, N. W., & Wrightsman, W. (1991). *The child witness: Legal issues and dilemmas.* Newbury Park, CA: Sage.

Peters, D. P. (1988). Eyewitness memory and arousal in a natural setting. In M. M. Gruneberg, P. E., Morris, & R. N. Sykes (Eds.), *Practical aspects of memory: Current research and issues. Vol. 1* (pp. 89–94). Chichester: Wiley.

Peterson, L. R., & Peterson, M. J. (1959). Short-term retention of individual verbal items. *Journal of Experimental Psychology, 58,* 193–198.

Pipe, M. E., & Wilson, J. C. (1994). Cues and secrets: Influences on children's event reports. *Developmental Psychology, 30,* 515–525.

Plaut, D. C., McClelland, J. L., Seidenberg, M. S., & Patterson, K. (1996). Understanding normal and impaired word reading: Computational principles in quasi-regular domains. *Psychological Review, 103,* 56–115.

Poole, D. A., & White, L. T. (1993). Two years later: Effects of question repetition and retention interval on the eyewitness testimony of children and adults. *Developmental Psychology, 29,* 844–853.

Posner, M. I. (1980). Orienting of attention. *Quarterly Journal of Experimental Psychology, 32,* 3–25.

Posner, M. I. (1993). Attention before and during the decade of the brain. In D. Meyer and S. Kornblum (Eds.), *Attention and performance XIV* (pp. 340–351). Cambridge, MA: MIT Press.

Posner, M. I., & Boies, S. J. (1971). Components of attention. *Psychological Review, 78,* 391–408.

Posner, M. I., & Petersen, S. E. (1990). The attention system of the human brain. *Annual Review of Neuroscience, 13,* 25–42.

Posner, M. I., Rafal, R. D., Choate, L. S., & Vaughn, J. (1985). Inhibition of return: Neural basis and function. *Cognitive Neuropsychology, 2,* 211–228.

Posner, M. J., & Mitchell, R. F. (1967). Chronometric analysis of classification. *Psychological Review, 74,* 392–409.

Poulton, E. C. (1956). Listening to overlapping calls. *Journal of Experimental Psychology, 52,* 334–339.

Power, M., & Dalgleish, T. (1997). *Cognition and emotion: From order to disorder.* Hove: Psychology Press.

Prabhakaran, V., Narayanan, K., Zhao, Z., and Gabrieli, J. D. (2000). Integration of diverse information in working memory within the frontal lobe. *Nature Neuroscience, 3,* 85–90.

Premack, D., & Premack, A. J. (1983). *The mind of an ape* (1st ed.). New York: Norton Press.

Pretz, J. E., Totz, K. S., & Kaufman, S. B. (2010). The effects of mood, cognitive style, and cognitive ability on implicit learning. *Learning and Individual Differences, 20,* 215–219.

Pullum, G. K. (1991). *The great Eskimo vocabulary hoax and other irreverent essays on the study of language.* Chicago, IL: University of Chicago Press.

QAA (2010) *Quality assurance agency benchmark for psychology.* London: Quality Assurance Agency.

Quinlan, P. T., & Wilton, R. N. (1998). Grouping by proximity or similarity? Competition between the Gestalt principles in vision. *Perception, 27,* 417–430.

Quinn, J. G., & McConnell, J. (1996). Irrelevant pictures in visual working memory. *Quarterly Journal of Experimental Psychology, 49A,* 200–215.

Rafal, R. D., & Posner, M. I. (1987). Deficits in human visual spatial attention following thalamic lesions. *Proceedings of the National Academy of Science, 84,* 7349–7353.

Raymond, M. J. (1964). The treatment of addiction by aversion conditioning with apomorphine. *Behaviour Research and Therapy, 1,* 287–91.

Rattner, A. (1988). Convicted but innocent. *Law and Human Behavior, 12,* 283 294.

Raven, J. C. (1982). *Revised manual for Raven's progressive matrices and vocabulary scale.* Windsor, UK: NFER Nelson.

Rich, E., & Knight, K. (1991). *Artificial intelligence* (2nd ed.). New York: McGraw-Hill.

Riener, C. R., Stefanucci, J. K., Proffitt, D., & Clore, G. (2003). An effect of mood on perceiving spatial layout. *Journal of Vision, 3,* Abstract 227. Available from http://www.journalofvision.org/3/9/227/

Robinson, J. A., & Swanson, J. A. (1993). Field and observer modes of remembering. *Memory, 1,* 169–184.

Rock, I., & Palmer, S. (1990). The legacy of Gestalt psychology. *Scientific American, 263,* 84–90.

Roediger, H. L. (1990). Implicit memory: A commentary. *Bulletin of the Psychonomic Society, 28,* 373–380.

Roediger, H. L., & McDermott, K. B. (1995). Creating false memories: Remembering words not presented in lists. *Journal of Experimental Psychology: Learning, Memory, & Cognition, 21,* 803–814.

Roediger, H. L., & Marsh, E. J. (2003). Episodic and autobiographical memory. In A. F. Healy & R. W.

Proctor, *Experimental psychology, Vol. 4, The handbook of psychology* (pp. 475–497). New York: Wiley.

Rogers, T. B., Kuiper, N. A., & Kirker, W. S. (1977). Self-reference and the encoding of personal information. *Journal of Personality and Social Psychology, 35*, 677–688.

Rosch, E. H. (1973) Natural categories. *Cognitive Psychology, 4*, 328–350.

Rubin, D. C., & Wetzler, S. E., & Nebes, R. D. (1986). Autobiographical memory across the lifespan. In D. C. Rubin (Ed.), Autobiographical memory (pp. 202–221). Cambridge, UK: Cambridge University Press.

Salamé, P., & Baddeley, A. D. (1989). Effects of background music on phonological short-term memory. *Quarterly Journal of Experimental Psychology, 41A*, 107–122.

Savage-Rumbaugh, S., Scanlon, J. L., & Rumbaugh, D. M. (1980). Communicative intentionality in the chimpanzee. Behavioral and Brain Sciences, 3(4), 620–623.

Saywitz, K. J., & Nathanson, R. (1993).Credibility of child witness: The role of communicative competence. *Topics in Language Disorders, 13*, 59–78..

Schachtel, E. (1947). On memory and childhood amnesia. *Psychiatry: Journal of the Biology and Pathology of Interpersonal Relations, 10*, 1–26.

Schachter, S., & Singer, J. E. (1962). Cognitive, social, and physiological determinants of emotional state. *Psychological Review, 69*, 379–399.

Schacter, D. L. (1987). Implicit memory: History and current status. *Journal of Experimental Psychology: Learning, Memory, and Cognition, 13*, 501–518.

Schacter, D. L. (1996). *Searching for memory: The brain, the mind, and the past.* New York: Basic Books.

Schacter, D. L., Church, B. A., & Bolton, E. (1995). Implicit memory in amnesic patients: Impairments of voice-specific priming. *Psychological Science, 6*, 20–25.

Schank, R. C., & Abelson, R. P. (1977). *Scripts, plans, goals, and understanding.* Hillsdale, NJ: Lawrence Erlbaum.

Scherer, K. R. (2001). Appraisal considered as a process of multilevel sequential checking. In K. R. Scherer, A. Schorr, & T. Johnstone (Eds.), *Appraisal processes in emotion: Theory, methods, research* (pp. 92–120). Oxford: Oxford University Press.

Schouten, J. F., Kalsbeek, J. W. H., & Leopold, F. F. (1960). On the evaluation of perceptual and mental load. *Ergonomics, 5*, 251–260.

Schroots, J. J. F., van Dijkum, C., & Assink, M. H. J. (2004). Autobiographical memory from a lifespan perspective. *International Journal of Aging and Human Development, 58*, 91–115.

Schultz, L. T., & Heimberg, R. G. (2008). Attentional focus in social anxiety disorder: Potential for interactive processes. *Clinical Psychology Review, 28*, 1206–1221.

Scoville, W. B., & Milner, B. (1957). Loss of recent memory after bilateral hippocampal lesions. *Journal of Neurology, Neurosurgery & Psychiatry, 20*, 11–21.

Seelau, S. M., & Wells, G. L. (1995). Applied eyewitness research: The other mission. *Law and Human Behavior, 19*, 319–324.

Segall, M. H., Campbell, D. T., & Herskovits, M. J. (1966). *The influence of culture on visual perception.* Indianapolis, IN: Bobbs-Merrill.

Shallice, T. (1988). *From neuropsychology to mental structure.* Cambridge, UK: Cambridge University Press.

Shallice, T., & Burgess, P. W. (1991). Deficits in strategy application following frontal lobe damage in man. *Brain*, 114(2), 727–741.

Shallice, T., & Warrington, E. K. (1970). Independent functioning of verbal memory stores: a neuropsychological study. *Quarterly Journal of Experimental Psychology, 22*, 261–273.

Shepard, R. N., & Metzler, D. (1971). Mental rotation of three-dimensional objects. *Science, 171*, 701–703.

Shibahara, N., Zorzi, M., Hill, M. P., Wydell, T., & Butterworth, B. (2003). Semantic effects in word naming: evidence from English and Japanese kanji. *The Quarterly Journal of Experimental Psychology, 56A(2)*, 263–286.

Shiffrin, R. M., & Schneider, W. (1977). Controlled and automatic human information processing: II. Perceptual learning, automatic attending, and a general theory. *Psychological Review, 84*, 127–190.

Simon, D., & Chabris, C. F. (1999). Gorillas in our midst: Sustained inattentional blindness for dynamic events. *Perception 28*, 1059–1074.

Skinner, B. F. (1938). The behavior of organisms. New York: Appleton-Century.

Skinner, B. F. (1953). *Science and human behavior.* New York: Macmillan.

Slamecka, N. J., & Graf, P. (1978). The generation effect: Delineation of a phenomenon. *Journal of Experimental Psychology: Human Learning and Memory, 4*, 592–604.

Slater, A., & Morison, V. (1985) Shape constancy and slant perception at birth. *Perception, 14*, 337–44.

Smith, C. A., & Kirby, L. D. (2001). Toward delivering on the promise of appraisal theory. In K. R. Scherer, A. Schoor, & T. Johnstone (Eds.), *Appraisal processes in emotion: Theory, methods, research.* Oxford: Oxford University Press.

Smith, C. A., & Lazarus, R. S. (1993). Appraisal components, core relational themes, and the emotions. *Cognition & Emotion, 7*, 233–269.

Smith, R. E. (2003). The cost of remembering to remember in event based prospective memory: Investigating the capacity demands of delayed intention performance. *Journal of Experimental Psychology: Learning, Memory & Cognition, 29*, 347–361.

Smith, R. E., & Bayen, U. J. (2004). A multinomial model of event-based prospective memory. *Journal of Experimental Psychology: Learning. Memory, & Cognition, 30*, 756–777.

Smith, S. M., & Vela, E. (1992). Environmental context-dependent eyewitness recognition. *Applied Cognitive Psychology, 6*, 125–139.

Somerville, S. C., Wellman, H. M., & Cultice, J. C. (1983). Young children's deliberate reminding. *Journal of Genetic Psychology, 143*, 87–96.

Spearman, C. (1923). *The nature of intelligence and the principles of cognition*. London: Macmillan.

Speisman, J. C., Lazarus, R. S., Mordkoff, A. M., & Davison, L. A. (1964). Experimental reduction of stress based on ego-defence theory. *Journal of Abnormal Psychology, 68*, 367–380.

Spelke, E., Hirst, W., & Neisser, U. (1976). Skills of divided attention. *Cognition, 4*, 215–230.

Sperling, G. (1960). The information available in brief visual presentations. *Psychological Monographs: General and Applied, 74*, 1–30.

Squire, L. (2009). Memory and brain systems: 1969–2009. *Journal of Neuroscience, 29*, 12711–12716.

Squire, L. R. (1987). *Memory and brain*. New York: Oxford University Press.

Stern, W. (1912). *Psychologische Methoden der Intelligenz-Prüfung*. Leipzig, Germany: Barth.

Sternberg, R. J. (1983). Criteria for intellectual skills training. *Educational Researcher, 12*, 6–12.

Sternberg, R. J. (1984). What should intelligence tests test? Implications for a triarchic theory of intelligence for intelligence testing. *Educational Researcher, 13*(1), 5–15.

Sternberg, R. J. (1993).The Sternberg triarchic abilities test (level H). Unpublished.

Stockhorst, U., Spennes-Saleh, S., Körholz, D., et al. (2000). Anticipatory Symptoms and Anticipatory Immune Responses in Pediatric Cancer Patients Receiving Chemotherapy: Features of a Classically Conditioned Response? *Brain, Behavior, and Immunity, 14*, 198–218.

Storbeck, J., & Clore, G. L. (2007). On the interdependence of cognition and emotion. *Cognition & Emotion, 21*, 1212–1237.

Stroop, J. (1935). Studies in interference in serial verbal reactions. *Journal of Experimental Psychology 18*, 643–661.

Stryker, M., & Sherk, H. (1975). Modification of cortical orientation selectivity in the cat by restricted visual experience: A reexamination. *Science, 190*, 904–906.

Sugita, Y. (2008). Face perception in monkeys reared with no exposure to faces. *Proceedings of the National Academy of Sciences of the United States of America, 105*, 394–398.

Talarico, J. M., & Rubin, D. C. (2003). Confidence, not consistency, characterizes flashbulb memories. *Psychological Science, 14*, 455–461.

Teasdale, J. D., & Barnard, P. J. (1993). *Affect, cognition and change: Re-modelling depressive thought*. Hove: Lawrence Erlbaum.

Terr, L. C., Bloch, D. A., Michel, B. A., Shi, H., Reinhardt, J. A., & Metayer, S. (1997). Children's thinking in the wake of Challenger. *American Journal of Psychiatry, 154*, 744–751.

Thorndike, E. L. (1911/2000), Animal intelligence (2nd ed.). New York: Transaction Publishers. (Original work published 1911.)

Thurstone, L. L. (1924). *The nature of intelligence*. London: Routledge

Thurstone, L. L. (1938). *Primary mental abilities*. Chicago, IL: University of Chicago Press.

Tractinsky, N., & Hassenzahl, M. (2005). Arguing for aesthetics in human-computer interaction. *i-com 4*, 66–68.

Treisman, A. (1960). Contextual cues in selective listening. *Quarterly Journal of Experimental Psychology, 12*, 242–248.

Treisman, A. (1964). Selective attention in man. *British Medical Bulletin, 20*, 12–16.

Treisman, A., & Gelade, G. (1980). A feature-integration theory of attention. *Cognitive Psychology, 12*, 97–136.

Tulving, E. (1966). Subjective organization and effects of repetition in multi-trial free-recall learning. *Journal of Verbal Learning and Verbal Behavior, 5*, 193–197.

Tulving, E. (1972). Episodic and semantic memory. In E. Tulving & W. Donaldson (Eds.), *Organization of memory* (pp. 382–402). New York: Academic Press.

Tulving, E. (1982). Synergistic ecphory in recall and recognition. *Canadian Journal of Psychology, 20*, 479–496.

Tulving, E. (1983). Echphoric processes in episodic memory. *Philosophical Transactions of the Royal Society, Series B, Biological Science, 302*, 361–370.

Tulving, E., & Osler, S. (1968). Effectiveness of retrieval cues in memory for words. *Journal of Experimental Psychology, 77*, 593–601.

Tulving, E., & Thomson, D. M. (1973). Encoding specificity and retrieval processes in episodic memory. *Psychological Review, 80*, 352–373.

Tulving, E., & Wiseman, S. (1975). Relation between recognition and recognition failure of recallable words. *Bulletin of the Psychonomic Society, 6*, 79–82.

Tulving, E., Schacter, D. L., & Stark, H. A. (1982). Priming effects in word-fragment completion are independent of recognition memory. *Journal of Experimental Psychology, 8*, 336–342.

Turing, A. M. (1950). Computing machinery and intelligence. *Mind, 59*, 433–60.

Ullman, S. (1980). Against direct perception. *Behavioral and Brain Sciences 3*, 333–81.

Underwood, G. (1974). Moray vs. the rest: The effect of extended shadowing practice. *Quarterly Journal of Experimental Psychology, 26*, 368–372.

Uttal, W. R. (2003). *The new phrenology: The limits of localizing cognitive processes in the brain*. Boston, MA: MIT Press.

Valentine, T., & Mesout, J. (2009). Eyewitness identification under stress in the London Dungeon. *Applied Cognitive Psychology, 23*, 151–161.

Vernon, P. A., Wickett, J. C., Bazana, P. G., & Stelmack, R. M. (2000). The neuropsychology and psychophysiology of human intelligence. In R. J. Sternberg (Ed.), *Handbook of intelligence* (pp. 245–264). New York: Cambridge University Press.

von Békésy G. (1960). *Experiments in hearing*. New York: McGraw-Hill.

von Wright, J. M., Anderson, K., & Stenman, U. (1975). Generalisation of conditioned GSR's in dichotic listening. In P. M. A. Rabbitt and S. Dornic (Eds.), *Attention and performance, V* (pp. 194–204). London: Academic Press.

Wada, J. (1949). A new method for the deterioration of the side of the cerebral speech dominance:

References

A preliminary report on the intracarotid injection of sodium amytal in man. *Medical Biology, 14,* 221–222.

Wagenaar, W. A. (1986). My memory: A study of autobiographical memory over six years. *Cognitive Psychology, 18,* 225–252.

Waldton, S. (1974). Clinical observations of impaired cranial nerve function in senile dementia. *Acta Psychiatrica Scandinavica, 50,* 539–547.

Walker, W. R., Vogl, R. J., & Thompson, C. P. (1997). Autobiographical memory: Unpleasantness fades faster than pleasantness over time. *Applied Cognitive Psychology, 11,* 399–413.

Warrington, E. K., Cipolotti, L., & McNeil, J. (1993). Attentional dyslexia: A single-case study. *Neuropsychologia, 31,* 871–885.

Wason, P. C. (1966). Reasoning. In B. Foss (Ed.), *New horizons in psychology* (pp. 135–51). Harmondsworth: Penguin Books.

Watson, J. B., & Raynor, R. (1920) Conditioned emotional reactions. *Journal of Experimental Psychology, 3*(1) 1–14.

Weingartner, H., Cohen, R. M., Murphy, D. L., Martello, J., & Gerdt, C. (1981). Cognitive processes in depression. *Archives of General Psychiatry, 38,* 42–47.

Weisenberg, M. Raz, T., & Hener, T. (1998). The influence of film-induced mood on pain perception. *Pain, 76,* 365–375.

Weiskrantz, L. (1986). *Blindsight: A case study and implications.* Oxford: Oxford University Press.

Welford, A. T. (1952). The psychological refractory period and the timing of high-speed performance: A review and a theory. *British Journal of Psychology, 43,* 2–19.

Wetzler, S. E., & Sweeney, J. A. (1986). Childhood amnesia: An empirical demonstration. In D. C. Rubin (Ed.), *Autobiographical memory* (pp. 191–201). Cambridge, UK: Cambridge University Press.

Wheeler, M., Stuss, D. T., & Tulving, E. (1997). Toward a theory of episodic memory: The frontal lobes and autonoetic consciousness. *Psychological Bulletin, 121,* 331–354.

Whorf, B. L. (1956). Science and linguistics. In J. B. Carroll (Ed.), *Language, thought and reliability: Selected writings of Benjamin Lee Whorf* (pp. 207–219). Cambridge, MA: MIT Press. (Originally published 1940.)

Wilkinson, J. (1988). Context effects in children's event memory. In M. M. Gruneberg, P. E. Morris, & R. N. Sykes (Eds.), *Practical aspects of memory: Current research and issues,* pp. 107–111. Chichester: Wiley.

Willerman, L., Schultz, R., Rutledge, J. N., & Bigler, E. D. (1992). Hemisphere size asymmetry predicts relative verbal and nonverbal intelligence differently in the sexes: An MRI study of structure–function relations. *Intelligence,* 16, 315–328.

Williams, J. M. G., & Broadbent, K. (1986). Autobiographical memory in suicide attempters. *Journal of Abnormal Psychology, 95,* 144–149.

Williams, J. M. G., Mathews, A., & MacLeod, C. (1996). The emotional Stroop task and psychopathology. *Psychological Bulletin, 120,* 3–24.

Witt, O., Grandt, M., & Küttelwesch, H. (2009). Direct perception displays for military radar-based air surveillance. *HCI*(17), 606–615.

Wolfe, J. M. (1994). Guided search 2.0: A revised model of visual search. *Psychonomic Bulletin and Review, 1,* 202–238.

Wolpe, J. (1958). *Psychotherapy by reciprocal inhibition.* Stanford, CA: Stanford University Press.

Woodworth, R. S., & Sells, S. B. (1935). An atmosphere effect in formal syllogistic reasoning. *Journal of Experimental Psychology, 18*(4), 451–460.

Wysocki, C. J., & Gilbert, A. N. (1989). The National Geographic smell survey: Effects of age are heterogenous. *Annals of the New York Academy of Sciences, 561,* 12–28.

Yuille, J. C., & Cutshall, J. L. (1986). A case study of eyewitness memory of a crime. *Journal of Applied Psychology, 71,* 291–301.

Zaidi, F. H., Hull, J. T., Peirson, S. N., et al. (2007). Short-wavelength light sensitivity of circadian, pupillary, and visual awareness in humans lacking an outer retina. *Current Biology, 17,* 2122–2128.

Zajonc, R. B. (1980). Feeling and thinking: Preferences need no inferences. *American Psychologist, 35,* 151–175.

Zajonc, R. B. (2000). Feeling and thinking: Closing the debate over the independence of affect. In J. P. Forgas (Ed.), *Feeling and thinking: The role of affect in social cognition* (pp. 31–58). Cambridge, UK: Cambridge University Press.

Zaragoza, M. S. (1987). Memory, suggestibility, and eyewitness testimony in children and adults. In S. J. Ceci, M. P. Toglia, & D. F. Ross (Eds.), *Children's eyewitness memory* (pp. 53–78). New York: Springer-Verlag.

Ziefle, M., & Bay, S. (2006). How to overcome disorientation in mobile phone menus: A comparison of two different types of navigation aids. *Human Computer Interaction, 21,* 393–432.

Index

Terms in **bold** refer to glossary entries

Index